Lecture Notes in Computer Science 11518

Commenced Publication in 1973
Founding and Former Series Editors:
Gerhard Goos, Juris Hartmanis, and Jan van Leeuwen

More information about this series at http://www.springer.com/series/7409

Ruifeng Xu · Jianzong Wang ·
Liang-Jie Zhang (Eds.)

Cognitive Computing – ICCC 2019

Third International Conference
Held as Part of the Services Conference Federation, SCF 2019
San Diego, CA, USA, June 25–30, 2019
Proceedings

 Springer

Editors
Ruifeng Xu (iD)
Harbin Institute of Technology Shenzhen
Shenzhen, China

Liang-Jie Zhang (iD)
Kingdee International
Software Group Co., Ltd.
Shenzhen, China

Jianzong Wang
Ping An Technology (Shenzhen) Co., Ltd.
Shenzhen, China

ISSN 0302-9743   ISSN 1611-3349   (electronic)
Lecture Notes in Computer Science
ISBN 978-3-030-23406-5   ISBN 978-3-030-23407-2   (eBook)
https://doi.org/10.1007/978-3-030-23407-2

LNCS Sublibrary: SL3 – Information Systems and Applications, incl. Internet/Web, and HCI

This Springer imprint is published by the registered company Springer Nature Switzerland AG
The registered company address is: Gewerbestrasse 11, 6330 Cham, Switzerland

Preface

The 2019 International Conference on Cognitive Computing (ICCC 2019) aimed to cover all aspects of Sensing Intelligence (SI) as a Service (SIaaS). Cognitive computing is a sensing-driven computing (SDC) scheme that explores and integrates intelligence from all types of senses in various scenarios and solution contexts. It is well beyond traditional human beings' senses, who have four major senses (sight, smell, hearing, and taste) located in specific parts of the body, as well as a sense of touch located all over a body.

ICCC 2019 was part of the Services Conference Federation (SCF). SCF 2019 had the following ten collocated service-oriented sister conferences: 2019 International Conference on Web Services (ICWS 2019), 2019 International Conference on Cloud Computing (CLOUD 2019), 2019 International Conference on Services Computing (SCC 2019), 2019 International Congress on Big Data (BigData 2019), 2019 International Conference on AI & Mobile Services (AIMS 2019), 2019 World Congress on Services (SERVICES 2019), 2019 International Congress on Internet of Things (ICIOT 2019), 2019 International Conference on Cognitive Computing (ICCC 2019), 2019 International Conference on Edge Computing (EDGE 2019), and 2019 International Conference on Blockchain (ICBC 2019). As the founding member of SCF, the First International Conference on Web Services (ICWS) was held in June 2003 in Las Vegas, USA. The First International Conference on Web Services—Europe 2003 (ICWS-Europe 2003) was held in Germany in October 2003. ICWS-Europe 2003 was an extended event of the 2003 International Conference on Web Services (ICWS 2003) in Europe. In 2004, ICWS-Europe was changed to the European Conference on Web Services (ECOWS), which was held in Erfurt, Germany. To celebrate its 16th birthday, SCF 2018 was held successfully in Seattle, USA.

This volume presents the accepted papers for the ICCC 2019, held in San Diego, USA, during June 25–30, 2019. The major topics of ICCC 2019 included but were not limited to: cognitive computing technologies and infrastructure, cognitive computing applications, sensing intelligence, cognitive analysis, mobile services, cognitive computing on smart home, cognitive computing on smart city.

We accepted 17 papers, including 14 full papers and three short papers. Each was reviewed and selected by three independent members of the ICCC 2019 international Program Committee. We are pleased to thank the authors, whose submissions and participation made this conference possible. We also want to express our thanks to the Program Committee members, for their dedication in helping to organize the conference and in reviewing the submissions. We look forward to your great contributions as a volunteer, author, and conference participant for the fast-growing worldwide services innovations community.

May 2019

Ruifeng Xu
Jianzong Wang
Liang-Jie Zhang

Organization

Program Chairs

Ruifeng Xu	Harbin Institute of Technology, Shenzhen, China
Jianzong Wang	Ping An Group, Shenzhen, China

Services Conference Federation (SCF 2019)

SCF 2019 General Chairs

Calton Pu	Georgia Tech, USA
Wu Chou	Essenlix Corporation, USA
Ali Arsanjani	8x8 Cloud Communications, USA

SCF 2019 Program Chair

Liang-Jie Zhang	Kingdee International Software Group Co., Ltd., China

SCF 2019 Finance Chair

Min Luo	Huawei, USA

SCF 2019 Industry Exhibit and International Affairs Chair

Zhixiong Chen	Mercy College, USA

SCF 2019 Steering Committee

Calton Pu (Co-chair)	Georgia Tech, USA
Liang-Jie Zhang (Co-chair)	Kingdee International Software Group Co., Ltd., China

SCF 2019 Operations Committee

Huan Chen	Kingdee International Software Group Co., Ltd., China
Jing Zeng	Kingdee International Software Group Co., Ltd., China
Yishuang Ning	Tsinghua University, China
Sheng He	Tsinghua University, China
Liping Deng	Kingdee International Software Group Co., Ltd., China

ICCC 2019 Program Committee

Luca Cagliero	Politecnico di Torino, USA
Yen-Hao Hsieh	Tamkang University, Taiwan
Eleanna Kafeza	Athens University of Economics and Business, Greece
Nagarajan Kandasamy	Drexel University, Pennsylvania, USA
Wenjia Li	New York Institute of Technology, USA
Supratik Mukhopadhyay	Louisiana State University, USA
Roberto Natella	Federico II University of Naples and Critiware, Italy
Rui André Oliveira	University of Lisbon, Portugal

Contents

Efficient Gene Assembly and Identification for Many Genome Samples

Zhichun Zheng[1,2], Ning Guo[1], Konda Mani Saravanan[1], and Yanjie Wei[1(✉)]

[1] Joint Engineering Research Center for Health Big Data Intelligent Analysis Technology, Center for High Performance Computing, Shenzhen Institutes of Advanced Technology, Chinese Academy of Sciences, Shenzhen 518055, Guangdong, People's Republic of China
yj.wei@siat.ac.cn
[2] University of Chinese Academy of Sciences, No.19(A) Yuquan Road, Shijingshan District, Beijing 100049, People's Republic of China

Abstract. The development of the next generation sequencing technology (NGS) has advanced the genomics research in many application domains. Metagenomics is one such powerful approach to study large community of microbial species. For the unknown species in the metagenomic samples, gene assembly and identification without a reference genome is a very challenging problem. To overcome this issue, distributed gene assembly software handling multiple metagenome samples can be used. In this paper, based on our previously developed highly scalable gene assembly software SWAP, we present a work flow called WFswap to assemble large genomic data based on many samples and to identify more genes. Our results suggested that WFswap is able to identify 94.2% of the bench-mark genes when tested on the 19 metagenomic samples that contain *Bifidobacterium animalis subsp. lactis* CNCM I-2494. Our proposed work-flow WFswap showed better performance than WFsoap, a similar workflow that used SOAPdenovo2 for gene assembly.

Keywords: Metagenomics · Gene assembly · Gene prediction · NGS

1 Background

The outcome of Next Generation Sequencing technologies (NGS) is featured by very short fragments and extremely high throughput. NGS technology can provide valuable biological information by sequencing DNA fragments of any species. With these outstanding features such as high throughput, NGS provides a broad platform for researchers in biological sciences. For the past few decades, NGS has been widely used in many research domains and application areas, such as metagenomics. For the species that lack reference genomes, de novo genome assembly is the first and most fundamental step for downstream analysis [1]. For example, researchers use de novo assembly for discovering variation by aligning sequencing data to a reference sequence.

Z. Zheng and N. Guo—Equal Contribution.

© Springer Nature Switzerland AG 2019
R. Xu et al. (Eds.): ICCC 2019, LNCS 11518, pp. 1–11, 2019.
https://doi.org/10.1007/978-3-030-23407-2_1

The reference sequences can be assembled with the help of various assembly methods. The methods such as SSAKE [2], VCAKE [3] and SHARGCS [4] use greedy algorithm to find pairs of reads with a large amount of overlaps and then merge them into longer sequences. These methods based on greedy algorithm are not efficient on genomes with more repeat regions [5]. Arachne [6], Celera Assembler [7], CAP3 [8], PCAP [9], Phrap [10], Phusion [11] and Newbler [12] adopt Overlap-Layout-Consensus (OLC) as the assembly algorithm. Overlap-Layout-Consensus algorithm builds the simplified overlap graph for generating contigs and is more suitable for the Sanger sequencing technology. While for NGS technology, de Bruijn graph [13] based assembly methods are widely used to assemble very short reads (much shorter than the ones from the Sanger sequencing technology).

SOAPdenovo2 [14] is a popular assembly software based on de Bruijn graph technology and can only run on a single computing node, hence the memory of the computing node limits its ability for assembling large dataset. IDBA-UD [15] is designed for sequences of single cell and metagenome. Megahit [16] can generate a large number of contigs, and is suitable for the assembly of complex samples (such as soil and water samples). For genomic data from massive parallel sequencing machines, the ability of genome assemblers to analyze these huge datasets plays a key role in genomic research. In our previous work, we developed a powerful scalable genome assembler called SWAP-Assembler 2 which runs on thousands of cores [17]. SWAP-Assembler 2 can assemble the Yanhuang genome dataset [18] in 26 min using 2,048 cores on TianHe 1A [19, 20], 99 s using 16,384 cores on Tianhe 2 [21–24] and 64 s using 65,536 cores on Mira [17, 25]. By improving its most time-consuming steps, such as input parallelization, kmer graph construction, and graph simplification, SWAP-Assembler 2 can scale to more than ten thousand of cores when assembling 4 terabyte genomic data [26].

In addition to gene assembly, gene identification/prediction is also very important for downstream analysis. Gene prediction attempts to identify a biological pattern in DNA sequences and predict the start and stop region of genes in the DNA sequence, or the location of protein coding regions. In eukaryotes, gene prediction and annotation are complicated due to the varying sizes of introns located between exons. Since proteins play all essential functions in the cellular environment, predicting/identifying genes that code the functional proteins in a sample is an important task. Considering the importance of gene identification, software like GENMARK [27], Glimmer [28] and Prodigal [29] respectively have been developed. These algorithms perform prediction by taking the advantage of compositional differences among coding regions, "shadow" coding regions (coding on the opposite DNA strand), and noncoding DNA. In gene prediction, there will be a large number of redundant sequences. Hobohm and Sander [30, 31] developed clustering algorithms for non-redundant gene sequences. The basic idea is to divide the gene sequence set into several classes, and then find a representative sequence for each class, and ultimately the set formed by these representative classes is the non-redundant reference gene set. The software for de-redundancy of biological gene data mainly includes NRDB90 [32], CD-HIT [33–35], PICSES [36], etc.

Analyzing metagenomic data has two challenges. One is the relatively low abundant species in the metagenomic samples without reference genome which leads to failure in identification of genes, and the other is the large size of the datasets.

Considering the rapid increase of huge data generated by NGS technology, we believe that the combining of big data technology and distributed gene assembly software can lead to assemble and identify genes accurately. By combining many samples together, the genomic information of low abundant species in the samples has been amplified, and thus better genome assembly results and more genes can be obtained. As a result, it is possible to discover more new genes.

Considering the above facts, based on our previously developed highly scalable gene assembly software SWAP-Assembler 2, we present a workflow, WFswap, which can assemble large genomic data based on many samples and more genes in the samples can be identified/predicted. The workflow has several steps including quality control, genome assembly, gene prediction etc. A similar workflow WFsoap that relies on SOAPdenovo2 for gene assembly is also used in the paper. The test experiments show that the proposed workflow WFswap achieved better performance both for N50 and the number of identified genes compared with WFsoap. WFswap is able to identify 94.2% of the benchmark genes when tested on the 19 metagenomic samples that contains *Bifidobacterium animalis subsp. lactis* CNCM I-2494 [37].

2   Methods

The proposed workflow aims at predicting and identifying genes from the NGS samples. For many metagenomic samples, the proposed method can better predict/identify the genes in the sample, especially for low abundant species, since the genomic information of the low abundant species is amplified with many samples.

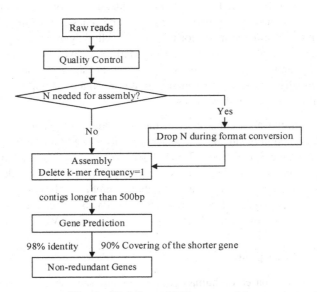

Fig. 1. Workflow of WFswap model

In order to improve the parallelism of the assembly algorithm and decouple the computational data dependence in the assembly algorithm, the method WFswap is proposed in this paper by using SWAP-Assembler 2 assembly software. SWAP-Assembler 2 proposed a mathematical model for assembly of highly extensible gene sequences called bidirectional multi-step graph model. Also, the "lock-computing-unlocking" mechanism is used to calculate the vertices or edges of a graph. Finally, optimization through input parallelization further reduces time usage.

The main workflow of the model is shown in the Fig. 1. Illumina raw sequencing reads from NGS genomic samples are filtered using fastp software [38]. The reads in fastq format are then converted into fasta format by FastX. High-quality reads are then assembled together. Gene prediction is performed for the assembled gene sequences that are longer than 500 bp using MetaGeneMark [39]. After that, predicted genes from all samples were clustered resulting in the non-redundant genes. Detailed descriptions about quality control, gene assembly and prediction are as follows,

- **Quality Control.** There are many errors in Illumina raw sequencing reads. In order to filter these errors for a high quality control, raw sequencing reads were filtered with a quality cutoff of 20 and reads shorter than 30 bp were discarded using fastp software. In WFswap, N base in reads would be dropped during format conversion using FastX.
- **Gene Assembly.** After quality control, reads were assembled into contigs with SWAP-Assembler 2 and SOAPdenovo2, which are all based on de Bruijn graph technology. Assembly parameter K-mer size was all set to 31. We dropped K-mers whose frequency is less than or equal to 1 for the purpose of reducing error information and improving assembly accuracy.
- **Gene Prediction.** Gene prediction attempts to identify a biological pattern in DNA sequences and predict the start and stop regions of genes in the DNA sequence, or the location of protein coding regions. In our workflow, genes were predicted from contigs longer than 500 bp using MetaGeneMark. Any two genes with greater than 98% identity and covering more than 90% of the shorter gene were clustered together. Finally, cluster representatives shorter than 100 bp were discarded resulting in the non-redundant genes.

Different assembly algorithms used in the workflow will generate different gene assembly and prediction results. In this paper we mainly use two assembly algorithms, SWAP-Assembler and SOAPdenovo2. SOAPdenovo2 is a popular assembly algorithm based on single computing node and thus is not able to assembly large datasets, while SWAP-Assembler 2 is a highly scalable/parallel assembly tool aiming at assembling genomic data of Terabytes. The workflow with SWAP-Assembler is referred as WFswap and the workflow with SOAPdenovo2 is referred as WFsoap in this paper.

2.1 Data Sets Description

Our experiments were based on human gut microbiome samples downloaded from the website of EBI [40]. All samples were subject to Illumina deep sequencing resulting in 4.5 Gb sequence per sample on average, and a total of 23.2 billion high-quality sequencing reads with an average length of 77 bp. Among all 396 samples, nineteen of the individuals consumed a defined fermented milk product containing the previously sequenced *Bifidobacterium animalis subsp. lactis* CNCM I-2494, and we used this species as a benchmark to assess the ability of our method to identify the benchmark genes. On average, only 0.3% of the sequence reads in the 19 samples originated from *B. animalis*.

2.2 Experiment Description

In order to evaluate the results, we take the following three metrics, N50 of contigs (referred as N50), the total number of predicted genes by MetaGeneMark and the total number of predicted genes in benchmark. In this paper, we evaluate the performance of our workflows in four steps.

In the first step, we test the workflow on 30 randomly selected single samples. Each sample is subject to the workflow and the results of WFswap and WFsoap are compared. In the second step, a total of four runs were conducted. Each run contains four samples from the 19 benchmark samples and each sample is selected by once. The third step contains three experiments with different sample sizes. We use three groups of samples, group 1 with 4 samples, group 2 with 8 samples and group 3 with 12 samples. Group 2 contains all the 4 samples of group 1, group 3 contains all the samples of group 1 and group 2. In the last experiment we use 6 groups to evaluate the performance of WFswap, with sample sizes ranging from 4 to 30. The aim is to study the effect of increasing number of samples on the results of gene assembly and prediction.

3 Results and Discussion

3.1 Results for Single Samples

The gene assembly and identification results of 30 samples randomly selected from the 396 samples are shown in Table 1. These samples were subject to the two different workflow analysis, WFsoap and WFswap respectively. In order to evaluate the results, we consider the following two metrics, N50 of contigs (referred as N50), and the total number of predicted genes by MetaGeneMark. Table 1 shows the difference in N50 and the difference in the total number of predicted genes between these two workflows. A positive value in Delta_$_{N50}$ and Delta_$_{NG}$ indicates that WFswap performs better than WFsoap. We observe that the difference in N50 ranges from 42 to 268, and for all the 30 randomly selected samples, N50 of WFswap is generally better than WFsoap.

For the non-redundant predicted genes by MetaGeneMark, an average of 2500 more genes are identified/predicted by WFswap compared with those of WFsoap. This clearly indicates the better performance of WFswap on randomly selected samples. On the other hand, 4 out of 30 samples showed negative results, indicating a poor performance for these samples by WFswap.

Table 1. Gene assembly and identification results for 30 single samples

SampleID	Delta_N50*	Delta_NG#	SampleID	Delta_N50*	Delta_NG#
1964914	103	4908	2042840	70	−23,411
1965906	268	12368	2042841	98	−30,116
2041926	188	4644	2042842	105	1,484
2042742	126	11269	2042911	283	8,419
2042828	176	10530	2042916	91	5,948
2042830	53	4838	2042918	112	6,516
2042831	56	5376	2042920	787	1,619
2042832	169	8227	2042982	130	6,173
2042833	212	6246	2042986	121	8,419
2042834	136	−17792	2042988	224	5,425
2042835	153	3193	2042990	93	6,781
2042836	162	9865	2042993	269	8,259
2042837	64	11238	2042995	179	7,822
2042838	42	−35536	2043043	71	11,773
2042839	43	160	2043046	593	6,123

Note: *indicates the difference in N50 value between WFswap and WFsoap workflows; #indicates the difference in total number of predicted genes by MetaGeneMark between WFswap and WFsoap.

3.2 Results for Four Combined Samples

In this section, we assemble the combined dataset of four samples in one run using WFswap and WFsoap. For each run, we selected four samples from the 19 benchmark samples of *B. animalis* and every sample can only be selected once. These 19 benchmark samples consumed a defined fermented milk product containing the previously sequenced *Bifidobacterium animalis subsp. lactis* CNCM I-2494. Overall a total of four runs were conducted, indicated by run1, run2, run3, run4 in Table 2 which shows the assembly and gene prediction results for both WFswap and WFsoap.

In addition to the metrics used in the previous section, we also evaluate results from the perspective of the total number of benchmark genes identified by the method. MetaGeneMark is used for predicting the gene catalogs from the assembly result and each benchmark gene in the *Bifidobacterium animalis subsp. lactis* CNCM I-2494 is mapped to the gene catalogs using BLAST [41]. We downloaded all genes of Bifidobacterium *animalis subsp. lactis* CNCM I-2494 and the total number is 1658. Finally, the identified benchmark genes can be calculated from the BLAST results.

BLAST is used for searching similar sequences during which default parameter were used other than the expected value set to 0.01. The expected value is a parameter that describes the number of hits one can expect to see by chance when searching a database of a particular size. It decreases exponentially as the score of the match increases. By BLAST comparison, we mapped each gene in the benchmark set to the gene catalogs predicted from MetaGeneMark and calculated the number of predicted benchmark genes (**Delta_NBG**).

Table 2. Results for 4 combined samples

	Delta_N50[*]	Delta_NG[#]	Delta_NBG[+]	NBG
Run1	336	69642	24	1538
Run 2	180	54497	10	1261
Run 3	452	59362	30	64
Run 4	373	72138	24	1370

Note:[*]indicates the difference in N50 value between WFswap and WFsoap; [#]indicates the difference in total number of predicted genes by MetaGeneMark between WFswap and WFsoap. [+]indicates the difference in total number of predicted genes by MetaGeneMark that are also in the benchmark between WFswap and WFsoap. NBG indicates the total number of identified benchmark genes.

Table 2 shows the results for 4 combined samples, including the difference in N50 (**Delta_N50**), the difference in the number of predicted genes (**Delta_NG**) and the difference in the number of predicted benchmark genes (**Delta_NBG**) between these two workflows. Our observations reveal WFswap performed better in terms of **Delta_N50**, **Delta_NG**, and **Delta_NBG**. On average, we found 60,000 more genes with WFswap, which corresponds to about 20% of the total number of predicted genes for WFsoap. Because some samples contain a very low amount of benchmark genes, the number of genes predicted is quite different. Despite this, we still found more mapped genes with WFswap. It should be noted that in run 3, only 64 benchmark genes were identified, much less than other runs. This is because two samples used in this run have much less genomic sequence information from the benchmark gene.

3.3   Results of Concatenated and Combined Datasets

Due to the larger memory consumption, some assembly algorithms cannot perform assembly and identification on the combined dataset (all samples assembled together which is referred as COMBINE mode in the paper). One possible strategy is to assemble each sample separately and then concatenate the results together (this is referred as CAT mode in the paper). For SWAP-Assembler, more samples can be assembled together in one run since it is highly parallel and more distributed memory can be used. Since WFsoap is not be able to analyze more than 4 combined samples, it is not tested in this section.

When assembling many samples, we need to compare the difference between the two modes, CAT and COMBINE. In this section, we use three groups of samples, group one with 4 samples, group two with 8 samples and group three with 12 samples. Group 2 contains all the 4 samples of group 1 and Group 3 contains all the samples of group 1 and group 2. Each of the groups are subject to the WFswap analysis, both in CAT and COMBINE modes.

Table 3 shows the detailed N50 values, total number of predicted genes and total number of identified benchmark genes. Generally, COMBINE mode performed better in all metrics. With the increasing number of samples used in each group, more and more genes have been predicted by MetaGeneMark and similar trend is observed for the total number of identified benchmark genes, which is true for both the CAT and COMBINE modes. The reason that COMBINE mode predicted more genes is that gene assembly with COMBINE mode is able to build the de Bruijn graph for all the low abundant genomic information at once, and thus more contigs and genes can be recovered.

Table 3. Comparison between CAT and COMBINE modes for WFswap

	N50	Total number of predicted genes	Total number of identified benchmark genes
4-CAT	454	326694	795
4- COMBINE	608	335604	1370
8-CAT	407	588619	1454
8- COMBINE	622	603474	1511
12-CAT	442	760141	1462
12- COMBINE	592	799174	1550

3.4 Results of Many Samples

From the previous analyses, we found more genes are predicted by WFswap for many samples. We want to further test the results of gene assembly and identification with even more samples. These runs are subjected to COMBINE mode since WFswap is able to assemble large dataset in one run.

We have started with 4 samples, for which WFswap was applied and the results of total numbers of predicted genes and benchmark genes are shown in Table 4. We also add 4 more samples to generate an 8 samples dataset. Similarly, datasets with 12 samples, 16 samples, 19 samples and 30 samples are generated. Each of a bigger dataset contains the samples of the smaller datasets. We performed six experiments in total and all of them are subject to the analysis in COMBINE mode. It should be noted that the first 19 samples correspond to the samples that consumed a defined fermented milk product containing the previously sequenced *Bifidobacterium animalis subsp. lactis* CNCM I-2494.

Table 4. Assembly results for different samples by WFswap

	Total number of predicted genes	Total number of genes in benchmark
4 samples	335064	1370
8 samples	603474	1511
12 samples	799174	1550
16 samples	922406	1549
19 samples	985221	1562
30 samples	1249570	1557

Table 4 shows the prediction for different samples by WFswap. As the number of samples increases, we were able to predict more genes. In terms of total number of genes in benchmark, the overall trend is also increasing. The total number of identified benchmark genes reached maximum of 1562 for 19 samples, corresponding to about 94.2% benchmark genes. This shows that many sample based method can help with gene assembly and prediction. However, for 30 samples, the total number of benchmark genes are reduced by 5 compared with that of 19 samples, this is because the added 11 samples don't contain *Bifidobacterium animalis subsp. lactis* CNCM I-2494 and noise is introduced to the combined dataset.

4   Conclusion

In this article, we have presented a workflow for efficient gene assembly and identification based on many genome samples. The presented workflow is systematically tested on many samples and found that performed better for gene assembly and identification. Also, we have shown combining multiple samples together makes the gene assembly and identification of low abundant species possible. The proposed workflow WFswap is able to analyze many samples in one run, and thus the de Bruijn graph built during the simulation contains more sequence information of the low abundant species than a run with less samples. The test on the 19 benchmark samples shows WFswap is able to identify 94.2% of the benchmark genes, thus the workflow can be effectively applied to large genomic projects with terabytes of data. In future, the presented workflow can be improved to identify more genes by analyzing the bottlenecks in the method.

Acknowledgements. This work was supported by National Key Research & Development Program of China under grant No. 2016YFB0201305, Shenzhen Basic Research Fund under grant no. JCYJ20160331190123578, JCYJ20170413093358429 & GGFW2017073114031767, National Science Foundation under grant no. 61702494 and U1813203. We would also like to thank the funding support by the Shenzhen Discipline Construction Project for Urban Computing and Data Intelligence, Youth Innovation Promotion Association, CAS to Yanjie Wei.

References

1. Qin, J., Li, R., Raes, J., et al.: A human gut microbial gene catalogue established by metagenomic sequencing. Nature **464**, 59–65 (2010)
2. Warren, R.L., Sutton, G.G., Jones, S.J.M., Holt, R.A.: Assembling millions of short DNA sequences using SSAKE. Bioinformatics **4**, 500–501 (2007)
3. Jeck, W.R., Reinhardt, J.A., Baltrus, D.A., et al.: Extending assembly of short DNA sequences to handle error. Bioinformatics **23**, 2942–2944 (2007)
4. Dohm, J.C., Lottaz, C., Borodina, T., Himmelbauer, H.: SHARCGS, a fast and highly accurate short-read assembly algorithm for de novo genomic sequencing. Genome Res. **17**, 1697–1706 (2007)
5. Bang-Jensen, G., Gutin, A., Yeo, A.: When the greedy algorithm fails. Discrete Optim. **1**, 121–127 (2004)

6. Batzoglou, S., Jaffe, D.B., Stanley, K., et al.: ARACHNE: a whole-genome shotgun assembler. Genome Res. **12**, 177–189 (2002)
7. Myers, E.W., Sutton, G.G., Delcher, A.L., et al.: A whole-genome assembly of Drosophila. Science **287**, 2196–2204 (2000)
8. Huang, X., Madan, A.: CAP3: a DNA sequence assembly program. Genome Res. **9**, 868–877 (1999)
9. Huang, X., Yang, S.P.: Generating a genome assembly with PCAP. Curr. Protoc. Bioinformatics **11** (2005). Unit11.3
10. de la Bastide, M., McCombie, W.R.: Assembling genomic DNA sequences with PHRAP. Curr. Protoc. Bioinformatics **11** (2007). Unit11.4
11. Mullikin, J.C., Ning, Z.: The phusion assembler. Genome Res. **13**, 81–90 (2003)
12. Marcel Margulies, M.E., William, E.A., Said, A., et al.: Genome sequencing in open microfabricated high density picoliter reactors. Nature **437**, 376–380 (2005)
13. Pevzner, P.A., Tang, H., Waterman, M.S.: An eulerian path approach to DNA fragment assembly. Proc. Natl. Acad. Sci. **98**, 9748–9753 (2001)
14. Luo, R., et al.: SOAPdenovo2: an empirically improved memory-efficient short-read de novo assembler. GigaScience **1**, 18 (2012)
15. Peng, Y., Leung, H.C.M., Yiu, S.M., et al.: IDBA-UD: a de novo assembler for single-cell and metagenomic sequencing data with highly uneven depth. Bioinformatics **28**, 1420–1428 (2012)
16. Li, D., Liu, C., Luo, R., et al.: MEGAHIT: an ultra-fast single-node solution for large and complex metagenomics assembly via succinct de Bruijn graph. Bioinformatics **31**, 1674–1676 (2015)
17. Meng, J., Seo, S., Balaji, P., et al.: SWAP-Assembler 2: optimization of de novo genome assembler at extreme scale. In: International Conference on Parallel Processing (2016)
18. Li, G., Ma, L., Song, C., et al.: The YH database: the first Asian diploid genome database. Nucleic Acids Res. **37**, D1025–D1028 (2009)
19. Meng, J., Wang, B., Wei, Y., et al.: SWAP-Assembler: scalable and efficient genome assembly towards thousands of cores. BMC Bioinformatics **15**(Suppl 9), S2–S2 (2014)
20. Yang, X.J., Liao, X.K., Lu, K., et al.: The TianHe-1A supercomputer: its hardware and software. J. Comput. Sci. Technol. **26**(3), 344–351 (2011)
21. Meng, J., Wei, Y., Seo, S., et al.: SWAP-Assembler 2: scalable genome assembler towards millions of cores – practice and experience. In: IEEE/ACM International Symposium on Cluster (2015)
22. Liao, X., Xiao, L., Yang, C., Lu, Y.: MilkyWay-2 supercomputer: system and application. Front. Comput. Sci. **8**, 345–356 (2014)
23. Xu, W., Lu, Y., Li, Q., et al.: Hybrid hierarchy storage system in MilkyWay-2 supercomputer. Front. Comput. Sci. **8**, 367–377 (2014)
24. Liao, X., Pang, Z., Wang, K., et al.: High performance interconnect network for Tianhe system. J. Comput. Sci. Technol. **30**, 259–272 (2015)
25. Kumaran, K.: Introduction to Mira, in Code for Q Workshop (2016)
26. Meng, J., Guo, N., Ge, J., et al.: Scalable assembly for massive genomic graphs. In: Proceedings of the 17th IEEE/ACM International Symposium on Cluster, Cloud and Grid Computing (CCGRID 2017), Madrid (2017)
27. Borodovsky, M., Mclninch, J.: GeneMark: parallel gene recognition for both DNA strands. Comput. Chem. **17**, 123–133 (1993)
28. Salzberg, S., Delcher, A., Kasif, S., White, O.: Microbial gene identification using interpolated Markov models. Nucleic Acids Res. **26**, 544–548 (1998)
29. Hyatt, D., Chen, G.L., Locascio, C.L., et al.: Prodigal: prokaryotic gene recognition and transla-tion initiation site identification. BMC Bioinformatics **11**, 119 (2010)

30. Hobohm, U., Scharf, M., Schneider, R., et al.: Selection of representative protein data sets. Protein Sci. **1**(3), 409–417 (2010)
31. Hobohm, U., Sander, C.: Enlarged representative set of protein structures. Protein Sci. **3**(3), 522–524 (2010)
32. Holm, L., Sander, C.: Removing near-neighbour redundancy from large protein sequence collections. Bioinformatics **14**(5), 423–429 (1998)
33. Li, W., Jaroszewski, L., Godzik, A.: Clustering of highly homologous sequences to reduce the size of large protein databases. Bioinformatics **17**(3), 282–283 (2001)
34. Li, W., Jaroszewski, L., Godzik, A.: Tolerating some redundancy significantly speeds up clustering of large protein databases. Bioinformatics **18**(1), 77–82 (2002)
35. Li, W.: Fast program for clustering and comparing large sets of protein or nucleotide sequences. In: Nelson, K.E. (ed.) Encyclopedia of Metagenomics. Springer, Boston (2015). https://doi.org/10.1007/978-1-4899-7478-5
36. Wang, G., Dunbrack Jr., R.L.: PISCES: a protein sequence culling server. Bioinformatics **19** (12), 1589 (2003)
37. Chervaux, C., Grimaldi, C., Bolotin, A., et al.: Genome sequence of the probiotic strain Bifidobacterium animalis subsp. lactis CNCM I-2494. J. Bacteriol. **93**(19), 5560–5561 (2011)
38. Shifu, C., Yanqing, Z., Yaru, C., et al.: fastp: an ultra-fast all-in-one FASTQ preprocessor. Bioinformatics **34**, i884–i890 (2018)
39. Zhu, W., Lomsadze, A., Borodovsky, M.: Ab initio gene identification in meta-genomic sequences. Nucleic Acids Res. **38**, e132 (2010)
40. Park, Y.M., Squizzato, S., et al.: The EBI search engine: EBI search as a service – making biological data accessible for all. Nucleic Acids Res. **45**, W545–W549 (2017)
41. Altschul, S., Warren, G., Miller, W., Eugene, M., Lipman, D.: Basic local alignment search tool. J. Mol. Biol. **215**, 403–410 (1990)

A Neural Framework for Joint Prediction on Intent Identification and Slot Filling

Jiawei Shan[1], Huayun Xu[1], Zeyang Gong[1], Hanchen Su[1], Xu Han[2], and Binyang Li[1(✉)]

[1] School of Information Science and Technology,
University of International Relations, Beijing, China
{jwshan,hyxu,zygong,hcsu,byli}@uir.edu.cn
[2] College of Information Engineering, Capital Normal University,
Beijing, China
hanxu@cnu.edu.cn

Abstract. In task-oriented dialog systems, understanding of users' queries (expressed in natural language) is a process of parsing users' queries and converting them into some structure that machine can handle. The understanding usually consists of two parts, namely intent identification and slot filling. To address this problem, we propose a neural framework, named SI-LSTM, that combines two tasks and integrates CRF into LSTM network, where the slot information is extracted by using CRF, and the intent will be identified by using LSTM. In our approach, the slot information is used for determining the intent, while the intent type is used to rectify the slot filling deviation. Based on the dataset provided by NLPCC 2018, SI-LSTM achieved 90.71% on intent identification, slot filling and error correction in terms of accuracy.

Keywords: Deep learning · Intent identification · Slot filling

1 Introduction

In task-oriented dialog systems, understanding of users' queries (expressed in natural language) is a process of parsing users' queries and converting them into some structure that machine can handle. The understanding usually consists of two parts, namely intent identification and slot filling. The textual strings, fed into a dialog system as input, are mostly the transcripts translated from spoken language by ASR (Automatic Speech Recognition) and thus subject to recognition errors.

Intent identification is to recognize the behavioral goals of the queries or sentences presented by users, such as playing music or booking tickets. Slot filling targets on extracting the semantic slot information related to the specific intents from conversation. Take the task of playing music as an example. When user intents to play music, the information of singer and song are the slots that are required to be extracted and filled. The former is considered as a classification problem, while the latter is a sequential labeling problem. Generally, as to the spoken language understanding in task-oriented dialog systems, intent identification and slot filling aim at converting

R. Xu et al. (Eds.): ICCC 2019, LNCS 11518, pp. 12–25, 2019.
https://doi.org/10.1007/978-3-030-23407-2_2

human natural language expressions into structured information. NLPCC 2018 [22] provides an annotated dataset which covers three domains, namely music, navigation and phone call.

There are much research on these two issues. Traditional approaches toward intent identification include rules matching and machine learning algorithms. These approaches was proved effective in some specific domains. However, as the size of the corpora grows dramatically, it is difficult to extract characteristics from general domain. Under this state, some deep learning techniques were applied, including convolutional neural networks (CNN) [19] and recurrent neural network (RNN) [20], especially long-short time memory (LSTM) [21], and so on. Similar situations occurred in slot filling task [14–16].

Our team tries to conduct a model to handle both tasks in spoken language understanding in task-oriented dialogue systems efficiently. We propose a neural framework, named SI-LSTM model, for tackling the intent identification and slot filling. SI-LSTM integrates CRF into an LSTM network, where the CRF will segment the words into different parts of entities and generate the sequential labels for slot filling; and the LSTM will maintain the semantics of each sentence for intent identification. SI-LSTM combines intent identification and slot filling together, and the slot information is used for determining the intent while each type of the intent is used to rectify the slot filling deviation.

Based on the dataset provided by NLPCC 2018, SI-LSTM successfully improves the accuracy of each task, and achieved 90.71% on intent identification, slot filling and error correction in terms of accuracy.

2 Related Works

In this paper, there are two main tasks that are intent identification and slot filling. It is required to firstly identify the intent and then fill the corresponding slot with respect to the specific intent. Intent identification is usually considered as a classification problem, which is to classify each query into a corresponding intent category, while slot filling is regarded as a sequential labeling issue. In this section, we will introduce the current studies on these two tasks.

Table 1. The samples of intent type and the slot information.

Intent	Slot
music.play	song, singer, theme, style, age, toplist, emotion, language, instrument, scene
navigation.navigation	destination, origin, custom_destination
phone_call.make_a_phone_call	phone_num, contact_name

2.1 Intent Identification

There are many previous researches on intent identification task, and most of them can be divided into three categories.

[1] presented a rule-based method and designed different templates for tackling this problem. For different intent categories, various thesauruses were constructed to facilitate to identify the intent in the specific domain. More specifically, based on the previous collected records, a list of intents will be listed that are computed by probability distribution. However, this method required too much professional knowledge to construct all the rules, and it is rather time-consuming.

[2, 3] proposed machine learning approaches for intent identification, and Support Vector Machine (SVM), Naive Bayesian, and Decision Trees (DT) [3]. Most of the approaches focused on either feature construction or model selection. These methods have been proved to be effective in the accuracy improvement on the identification. Yet since corpora have become more and more random, it is difficult to find uniform features to figure out all intents.

More recently, researchers attempted to utilize deep learning technology to classify the intent, since the attributes of each sentence can be represented well. For instance, CNN [4], RNN [20], LSTM [5] were widely applied. Also, user profiling tried to guide the intent identification and perform the determination [6]. It was proved that these neural network models worked better on intent identification and speeded up the training process.

2.2 Slot Filling

Since our model also targets at the slot filling, we review the related works on slot filling from the following three aspects as well.

Firstly, rule-based methods are proposed. Based on linguistic rules, slot filling was usually accomplished by matching different rules. Despite a high accuracy, much time and abundant knowledge in specific field are required. After that, many statistical models were applied to solve the problem, which was proved efficient and effective. Hidden Markov Model (HMM) [7] and CFG [8] and Conditional Random Field (CRF) [9] are widely used for the sequential tagging problems. Then, researchers today begin to apply RNN [10] into slot filling, and many advantages are explored, including faster training process, a flexible architecture, effective performance, and so on. More importantly, these neural network models can be integrated by the sequential tagging model, such as HMM, CRF, which will further improve the performance.

Our work is inspired by the studies above, and we design a SI-LSTM model for intent identification and slot filling, which will be described in the following section.

3   Joint Prediction on Intent Identification and Slot Filling

In task-oriented dialog systems, the comprehension of users' queries is a process of parsing users' queries and converting them into some structures that machine can handle. This comprehension usually consists of two parts, namely intent identification and slot filling.

It is obvious that there is a strong correlation between intent identification and slot filling, and both of them can be mapped into a certain scope, especially in the dataset provided by NLPCC [22]. For example, some specific slot categories such as *song*, *language, toplist*, etc. will only appear in the sentences about *music.play*, rather than *navigation.navigation*. The correlations between the intention and the slot are shown in Table 1.

Besides, the dataset can be seen as a stream of user queries ordered by time stamp. The stream is further split into a series of segments according to the gaps of time stamps between queries and each segment is denoted as a 'session'. Instead of being separated contexts, the contexts within a session is correlated with previous ones. For example, given the input text "张三 (Zhang San)" (a singer's name), only when the latest intention is *phone_call.make_a_phone_call*, the current intent will be recognized as *phone_call.make_a_phone_call*, and the slot information will be "<contact_-name> 张三 <contact_name>". Otherwise, the intent will be classified into *OTHERS* and the slot information is empty.

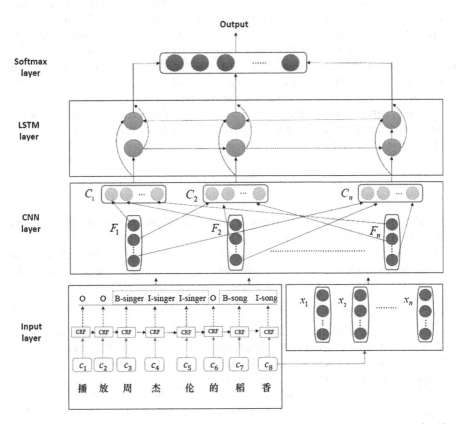

Fig. 1. The structure of SI-LSTM. (The Chinese sentence in the example means that play the song by Jay Chou.)

Based on the above observation, we design a neural framework to tackle two tasks at the same time, named SI-LSTM. The structure of the SI-LSTM is shown in Fig. 1. SI-LSTM is a four-layer neural framework, consisting of a CRF layer, a CNN layer, a LSTM layer and n fully connected layer Firstly, each word in a sentence is regarded as the input to the CRF layer to generate the sequential label. After the CRF layer, slot filling results are obtained. Then the output of CRF layer together with the vectorized representation is putted into the CNN layer to extract rich semantics feature. On top of that, the LSTM layer enhances the use of text word order and time information. In the end, the fully connected layer will output the prediction result of the intent identification. Since the contexts within a session are taken into, we set up a memory cell to store the latest user intent. In this way, SI-LSTM will take the memory cell as a reference when it outputs the final result of the classification.

3.1 Conditional Random Field Layer

In our Conditional Random Field (CRF) layer, we utilize the classic CRF [11] model for sequential labeling, which attempts to model the conditional probability distribution P(Y|C). Our model first uses CRF for named entity recognition and slot filling.

Based on the given sentence, the CRF layer will firstly segment the words into different parts of entities, and then classify each entity according to the type, such as person, organization, location, and so on. To avoid of the limitations of the data bias towards the states with few successor states, our CRF layer is designed to have the ability to relax strong independence assumptions made in other models.

Given the observation C, the model based on the assumption of first order Markov chain predicts the hidden sequence Y represent the attributes of the entities.

Conditional distribution is computed by Eq. (1):

$$P(Y|C) = \frac{1}{Z(c)} e^{\sum_i \sum_j \lambda_j f_j(y_{i-1}, y_i, c, i)} \tag{1}$$

where $Z(c)$ is a normalizing constant, and λ_j is the bias weight learned from the training data, and f_j is the feature function.

In our CRF layer, the output will be considered as the input for the CNN layer, in this way both the sequential label and the semantics information will be maintained.

3.2 CNN Layer

Inspired by the good feature extraction capabilities of CNN [12], we also use a CNN layer to extract features from texts. Meanwhile in this layer we will combine the slot filling categories with intent identification for the further processing.

Without the loss of generality, for each sentence s, it can be formulated as a word sequence $s = \{w_1, w_2, \ldots, w_L\}$, where L denotes the length of s. The objective of intent identification is produce y_i for each s_i, and y_i is belonging one of the intent type. Then in the CNN layer, an n-dimensional vector is obtained by the combination of the whole words in the sentence shown in Eq. (2).

$$x_{1:n} = x_1 \oplus x_2 \oplus x_3 \oplus \ldots \oplus x_n \tag{2}$$

The convolutional layer is mainly used to capture the local information between words based on a sliding window. In our CNN layer, the length is denoted by h and the size is denoted by $\omega \in \mathbb{R}^{hk}$, which means that from i_{th} word to the $i + h - 1_{th}$ word will be covered. Then the convolution kernel obtains a characteristic representation by Eq. (3).

$$f_i = f(\omega_i \cdot x_{i:i+h-1} + b) \tag{3}$$

The convolution kernel sequentially convolves all the windows in the sentence to get a feature map $F \in \mathbb{R}^{n-h+1}$ shown in Eq. (4).

$$F = [f_1, f_2, \ldots, f_{n-h+1}] \tag{4}$$

A max pooling is used to get the max dimension from each feature map as the final feature and retains only the most representative features in the feature vector.

The *Softmax* function is used to output the results which can be seen as the conditional probability distribution shown in Eq. (5), and it help us determine the most likely intent shown in Eq. (6).

$$P_\theta(y_j | h_{s_i}) = softmax(h_{s_i}\omega + b) \tag{5}$$

$$Y_{pred} = argmax P_\theta \tag{6}$$

In our CNN layer, by using the classic CNN model, the input vector will be converted into a new fixed-length global vector which contains the most representative feature. Meanwhile, the training process is accelerated.

3.3 Long Short-Term Memory Layer

In LSTM layer, our model will encode the information from the vector converted by CNN into a fixed-length vector representation. In our task, the dialogue is a hierarchical sequence of data: each sentence is a sequence of words, and each session is a list of sentences.

The long and short term memory layer consists of several repeated cells, and each of them receives the output of the hidden layer h_{t-1} at the previous time and the current input h_t. Each cell is made up of an input gate i_t, an oblivion gate f_t and an output gate o_t. For every neuron in LSTM, the whole working process is as follows:

$$i_t = \sigma(w_t^i \cdot x_t + w_t^i \cdot h_{t-1} + b_t) \tag{7}$$

$$f_t = \sigma(w_t^f \cdot x_t + w_t^f \cdot h_{t-1} + b_t) \tag{8}$$

$$q_t = tanh(w_t^q \cdot x_t + w_t^q \cdot h_{t-1} + b_q) \tag{9}$$

$$o_t = \sigma(w_o \cdot x_t + w_o \cdot h_{t-1} + b_o) \tag{10}$$

$$c_t = f_t \odot c_{t-1} + i_t \odot q_t \tag{11}$$

$$h_t = o_t \odot tanh(c_t) \tag{12}$$

Each vector of the feature combination layer is obtained by sequentially connecting the elements corresponding to the i_{th} dimension of each convolutional feature map shown in the Eq. (13).

$$C_i = F_1^i \oplus F_2^i \oplus F_3^i \oplus \ldots \oplus F_{n-h+1}^i \tag{13}$$

We will get $n - h + 1$ combination vectors so that each vector is recombined according to the convolution order to ensure the temporality of the text. Then the vectors are sequentially sent to the LSTM cell. The output of the last hidden layer is obtained as the final sentence representation and finally, the prediction result would be identified by the Softmax layer.

4 Spelling Correction

Among the process of slot filling, we need to handle the Chinese typos in the slot, thus the work of spelling correction is needed. Spelling correction has two requirements: to recognize the typos and to find the correct answers. For this consideration, we should design our method to calculate the string similarity such as Edit Distance and determine whether the lot is a typo by using the corresponding thesaurus and find the correct answer for each typo.

4.1 Preprocessing

Since the training corpus and test corpus in this task both contain multiple languages and some other characteristics may impose obstacles to the result, data preprocessing is supposed to be necessary.

There are a few obstacles. First of all, given the fact that Arabic numbers and Chinese numbers are considered as completely different character in this research, the conversion between Arabic numbers and Chinese numbers is necessary. When it comes to the expression of exact years such as '2002', the conversion should follow the Chinese traditional expression.

Then the multiple languages could be another problem not only in the process of comparing the similarity between strings, but also in the process of getting each word's Chinese Pinyin. In order to reduce the negative influence from the foreign languages on comparing Chinese Pinyin, all consecutive foreign characters in each slot are regarded as one Pinyin.

4.2 Congruent Length in String Order

We design our approach to compute the string similarity, especially when the string is missing one or two characters. Since the lengths of two strings are crucial for the similarity computation, we use the following equation to compute the similarity when the congruent length(Cl) is not less than a predefined value.

$$Sim = 0.8 + 0.01 * Cl \quad \text{where} \quad Cl \geq k \tag{14}$$

The parameter k is the congruent length, which is defined as follows.

$$k = \begin{cases} 2 & 2 \leq slotlength \leq 4 \\ slotlength - [0.4 * slotlength] & 5 \leq slotlength \leq 7 \\ 6 & slotlength \geq 8 \end{cases} \qquad (15)$$

4.3 Edit Distance

We also treat the edit distance [13] as another measurement to calculate similarity between two strings. We regard the edit distance as the minimum number of times needed to edit a single character (such as modify, insert, delete) when changing from one string to another. The smaller the edit distance is, the higher the similarity will be. This time complexity of this algorithm is $O(m * n)$ and space complexity is $O(m * n)$. m and n stand for the length of string a and b.

4.4 Spelling Correction

In this task, the content and the category of input slots are the two variables. At first, the content will be matched to the thesaurus in accordance with the specific category. If the content is appeared in the corresponding thesaurus, this content is not a spelling error. On the contrary, the algorithm will calculate its possibility of becoming a spelling error. Then the remaining slots will be compared with all the strings comparing to the thesaurus and then we obtain the highest similarity.

In our model, we design three ways to calculate the similarity of two strings. The first measurement is congruent length in string order. If there are qualified strings in corresponding thesaurus we will achieve the first similarity. The second measurement is edit distance(lev). This could be used to calculate the similarity in this way.

$$sim = 1 - \frac{lev}{slotlength} \qquad (17)$$

The third measurement is the edit distance(lev) between Chinese Pinyins. We define a parameter m to measure the similarity of the conversion between the character to Pinyin. Then the similarity can be computed by the following equation.

$$sim = 1 - \frac{m * lev}{slotlength} \qquad (18)$$

In our experiment, based on the performance on training dataset, we set $m = 1.8$.

With the incensement of the similarity, the corresponding slot is more likely a typo. On the contrary, this means that this slot is not similar to any strings in the corpus and is not likely to be a typo. We set a variable $p = 0.55$ to help us determine whether the slot is a typo. We take the biggest measurement among these three to represent the overall possibility. When the biggest measurement is bigger than p, then this slot is a spelling error and the corresponding string is the correct answer.

5   Experiment

In this section, we will report the performance of our proposed approach SI-LSTM based on the dataset provided by NLPCC 2018 [22].

5.1   Experiment Setup

NLPCC 2018 [22] provides a dialogue dataset focusing on three scenarios, namely music, navigation and telephone. The training dataset is consisted of 4,707 real annotated dialogue sessions, including 21,350 sentences and 11 intents. According to our statistics, there are 4.5 sentences in per session in average. As to the test dataset, 1,177 dialogue sessions containing 5,349 sentences are involved, and there are 4.5 sentences in per session on average as well. The training and test dataset information is shown in Table 2.

Table 2. The description of training and test dataset.

	Sessions	Sentences	Intents	Avg # of sentences in per session
Training set	4707	21350	11	4.5
Test set	1177	5349	11	4.5

To better demonstrate the dataset, we also list some statistics in Table 3. There are 11 types of intent in total, and the type of *music.play* contains the most sessions except for *OTHERS*. Note that, for some types of the intents, a corresponding thesaurus is also provided, which can help us to extract the slot information and spelling correction.

Table 3. The statistics of the dataset.

Intent	Training set	Test set
music.play	6,403	1,641
music.pause	298	75
music.prev	5	4
music.next	132	34
navigation.navigation	3,961	1,039
navigation.open	245	56
navigation.start_navigation	33	4
navigation.cancel_navigation	836	206
phone_call.make_a_phone_call	2,789	674
phone_call.cancel	22	18
OTHERS	6,628	1,641

In our training process, the dataset was randomly divided into 9:1, with training set (90%), validation set (10%), to train our model and tune some parameters.

In this task, $F1_{macro}$ is used as the evaluation metrics.

$$P_{macro} = \frac{1}{N} \sum_{i=1}^{N} \frac{\text{\# of queries correctly predicted as intent } c_i}{\text{\# of queries predicted as intent } c_i}$$

$$R_{macro} = \frac{1}{N} \sum_{i=1}^{N} \frac{\text{\# of queries correctly predicted as intent } c_i}{\text{\# of queries labelled as intent } c_i}$$

$$F1_{macro} = \frac{2}{\frac{1}{P_{macro}} + \frac{1}{R_{macro}}}$$

5.2 Experimental Results

We deal with all the three tasks, intent identification, slot filling and spelling correction, and we will report the results in this subsection. Moreover, other approaches, such as SVM, LSTM, etc., are also implemented for the comparison with SI-LSTM on the provided dataset.

Intent Identification. SI-LSTM was implemented based on the open source library Keras in Python which was backended by Tensorflow. In SI-LSTM, we trained our word embedding by using word2vec based on the whole dataset, and set the dimensionality as 50. 50 epochs were run in total, and the parameters were updated after each batch. We finally set the parameter with the value when the model achieved highest accuracy.

To better demonstrate the performance of our model, we also redesign some classic models for intent identification, including SVM [17], FastText [18], and LSTM. SVM is a classic supervised machine learning algorithm and LSTM is a representative deep learning algorithm. FastText is a classifier developed by Facebook that provides a simple and efficient way to represent textual information. These three models are widely used in NLP research and can provide basic support. Besides, since the slot information works as an important factor, we also integrate it into the three traditional models, and get S-SVM, S-FastText, S-LSTM.

The performance of each model on test set was shown in Table 4.

From Table 4, we can find that our proposed model SI-LSTM achieved the best run in both metrics, which proved the effectiveness of our model. Although SVM is non-deep learning model, the accuracy was 90.43% and the $F1_{macro}$ was 81.97%, that were comparable with other deep learning models. To the contrary, FastText performed poor in both accuracy and $F1_{macro}$. We can also find that compared with basic models, the $F1_{macro}$. The accuracy and $F1_{macro}$ were both improved when putting the slot information into the model. In Table 4.

What's more, the combination of CNN and LSTM accelerates the training process greatly. Also, if we eliminate some minimum categories which contain only a few number of sentences, we are able to see a more surprising output from SI-LSTM.

Table 4. The comparison between different models.

Model	Accuracy	$F1_{macro}$
SVM	90.43%	81.97%
FastText	87.90%	82.27%
LSTM	90.60%	86.26%
S-SVM	91.30%	78.41%
S-FastText	94.10%	85.47%
S-LSTM	93.64%	87.49%
SI-LSTM	**94.52%**	**87.73%**

In our experiment, we also list the accuracy and recall of each type of intent as shown in Table 5.

Table 5. The results of each type of intent.

Intent	Accuracy	Recall
music.play	94.30%	98.78%
music.pause	80%	64%
music.prev	100%	75%
music.next	91.18%	91.18%
navigation.navigation	95.11%	99.13%
navigation.open	100%	91.07%
navigation.start_navigation	100%	100%
navigation.cancel_navigation	89.89%	86.41%
phone_call.make_a_phone_call	87.65%	97.92%
phone_call.cancel	100%	16.67%

Spelling Correction. Since the typos only appear in the slots, the spelling correction is based on the result of slot filling. Besides, we will focus on the errors that are related to *music* and *navigation*, and other fields, e.g. *phone calls*, are not considered. The experimental results are shown in Tables 6 and 7.

Table 6. The confusion matrix of spelling correction on both training set and test set.

Table head		Predict	
		Non-typos	Typos
Training data	Non-typos	5,913	51
	Typos	46	252
Test data	Non-typos	1,485	13
	Typos	6	82

Table 7. The result of spelling correction.

Types	# of typos	# of correction	Accuracy
Song	71	63	88.73%
Singer	11	7	63.63%
Total	82	70	85.37%

Intent Identification and Slot Filling Results. We evaluated the performance on both intent identification and slot filling (with spelling correction) on the SVM, FastText, basic LSTM and SI-LSTM, and the results are shown in Table 8.

Table 8. The comparison between different models on intent identification with slot filling.

Model	Accuracy
SVM	84.49%
FastText	84.90%
LSTM	84.56%
S-SVM	72.67%
S-FastText	89.25%
S-LSTM	89.08%
SI-LSTM	**90.71%**

It is obviously that the accuracy of model for the joint prediction on slot filling and intent recognition achieved the best performance.

5.3 Discussion

Based on the above experimental results, we summarized some characteristics of our approach and made some error analysis.

SI-LSTM achieved a high accuracy in intent identification, but performed not as good in the metric of $F1_{macro}$. In Table 5, we can see the recall of our model is very low under '*phone_call.cancel*' intent which in turn imposes negative effect on $F1_{macro}$, although the size of that type is quite small, i.e. 18. In fact, many contents under this type '*phone_call.cancel*' only express the instruction of cancel or stop, but few mention the specific objection of the instruction. So the classification of this specific intent needs to account for the previous content and it is difficult for the model to distinguish between '*music.pause*', '*navigation.cancel_navigation*' and '*phone_call.cancel*'. Regarding that there are only 22 data in training set and 18 data in test set under the intent '*phone_call.cancel*', the volume of data does greatly affect the final result of the model.

Besides, in the task of spelling correction, multiple languages occur in a session. Due to limited resources, the result of typo detection is susceptible by the volume and quality of thesauruses. Therefore, for the slots beyond the thesaurus, it is difficult for our model to distinguish the intent accurately.

6   Conclusions

In this paper, we propose a neural framework, named SI-LSTM, for intent identification and slot filling. SI-LSTM combines two tasks and integrates CRF into a LSTM network, where the slot information is extracted by using CRF, while the intent will be identified by using LSTM. In our approach, the slot information is used for determining the intent, and the intent type is used for slot filling. Based on the dataset provided by NLPCC 2018, SI-LSTM achieved 90.71% on intent identification, slot filling and error correction in terms of accuracy.

Acknowledgement. This work is partially funded by the National Natural Science Foundation of China (61602326, U1636103, 61672361, and U1536207) and the Fundamental Research Fund for the Central Universities (3262019T29 and 3262019T54).

References

1. De, A., Kopparapu, S.K.: A Rule-Based Short Query Intent Identification System. Submitted on 25 Mar 2015
2. Song, X., Zheng, Y., Cao, H.: Research on driver's lane change intention recognition based on HMM and SVM. J. Electron. Meas. Instrum. **30**(1), 58–65 (2016)
3. Worachartcheewan, A., Nantasenamat, C.: Identification of metabolic syndrome using decision tree analysis. Diabetes Res. Clin. Prac. **90**(1), e15–e18 (2010)
4. Turra, G., Arrigoni, S., Signoroni, A.: CNN-based identification of hyperspectral bacterial signatures for digital microbiology. In: Battiato, S., Gallo, G., Schettini, R., Stanco, F. (eds.) ICIAP 2017. LNCS, vol. 10485, pp. 500–510. Springer, Cham (2017). https://doi.org/10.1007/978-3-319-68548-9_46
5. Ren, J., et al.: Look, Listen and Learn - A Multimodal LSTM for Speaker Identification. Accessed 13 Feb 2016
6. Rezaei, B.A., Roychowdhury, V., Ghate, S., Khajehnouri, N., Boscolo, R., Mracek, J.: Concept-level user intent profile extraction and applications. Accessed 03 June 2014
7. Rabiner, L.R., Juang, B.H.: An introduction to HMMs. IEEE ASSP Mag. **3**(1), 4–16 (1986)
8. Wang, Y.-Y., Acero, A.: Combination of CFG and n-gram modeling in semantic grammar learning. In: European Conference on Speech Communication & Technology, pp. 2809–2812 (2003)
9. SUN, X., WANG, H.: Intent determination and slot filling in question answering. J. Chin. Inf. Process. **31**(6), 132–139 (2017)
10. Pollack, J.B.F.: Recursive distributed representations. Artif. Intell. **46**(1–2), 77–105 (1990)
11. Lafferty, J., McCallum, A., Pereira, F.C.: Conditional random fields: probabilistic models for segmenting and labeling sequence data. In: Proceedings 18th International Conference on Machine Learning, pp. 282–289. Morgan Kaufmann (2001)
12. Collobert, R., Weston, J.: A unified architecture for natural language processing: deep neural networks with multitask learning. In: Proceedings of the 25th International Conference on Machine Learning. ICML 2008, pp.160–167. ACM, New York, 01 January 2008
13. Levenshtein, V.I.: Binary codes capable of correcting deletions, insertions, and reversals. Sov. Phys. Dokl. **10**(8), 707–710 (1966)
14. Huang, Z., Xu, W., Yu, K.: Bidirectional LSTM-CRF Models for Sequence Tagging. Computer Science (2015)

15. Mesnil, G., Dauphin, Y., Yao, K.: Using recurrent neural networks for slot filling in spoken language understanding. IEEE/ACM Trans. Audio Speech Lang. Process. **23**(3), 530–539 (2015)
16. Yao, K., Peng, B., Zweig, G., Yu, D., Li, X., Gao, F.: Recurrent conditional random fields for language understanding. In: ICASSP (2014)
17. Cortes, C., Vapnik, V.: Support-vector networks. Mach. Learn. **20**, 273–297 (1995)
18. Joulin, A., Grave, E., Bojanowski, P., Mikolov, T.: Bag of Tricks for Efficient Text Classification. arXiv preprint arXiv:1607.01759 (2016)
19. Lecun, Y., Boser, B., Denker, J.S., et al.: Backpropagation applied to handwritten zip code recognition. Neural Comput. **1**(4), 541–551 (1989)
20. Graves, A., Mohamed, A., Hinton, G.: Speech Recognition with Deep Recurrent Neural Networks. arxiv (2013)
21. Hochreiter, S., Schmidhuber, J.: Long short-term memory. Neural Comput. **9**(8), 1735–1780 (1997). https://doi.org/10.1162/neco.1997.9.8.1735. PMID 9377276
22. Zhao, X., Cao, Y.: Overview of the NLPCC 2018 shared task: spoken language understanding in task-oriented dialog systems. In: Zhang, M., Ng, V., Zhao, D., Li, S., Zan, H. (eds.) NLPCC 2018. LNCS (LNAI), vol. 11109, pp. 468–478. Springer, Cham (2018). https://doi.org/10.1007/978-3-319-99501-4_46

Conditional Joint Model for Spoken Dialogue System

Changliang Li[1]([✉]), Yan Zhao[2], and Dong Yu[2]

[1] Kingsoft AI Lab, Beijing, China
`lichangliang@kingsoft.com`
[2] Beijing Language and Culture University, Beijing, China
`zhaoyan.nlp@gmail.com`, `yudong@blcu.edu.cn`

Abstract. Spoken Language Understanding (SLU) and Dialogue Management (DM) are two core components of a spoken dialogue system. Traditional methods model SLU and DM separately. Recently, joint learning has made much progress in dialogue system research via taking full advantage of all supervised signals. In this paper, we propose an extension of joint model to a conditional setting. Our model does not only share knowledge between intent and slot, but also efficiently make use of intent as a condition to predict system action. We conduct experiments on popular benchmark DSTC4, which includes rich dialogues derived from real world. The results show that our model gives excellent performance and outperforms other popular methods significantly, including independent learning methods and joint models. This paper gives a new way for spoken dialogue system research.

Keywords: Joint learning · Spoken language understanding ·
Dialogue management

1 Introduction

One long-term goal in artificial intelligence field is to build an intelligent human-machine dialogue system, which is capable of understanding human's language and giving smooth and correct responses. Especially with the success of new speech- based human-computer interfaces, there is a great need for effective dialogue agents, such as digital personal assistants, which can handle everyday tasks such as booking flights. SLU and DM are two essential parts in building a spoken dialogue system [1].

A typical dialogue system is designed to execute the following components: (i) automatic speech recognition converts a spoken query into transcription; (ii) spoken language understanding (SLU) component analyzes the transcription to extract semantic representations; (iii) dialogue manager (DM) interprets the semantic information and decides the best system action, according to which the system response is further generated either as a natural language output or a result page.

© Springer Nature Switzerland AG 2019
R. Xu et al. (Eds.): ICCC 2019, LNCS 11518, pp. 26–36, 2019.
https://doi.org/10.1007/978-3-030-23407-2_3

SLU aims to obtain semantic representations in user utterances. In SLU, there are two main tasks: slot filling and intent detection. Slot filling aims to assign a semantic concept to each word in an utterance. Intent detection aims to identify the intent that users express. DM is responsible for controlling the dialogue flow, tracking the dialogue states and deciding what actions the system should take to handle the interaction between users and system. For DM, we focus on system action prediction (SAP) in this work.

Traditional approaches train SLU model and SAP model separately, which may have restrictions on knowledge sharing. In order to take full advantage of all supervised signals and utilize the information from both tasks, some joint models have been explored [2,3]. However, the traditional way of joint learning is just combining the loss functions of slot filling and intent detection, which brings the limitation that the information is hard to be used and transmitted effectively. We consider that intent labels, slot tags and actions are correlated, and intent information is helpful for slot filling and SAP. We use intent information as condition to integrate with semantic representations for slot filling and SAP.

In this paper, we propose a conditional joint model that can be used to perform SLU and SAP. In our model, we obtain the semantic representations by a shared Bi-LSTM layer. Meanwhile, intent information is provided to predict slot tags, and is used as a condition to predict system action. Moreover, knowledge between the three supervised signals can be shared implicitly by joint learning. We evaluate our model on the popular benchmark DSTC4 dataset. The results show that our model has a great performance and outperforms other popular methods significantly.

The rest of our paper is structured as follows: Sect. 2 discusses related work, Sect. 3 gives a detailed description of our model, Sect. 4 presents experiments results and analysis, and Sect. 5 summarizes this work and the future direction.

2 Related Work

In this section, we introduce some previous work on SLU and SAP.

Firstly, SLU consists of two tasks: slot filling and intent detection. Traditionally, slot filling can be viewed as a sequence labeling task and intent detection can be viewed as an utterance classification task. These two tasks are usually processed by different models separately.

Machine learning methods such as hidden Markov models (HMM) [4] or conditional random fields (CRF) [5] have been widely employed for slot filling. These methods need complicated feature engineering. However, models with neural network architectures show advantages in feature generation and have a good performance on slot filling task. RNNs are applied in [6–8]. [9] utilized LSTM to generate context-aware distributions for capturing temporal dependencies. [10] enhanced the LSTM-based slot filling to model label dependencies.

Several classifiers such as SVM [11], Adaboost [12] and maximum entropy [13] have been employed for intent detection. With the development of deep learning, deep belief networks (DBNs) have been applied [14]. [15] proposed an RNN architecture to improve intent detection.

In recent years, joint learning of slot filling and intent detection are explored for utilizing some shared knowledge. [16] utilized CNN based triangular CRF to extract features for joint learning slot filling and intent detection. [17,18] adapted RNNS for joint learning of SF and ID. [19] presented a contextual method to exploit possible correlations among intent detection and slot filling. [20] utilized explicit alignment information in the attention-based encoder-decoder neural network models.

For SAP, [21] explored a partially observable Markov decision process (POMDP) to control the system actions. Furthermore, RNN based dialog state tracking models for monitoring the dialogue progress was proved [22]. [2] provided conjoint representations among the utterances, slot- value pairs and knowledge graph representations to overcome current obstacles of deploying dialogue systems. [23] implemented an online learning framework to jointly train actions and the reward model with a Gaussian process model. [24] employed a value iteration method of reinforcement learning framework. [25] described a novel framework using genetic algorithm to optimize system actions. [3] proposed an end-to-end deep recurrent neural network with limited contextual dialogue history to train SLU and SAP jointly.

3   Model

The structure of our conditional joint model is shown in Fig. 1. It consists of SLU model and SAP model. Firstly, SLU model takes user utterances as inputs and obtains the context-aware distribution of each word by a shared Bi-LSTM layer. Then it performs slot filling and intent detection through task-specific output layers. Using the hidden outputs from SLU model, a sentence-level distribution for each utterance is produced in SAP model, and the distribution is combined with intent information for predicting system actions.

3.1   SLU Model

As is shown in Fig. 2, SLU model consists of embedding layer, shared Bi-LSTM layer and task-specific output layers for slot filling and intent detection.

Embedding Layer. Given a sequence of words $w_1, w_2, ..., w_T$ as inputs, we map them into a vector space to produce embeddings $x = \{x_1, x_2, ..., x_T\}$, where x_t means the word embedding of the t-th word.

Shared Bi-LSTM Layer. We employ Bi-LSTM network to obtain the context-aware distribution of each word. Since we have x_t as the t-th word embedding,

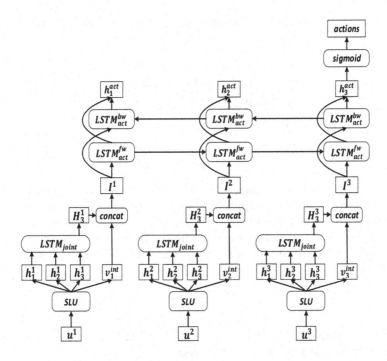

Fig. 1. Conditional joint model

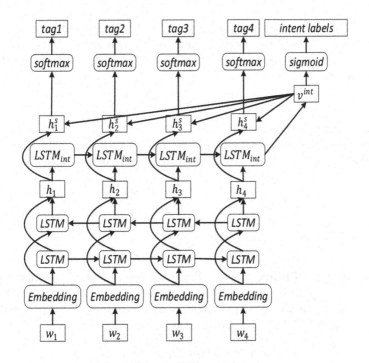

Fig. 2. SLU model

we calculate the forward and backward hidden states $\overrightarrow{h_t}$ and $\overleftarrow{h_t}$ respectively by the following equations,

$$
\begin{aligned}
i_t &= \sigma(W_{it}x_t + W_{hi}h_{t-1} + b_i) \\
f_t &= \sigma(W_{ft}x_t + W_{hf}h_{t-1} + b_f) \\
o_t &= \sigma(W_{ot}x_t + W_{ho}h_{t-1} + b_o) \\
\hat{c}_t &= tanh(W_{ct}x_t + W_{hc}h_{t-1} + b_c) \\
c_t &= f_t \odot c_{t-1} + i_t \odot \hat{c}_t \\
h &= o \odot tanh(c_t)
\end{aligned}
\tag{1}
$$

where σ is the sigmoid function, $\odot$ is element-wise multiplication, and i, f, o and c represent input gate, output gate, forget gate and cell state respectively. W and b are trainable parameters. c_{t-1} means previous cell state; h_{t-1} means previous hidden state. Finally, we can obtain the final state h_t by concatenating the forward and backward hidden states. In this way, the context information is integrated from two directions as:

$$
h_t = [\overrightarrow{h_t}, \overleftarrow{h_t}]
\tag{2}
$$

Intent Detection Layer. We stack another LSTM layer $LSTM_{int}$ on top of the shared Bi-LSTM layer for intent detection,

$$
h_t^{int} = LSTM_{int}(h_{t-1}^{int}, h_t)
\tag{3}
$$

where h_t is the hidden state at time step t. We take the last hidden state h_T^{int} for intent detection. Sometimes, there are more than one intents in a user utterance. In such a situation, we use a sigmoid function to calculate the probability over all intent labels,

$$
p^{int} = sigmoid(W_T^{int} h_T^{int})
\tag{4}
$$

where W_T^{int} is a weight matrix.

Similar with the intent detection layer, we obtain a threshold. The system action label is predicted if its probability is no less than the threshold,

$$
y_n^{int} = \begin{cases} 1, & p_n^{int} \geq threshold \\ 0, & otherwise \end{cases}
\tag{5}
$$

$n \in [1, N]$ is the index of intent labels.

Conditional Slot Filling Layer. Since we have already obtained the last hidden state h_T^{int} from the layer $LSTM_{int}$, we use it as an intent vector v^{int}. The probability p_t^s is calculated as an attention weight to evaluate the contribution of the intent vector v^{int} to each hidden state h_t from the shared Bi-LSTM layer.

$$
p_t^s = softmax(h_t \odot v^{int})
\tag{6}
$$

Then, we add the hidden state and weighted intent vector together for predicting slot labels.

$$h_t^s = h_t + v^{int} * p_t^s \tag{7}$$

Finally, we choose the maximum of the probability as the predicted slot label,

$$y_t^s = argmax(softmax(W_t^s h_t^s + b^s)) \tag{8}$$

where W_t^s is a weight matrix.

3.2   Conditional Joint Model

To predict system actions, we joint SLU and SAP model together to make full use of information from each other. In multi-turn dialogues, history utterances play an important role in system actions. We recombine the utterances in a window size $u = \{u^1, u^2, ..., u^k\}$, where u^k is the k-th utterance in the window. Then we put them into SLU model for slot filling and intent detection. For each utterance, we can obtain the hidden outputs $h_t^k (t = 1, ...T, k = 1, ...K)$ and the intent vector v_k^{int} from SLU model, then we take h_t^k as inputs to a LSTM layer $LSTM_{joint}$ and use the last hidden state H_T^k to produce a sentence-level distribution.

$$H_t^k = LSTM_{joint}(H_{t-1}^k, h_t^k) \tag{9}$$

We concatenate the sentence-level distribution H_k with the intent vector v_k^{int} to utilize intent information.

$$l^k = [H_T^k, v_k^{int}] \tag{10}$$

Then the concatenated vector I^k is used as the input to the top Bi-LSTM layer for computing system action h_k^{act},

$$\left\{ \begin{array}{l} \overrightarrow{h_k^{act}} = LSTM_{act}^{fw}(\overrightarrow{h_{k-1}^{act}}, I^k) \\ \overleftarrow{h_k^{act}} = LSTM_{act}^{fw}(\overleftarrow{h_{k-1}^{act}}, I^k) \\ h_k^{act} = [\overrightarrow{h_k^{act}}, \overleftarrow{h_k^{act}}] \end{array} \right. \tag{11}$$

where $LSTM_{act}^{fw}$ and $LSTM_{act}^{bw}$ stand for forward and backward LSTM network for SAP respectively.

The last hidden state h_K^{act} is used for predicting system actions. System can make more than one actions for an user utterance. Therefore, we use a sigmoid function to calculate the probability overall system action labels,

$$p^{act} = sigmoid(W_K^{act} h_K^{act}) \tag{12}$$

where W_K^{act} is a weight matrix.

Similar with the intent detection layer, we obtain a threshold. The system action label is predicted if its probability is no less than the threshold,

$$y_m^{act} = \begin{cases} 1, & p_m^{act} \geq threshod \\ 0, & otherwise \end{cases} \tag{13}$$

where $m \in [1, M]$ is the index of system action labels.

The loss function for SAP is defined as:

$$\mathcal{L}_{act} = -\sum_{m=1}^{M} a_m^{act} log y_m^{act} \tag{14}$$

where a_m^{act} means the ground truth label of system action.

In this joint model, the losses for slot filling and intent detection are defined as,

$$\mathcal{L}_{int} = -\sum_{n=1}^{N} g_n^{int} log y_n^{int}$$
$$\mathcal{L}_{slot} = -\sum_{t=1}^{T} s_t^s log y_t^s \tag{15}$$

where N is the number of intent labels. For joint learning of SLU model and SAP model, we add the three losses together. The total loss is as follows.

$$\mathcal{L}_{total} = \sum_{D} (\mathcal{L} + \mathcal{L}_{int} + \mathcal{L}_{slot}) \tag{16}$$

where $\mathcal{D}$ means the number of sequences in the total dataset. Via joint learning with the united loss function, the shared hidden states can combine two tasks jointly. Furthermore, the correlations of the two tasks can be learned and promote each other.

4   Experiment

In this section, we conduct experiment on benchmark DSTC4 and give the experiment result and analysis.

4.1   Corpus

DSTC4 corpus contains several multi-turn dialogues collected from Skype calls between tour guides and tourists. It involves touristic information for Singapore in five aspects: accommodation, attraction, food, shopping, and transportation. In this paper, we use the DSTC4 corpus setting following [3]. The training set contains 5648 utterances, the validation set contains 1939 utterances, and test set contains 3178 utterances. The number of slot labels, intent labels and system action labels are 87, 68, 66 respectively. The statistic of DSTC4 is shown in Table 1.

Table 1. DSTC4 corpus setup in this work

Contents	Train	Dev	Test
Utterances	5648	1939	3178
Slot labels	87	79	75
Intent types	68	54	58

4.2 Training Details

For comparison purpose, we used the same training configurations as work [3]. The model is trained on all of the training data with its learning rate initialized to be 0.01. In order to enhance the model, we set the maximum norm for gradient clipping to 5 and dropout rate to 0.5

Table 2. Results for slot filling and intent detection

Model	Slot Filling(SF)				Intent Detection(ID)				SLU(SF+ID)
	F1	P	R	FrmAcc	F1	P	R	FrmAcc	FrmAcc
CRF+SVMs	40.50	61.41	30.21	77.31	49.75	52.56	47.24	37.19	33.13
BiLSTMs	46.15	54.63	39.96	76.84	47.48	52.19	43.55	39.96	36.38
JointModel	45.04	53.35	38.97	76.49	49.67	52.22	47.35	**42.20**	37.38
Con-Joint model	**49.32**	53.62	**45.65**	**78.41**	**49.81**	50.04	**49.59**	**42.20**	**38.01**

4.3 Metrics

Following the work [3], the performance of slot filling, intent detection and system action prediction are measured by token- level micro-average F1-score and frame-level accuracy(calculated only when the whole frame is correct).

4.4 Experiment Results and Analysis

We compare our model with the results from [3]. Table 2 shows results for slot filling and intent detection. There are previous works for SLU on DSTC4:

- CRF+SVMs: CRF for slot filling and LinearSVM for intent detection are training separately.
- BiLSTMs: A shared Bi-LSTM layer is provided for joint learning of slot filling and intent detection.
- JointModel: A SAP model stacks on top of a history of SLU models simply.

From Table 2, we can see that our model gains much increase in slot filling task. In term of F1 score, our model outperforms previous best result (BiLSTMs) by 3.17%. In term of frame-level accuracy, our model achieves 1.1% improvement compared with previous best result (CRF+SVMs). In intent detection task, our model also shows good performance. It outperforms previous best result (CRF+SVMs) by 0.06% in term of token-level F1 score, and achieves the same score in term of frame-level accuracy. For both slot filling and intent detection, our model outperforms previous best result (JointModel) by 0.63% in term of the frame-level accuracy.

From all the results above, we can conclude that with conditioned intent information, our joint model performs well in SLU. This can be explained that intent labels can provide more effective information for predicting slot tags. Table 3 gives the results for SAP. The models in the table are introduced as follows.

- SVMs: LinearSVM with features of one-hot vectors of aggregated slots and intents.
- BiLSTMs: A Bi-LSTM layer which takes the predicted slot label and intent label from NLU model as input for system action prediction.
- OraSAP (SVMs): LinearSVM with human annotated slot tags and user intents.
- OraSAP (biLSTM): A Bi-LSTM layer whose inputs are the same as Oracle-SAP.

Our conditional joint model outperforms all other models in token-level F1 score, especially in the recall value. Compared with the best result (SVMs), our model obtains 2.54% improvement in F1 score and 10.05% improvement in the recall value especially. Through combining intent information for SAP, the model can identify the most accurate action labels, which brings the recall value with obvious increase.

Table 3. Results for system action prediction

Models	F1	P	R	FAcc
SVMs	31.15	29.92	32.48	7.71
BiLSTMs	19.89	14.87	30.01	11.96
JointModel	19.04	18.53	19.57	**22.84**
OraSAP(SVMs)	30.61	**30.20**	31.04	7.65
OraSAP(biLSTM)	23.09	22.24	24.01	19.67
Con-Joint Model	33.69	**27.88**	**42.53**	18.25

We found that most user utterances in the dataset have more than one action labels (the maximum is 20). It is difficult to predict all the actions correctly. To purse high F1 score, we make a trade-off between token-level F1 score and frame-level. We found that most user utterances in the dataset have more than one action labels (the maximum is 20). It is difficult to predict all the actions correctly. To purse high F1 score, we make a trade-off between token-level F1 score and frame-level accuracy. Therefore, it is reasonable that our model ranks a little lower in term of frame-level accuracy.

Above all, our conditional joint model has a great performance on both SLU and SAP. It can be interpreted that slot tags, intent labels and actions share knowledge with each other, and they promote each other via joint learning.

5   Conclusion

In this paper, we proposed a conditional joint model that can be used to perform spoken language understanding and dialogue management. Our model is capable of achieving knowledge sharing between slot tags, intents and system actions by utilizing intent information. Experiments on dataset DSTC4 demonstrate that our model has an excellent performance and outperforms other popular methods significantly. In future work, we intend to explore how to integrate information from the three different tasks explicitly for an enhanced joint model. Besides, we plan to extend our work to spoken language generation task for a more complete spoken dialogue system.

Acknowledgements. This research is supported by The National Key Research and Development Program of China (2016QY03D0501).

References

1. Chen, Y.-N., Celikyilmaz, A., Hakkani-Tur, D.: Deep learning for dialogue systems. In: ACL 2017, Tutorial, pp. 8–14 (2017)
2. Mrksic, N., OSeaghdha, D., Wen, T., Thomson, B., Young, S.: Neural belief tracker: data-driven dialogue state tracking. In: ACL 2017 (2017)
3. Yang, X., et al.: End-to-end joint learning of natural language understanding and dialogue manager. In: 2017 IEEE International Conference on Acoustics, Speech and Signal Processing (ICASSP), pp. 5690–5694 (2017)
4. Wang, Y.-Y., Deng, L., Acero, A.: Spoken language understanding. IEEE Signal Process. Mag. **22**(5), 16–31 (2005)
5. Lafferty, J.D., McCallum, A., Pereira, F.C.N.: Conditional random fields: probabilistic models for segmenting and labeling sequence data. In: Proceedings of the International Conference on Machine Learning, ICML, pp. 282–289 (2001)
6. Yao, K., Zweig, G., Hwang, M.-Y., Shi, Y., Yu, D.: Recurrent neural networks for language understanding. In: Interspeech, pp. 2524–2528 (2013)
7. Mesnil, G., He, X., Deng, L., Bengio, Y.: Investigation of recurrent-neural-network architectures and learning methods for spoken language understanding. In: Interspeech, pp. 3771–3775 (2013)
8. Yao, K., Peng, B., Zweig, G., Yu, D., Li, X., Gao, F.: Recurrent conditional random field for language understanding. In: 2014 IEEE International Conference on Acoustics, Speech and Signal Processing (ICASSP), pp. 4077–4081 (2014)

9. Yao, K., Peng, B., Zhang, Y., Yu, D., Zweig, G., Shi, Y.: Spoken language under-standing using long short-term memory neural networks. In: Spoken Language Technology Workshop (SLT), 2014 IEEE, pp. 189–194 (2014)
10. Kurata, G., Xiang, B., Zhou, B., Yu, M.: Leveraging sentence-level information with encoder LSTM for natural language understanding. In: EMNLP 2016, pp. 2077–2083 (2016)
11. Haffner, P., Tur, G., Wright, J.H.: Optimizing SVMs for complex call classifica-tion. In: 2003 IEEE International Conference on Acoustics, Speech, and Signal Processing, 2003. Proceedings. (ICASSP 2003), pp. I–I (2003)
12. Schapire, R.E., Singer, Y.: BoosTexter: a boosting-based system for text catego-rization. Mach. Learn. **39**, 135–168 (2000)
13. McCallum, A., Freitag, D., Pereira, F.CN.: Maximum entropy Markov models for information extraction and segmentation. In: ICML, vol. 17, pp. 591–598 (2000)
14. Sarikaya, R., Hinton, G.E., Ramabhadran, B.: Deep belief nets for natural language call-routing. In: 2011 IEEE International Conference on Acoustics, Speech and Signal Processing (ICASSP), pp. 5680–5683 (2011)
15. Ravuri, S., Stolcke, A.: Recurrent neural network and LSTM models for lexi-cal utterance classification. In: Sixteenth Annual Conference of the International Speech Communication Association, pp. 135–139 (2015)
16. Xu, P., Sarikaya, R.: Convolutional neural network based triangular CRF for joint intent detection and slot filling. In: 2013 IEEE Workshop on Automatic Speech Recognition and Understanding (ASRU), pp. 78–83 (2013)
17. Guo, D., Tur, G., Yih, W., Zweig, G.: Joint semantic utterance classification and slot filling with recursive neural networks. In: IEEE Spoken Language Technology Workshop (SLT), pp. 554–559 (2014)
18. Zhang, X., Wang, H.: A joint model of intent determination and slot filling for spoken language understanding. In: Proceedings of the Twenty-Fifth International Joint Conference on Artificial Intelligence (IJCAI-16) (2016)
19. Shi, Y., Yao, K., Chen, H., Pan, Y., Hwang, M.Y., Peng, B.: Contextual spoken lan-guage understanding using recurrent neural networks. In: 2015 IEEE International Conference on Acoustics, Speech and Signal Processing (ICASSP), pp. 5271–5275 (2015)
20. Liu, B., Lane, I.: Attention-based recurrent neural network models for joint intent detection and slot filling. Interspeech **2016**, 685–689 (2016)
21. Young, S., Gasic, M., Thomson, B., Williams, J.D.: POMDP-based statistical spo-ken dialog systems: a review. Proc. IEEE **101**(5), 1160–1179 (2013)
22. Henderson, M., Thomson, B., Young, S.: Deep neural network approach for the dialog state tracking challenge. In: Proceedings of the SIGDIAL 2013 Conference, pp. 467–471 (2013)
23. Su, P.-H., et al.: On-line active reward learning for policy optimisation in spoken dialogue systems. In: ACL 2016, pp. 2431–2441 (2016)
24. Xu, Y., et al.: Policy optimization of dialogue management in spoken dialogue system for out-of-domain utterances. In: 2016 International Conference on Asian Language Processing (IALP) (2016)
25. Hang, R., Xu, W., Yan, Y.: Optimizing human-interpretable dialog management policy using genetic algorithm. In: 2015 IEEE Workshop on Automatic Speech Recognition and Understanding (ASRU) (2015)

Small Traffic Sign Detection and Recognition in High-Resolution Images

Lei You[1], Yu Ke[1], Hongpeng Wang[1(✉)], Wenhu You[2], Bo Wu[3], and Xinghao Song[1]

[1] HIT Campus of University Town of Shenzhen, Shenzhen 518055, China
wanghp@hit.edu.cn
[2] No. 92 West Da Jie, Nangang District, Harbin 150001, China
[3] No. 2190, Liuxian Street Nanshan, District, Shenzhen 518055, China

Abstract. Traffic sign detection and recognition is a research hotspot in the computer vision and intelligent transportation systems fields. It plays an important role in driver-assistance systems and driverless operation. Detecting signs, especially small ones, remains challenging under a variety of road traffic conditions. In this manuscript, we propose an end-to-end deep learning model for detecting and recognizing traffic signs in high-resolution images. The model consists of basic feature extraction and multi-task learning. In the first part, a network with fewer parameters is proposed, and an effective feature fusion strategy is adopted to gain a more distinct representation. In the second part, multi-task learning is conducted on different hierarchical layers by considering the difference between the detection and classification tasks. The detection results on two newly published traffic sign benchmarks (Tsinghua-Tencent 100K and CTSD) demonstrate the robustness and superiority of our model.

Keywords: Traffic Sign Detection · Traffic Sign Recognition · Small traffic sign detection · End-to-end detection and recognition

1 Introduction

Traffic sign detection (TSD) and traffic sign recognition (TSR) are important components of autonomous driving and assisted driving, which are designed to help drivers avoid traffic accidents. Traffic sign detection aims to find areas that contain a traffic sign. Traffic sign recognition aims to determine the specific categories of these areas. The automatic detection and recognition of traffic signs can improve driving safety and comfort. However, effective traffic sign detection is not easy to achieve when faced with complex natural scenes. On the other hand, as the speed increases, distant traffic signs, which are relatively small and very difficult to detect, need to be detected in advance.

Many approaches have been proposed to address TSD and TSR; a good review [1] shows the efforts that have been made in recent years. Convolutional neural network (CNN) methods [2–5] have achieved perfect or near-perfect results on the German Traffic Sign Detection Benchmark (GTSDB) [6] and German Traffic Sign Recognition Benchmark (GTSRB) [7]. The reason for this is that CNNs generate more discriminative

R. Xu et al. (Eds.): ICCC 2019, LNCS 11518, pp. 37–53, 2019.
https://doi.org/10.1007/978-3-030-23407-2_4

features than traditional methods, such as color segmentation [8–10] and shape detection [11, 12]. However, the number of datasets for TSD and TSR is relatively small and not representative of a real environment. For example, the GTSDB contains only 900 images, while most of the images in the GTSRB contain traffic signs; thus, we need only to perform image classification. Similar to other computer vision tasks, deep learning algorithms [13–15] are also used to detect and recognize traffic signs.

At present, the proportion of traffic signs in most benchmarks is relatively large, which indicates that when a vehicle is close to a traffic sign, the remaining driver reaction time will be very short. In this work, we focus on relatively small traffic signs in the distance. We propose a multi-task deep learning framework to simultaneously detect and recognize traffic signs in an image. Compared with previous work [16], our method performs better in terms of recall and accuracy. As illustrated in Fig. 3, our model consists of feature extraction and multi-task learning. In the first part, the model gains a more distinct representation via feature fusion from multiple layers. In the second part, multi-task learning based on detection and classification, which includes three branches: bbox branch, type branch and pixel branch, is carried out.

We perform experiments on the Tsinghua-Tencent 100K (TT100K) [16] and Chinese Traffic Sign Dataset (CTSD) [17] to illustrate the effectiveness and efficiency of our proposed method. The size of many traffic signs in TT100K is approximately 20 * 20 pixels, and the signs occupy less than 1/10000 of the area of their respective images. Image samples from the TT100K benchmark are shown in Fig. 1. The sizes of traffic signs in the CTSD are relatively larger; samples of the CTSD are shown in Fig. 2.

Our main contributions are as follows. First, we propose a feature extraction network with fewer parameters that outperforms the work in [16]. Second, we add a

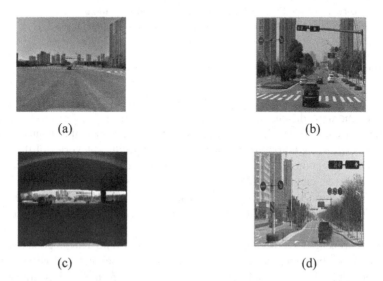

(a)   (b)

(c)   (d)

Fig. 1. TT100K image samples. (a) (c) Original images: the green rectangle represents the area that contains small traffic signs. (b) (d) Image patches that contain the small traffic signs corresponding to the original images "bottleneck" layer, which is similar to ResNet [18], to fuse the feature maps from different layers, which improves the recall of the TSD. Third, multi-task learning on different hierarchical feature maps is conducted to further improve the result, especially for small traffic signs. Finally, the proposed method is shown to achieve state-of-the-art results on TT100K and comparable results on the CTSD.

The remainder of this paper is organized as follows. In Sect. 2, we review previous work. In Sect. 3, we describe the network structure of the model. Detailed experiments are introduced in Sect. 4, and we conclude this paper in Sect. 5.

(a)   (b)

Fig. 2. CTSD image samples. The benchmark includes images at two different resolutions.

2 Related Work

2.1 Traffic Sign Detection

Traffic Sign Detection Traffic sign detection aims to segment the regions of an image that may contain traffic signs. Three main approaches to TSD exist: the color-based, shape-based and sliding-window methods. The color-based method is used to identify specific regions in various color spaces. Since the original RGB color space is sensitive to changing light, other color spaces, such as the HSI color space [8, 19] and Lab color space [9], are adopted to improve performance. For example, the authors of [20, 21] adopt color enhancement in the three channels of the RGB color space to filter regions that do not contain traffic signs. The author of [17] uses color probability maps and maximally stable extremal regions to generate candidates. The shape-based method detects specific circular, triangular and octagonal regions. The Hough transform [12], fast radial symmetry [11], log-polar transformation [22] and distance to the border [23] are commonly used to detect the shape information of traffic signs. For example, [24] proposes a saliency model for identifying sign-specific color, shape and spatial location information to facilitate detection. The sliding-window method goes through all possible positions of the traffic signs. The shortcoming of these methods is that they are usually time-consuming. For example, a coarse-to-fine algorithm for TSD is presented in [25]. The algorithm roughly identifies all candidates by using a small sliding window and relocates these candidates to a larger window for further verification. Although this method achieves state-of-the-art detection results on the GTSDB, it is extremely time-consuming when the images have high resolution.

2.2 Traffic Sign Recognition

Traffic sign recognition aims to classify candidate regions into subclasses. The traditional methods based on handcrafted features, the HOG [8, 26, 27] and the LBP [28] are used to train classifiers such as the SVM [23, 28, 29], k-NN [19], ELM [30] and sparse representation [31, 32]. Compared with handcrafted features, the features learned by neural networks from a large amount of data are more discriminative. Most methods that achieve state-of-the-art results on the GTSRB utilize neural networks for classification. For example, a committee of CNNs is used to perform classification in [3]. Several CNNs trained on differently preprocessed data are combined into a multi-column CNN to perform classification in [4]. The authors of [5] use a CNN with a hinge loss stochastic gradient descent function to perform classification and achieve a nearly perfect result that is better than human performance. Most of the methods above consider only classification and do not involve end-to-end detection and recognition.

2.3 Object Detection Based on Deep CNNs

Deep convolutional neural networks have attracted substantial attention because of their outstanding performance in object detection and classification. We classify deep CNNs into region-proposal-based methods and others. Region-proposal-based methods predict the number of candidates that contain targets and then perform classification and regression on these candidates. For example, in Fast-RCNN [33], selective search is used to generate approximately 1000 candidates. Based on Fast-RCNN, Faster-RCNN [15] integrates the region proposal network (RPN) into the entire network to accelerate detection. R-FCN [14] is a region-based method that improves the detection and recognition accuracy by generating position-sensitive maps and has achieved state-of-the-art results on PASCAL VOC 2012. Other methods that are not based on a region proposal, such as YOLO [34] and SSD [13], aim at real-time detection performance. These methods are much faster than region-based methods and have relatively lower detection and recognition accuracy.

Deep CNNs have also been used in intelligent transportation systems. For example, the authors of [35] propose a deep neural network based on Overfeat [36] to detect cars and lanes on a highway. Based on [35], the authors of [16] propose multi-task learning to simultaneously detect and recognize small traffic signs in images. A fully convolutional network (FCN) is used in [37] to generate a heat map of the traffic signs. The candidates are generated on these heat maps and are then classified by a shallow CNN.

Small object detection is an open challenge, with few methods showing good performance. In [38], the authors design a detector to detect tiny faces in an image. The contextual information and resolution information are fully used to enhance the accuracy of small face detection. A network based on SSD [13] is used to detect small traffic signs in [39]. Based on an image pyramid strategy and SOS-CNN, this method has achieved state-of-the-art results on TT100K. Perceptual generative adversarial networks (GANs) [40] are used to learn more discriminative feature representations of small traffic signs. GANs effectively detected small traffic signs on TT100K.

We propose an end-to-end learning structure to solve the problem of small traffic sign detection and recognition. The performance of the proposed method is evaluated

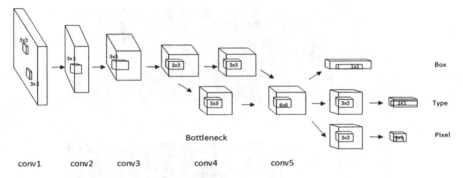

Fig. 3. The architecture of our network, which consists of four convolution blocks, a "bottleneck" block and three branches after the fifth block.

on the TT100K dataset. The CTSD is used to evaluate the generality of our model. Our work is based on the method in [16] but with several significant modifications. The implementation details and experimental results are described later.

3   Our Work

Our proposed network has an architecture similar to that of FCNs, as shown in Fig. 3, with fewer parameters and being insensitive to image size. The first half of the network is a feature extraction subnetwork similar to the VGG net [41]; a new feature fusion strategy that is similar to ResNet is also adopted. The second half of the network is a multi-task learning subnetwork that includes three branches: the bbox branch, pixel branch and type branch. For the bbox branch, each result represents the distance between the original 4 * 4 pixel region and the four sides of the predicted bounding box of the target. The pixel branch represents the probability that a certain 4 * 4 pixel region in the input image contains a target object. The type branch represents the probability of a specific class. The visualization results of the type branch and pixel branch are shown in Fig. 4. Both general traffic signs and small traffic signs can be detected on the heat maps.

3.1   Feature Extraction Network

For the first part of the network, we proposed a feature extraction network with fewer parameters, which has better performance than that in [16]. To some extent, the good performance of deep learning depends on a large number of data sets. Some commonly used benchmarks for deep learning are shown in Table 1, and the sizes of some deep learning models are shown in Table 2. Clearly, the amount of data and the size of each model are unbalanced. In general, models with larger parameters require more training data. Considering the design of the VGG network, we propose a feature extraction network with fewer parameters. The parameters of the new model reflect a reduction of 75% compared with the previous model. The sizes of the convolution kernel are mainly 3 * 3 and 1 * 1. The fifth convolution layer adopts a relatively large convolution

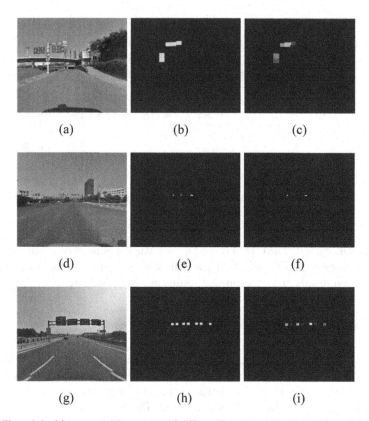

Fig. 4. The original images and heat maps of different branches. (a) (d) (g) The original testing image. (b) (e) (h) Heat maps of the pixel branch, which represents the probability that the corresponding position contains the target. (c) (f) (i) Heat maps of the type branch, which represents the probability that the corresponding position belongs to a specific class

Table 1. Open deep learning benchmarks

Benchmark	Number (k)	Labels
ILSVRC 2012	1200	1000
Open Images Dataset	9000	6000
Microsoft COCO	330	80
PASCOL VOC	22	20
TT100K	9.7	200
CTSD	1.1	48

kernel size of 6 * 6 to learn more contextual information and own larger receptive fields. These two tricks are proven to be effective for detecting small objects in [38]. The number of convolution steps of the feature extraction network is 16, and the final feature maps are twice as large as before.

Table 2. Commonly used deep learning model size

Model	Faster-RCNN	R-FCN	YOLO	SSD	Model [1]
Size (MB)	528	203	257	114	446

3.2 Feature Fusion Strategy

The sizes of traffic signs in TT100K vary widely, with most being of small size. The size distribution is shown in Fig. 5. We show the visualization results of the last two convolutional feature maps for two different sizes of traffic signs in Fig. 6. In general, we need more detailed information to detect small targets, which is not always true for large targets. Though the model can detect more small traffic signs if we use the information of convolution layer conv4, the accuracy of the classification will decrease. Considering the difference between small traffic sign detection and large traffic sign detection, we propose a feature fusion strategy that is similar to ResNet [18]. A "bottleneck" layer, which is used to fuse the feature maps of the last two convolution layers, is added to the feature extraction network. The final feature maps retain more details. In addition, our feature fusion strategy detects more traffic signs while ensuring classification accuracy.

3.3 Hierarchical Multi-task Learning

In deep learning, differences exist in the characteristic information needed by the target detection and classification tasks. In general, the larger the number of convolutional networks, the smaller the size of the convolutional feature maps. The classification task requires high-level features that are more representative. However, this is not true for the small target detection task. If the size of the feature maps is too small, it will not be conducive to the detection of small traffic signs. Considering the difference, we perform multi-task learning on different hierarchical feature maps. The detection task is based on relatively larger feature maps, while the classification task is based on higher feature maps. Specifically, the convolution step of the pixel branch and the type branch is 32, while the convolution step is 16 for the box branch. We add additional convolutional layers to the pixel branch and type branch. Based on this strategy, we further improve the detection recall rate of small traffic signs. The overall recall rate and accuracy rate on the TT100K benchmark are 94% and 91%, respectively, which are 3% and 3% higher than before.

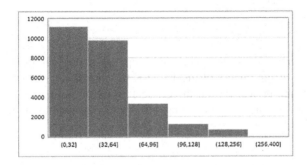

Fig. 5. The size distribution of traffic signs in TT100K.

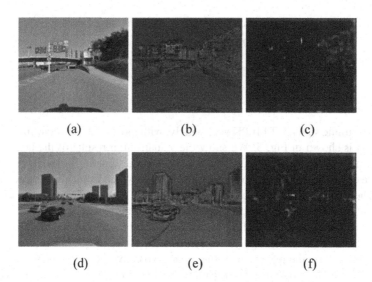

(a)   (b)   (c)

(d)   (e)   (f)

Fig. 6. The visualization results of the last two convolutional feature maps. (a) (d) The original testing image. (b) (e) The visualization results of conv4. (c) (f) The visualization results of conv5.

3.4   Training

Our experimental environment is a Linux PC with a single NVIDIA Tesla K40 GPU and 12 GB of memory. Our deep learning framework is Caffe. Images in the TT100K benchmark cannot be trained directly because of the image sizes and imbalance among traffic sign classes. To address the first problem, we randomly resize the original images within a certain range. A rectangle of 640 * 480 is utilized to segment the resized image according to the ground truth, which represents the position of the bounding box. For the second problem, we place the standard template of each traffic sign on a background of 640 * 480. These standard templates are rotated and scaled, and some Gamma color noise is added to obtain adequate training instances. We use a data augmentation technique that combines the generated images and original images in the benchmark. The final network input is image patches with a fixed size of 640 * 480. We start training networks from scratch. The loss function of the pixel branch and type branch is Softmax loss, while the bbox branch uses L1 loss on the bounding box regression.

3.5   Testing

We adopt the same multi-scale testing and cropping strategy as used in the testing phase. The input testing images of the TT100K benchmark are 1280 * 1280, and the detection results are projected onto the original image according to the scale. In the projected images, we apply a bounding box merge method to remove redundant images.

4 Experiments

We describe the experimental details in this section. First, we provide a brief introduction to the two benchmarks. Then, the comparative experiments are introduced in detail.

4.1 Datasets and Evaluation Metrics

Tsinghua-Tencent 100K [16] is a large traffic sign benchmark that consists of 10,000 images collected from 10 regions of 5 cities in China (including both downtown regions and suburbs for each city). A total of 30,000 traffic sign instances are included in this benchmark, with detailed annotations for each sign, such as its bounding box, pixel mask and class. Each image is 2048 * 2048 pixels in size, which is larger than the high-resolution images considered in [7]. Common traffic conditions, such as illumination changes and weather changes, are included in this benchmark, but a data imbalance exists among classes.

Following [16], we ignore classes with fewer than 100 instances and implement our method on the remaining 45 classes. The evaluation metrics include accuracy and recall. Since many small traffic signs exist in the benchmark, the performance is also evaluated using the same detection metrics as used for the Microsoft COCO benchmark. The performance is evaluated on objects of different size, including small objects (area < area 96 * 96). The CTSD benchmark contains 1100 images (700 for training and 400 for testing) of different sizes (typical sizes are 1024 * 768 and 1280 * 720). The benchmark has 48 classes, and the proportion of traffic signs is relatively large. In this paper, we focus on the more challenging TT100K benchmark and utilize CTSD as a supplement to evaluate the generalizability of our model.

4.2 Experimental Details

Our experiments are divided into two parts to evaluate the performance of the proposed method. In the first part, we test the performances of several classic models on the TT100K dataset to identify the weaknesses of directly applying these models to TSD and TSR. The classic models used in our work include Fast-RCNN [33], Faster-RCNN [15], YOLO [34], and R-FCN [14]. The experimental results of Fast-RCNN and Faster-RCNN on TT100K are published in [16] and [40]. We focus only on YOLO and R-FCN in this section. In the second part, our experiments are based on the three design points mentioned above. The first is the feature extraction network, the second is the feature fusion strategy and the third is the hierarchical multi-task learning strategy. We initially convert the TT100K dataset into VOC format and fine-tune the YOLO model and R-FCN model. The results are shown in Table 3, which reveals that these two traditional models have poor performance in terms of small traffic sign detection.

YOLO [34] is a fast object-detection framework that does not require region proposal generation. We choose the model that is pre-trained on the Pascal VOC dataset and fine-tune it using the TT100K benchmark. The network is trained over 45,000 iterations. The images are resized to 416 * 416 and sent to the network. The network has a stride of 32 pixels; thus, small traffic signs cannot be effectively expressed in the final feature map, resulting in poor detection results for small objects. R-FCN [14] performs well on the Pascal VOC dataset. We choose ResNet-101 as the basic feature extraction network and initialize our network with a model that is pre-trained on ImageNet. Since ResNet-101 is deeper, we train the network over 200,000 iterations.

R-FCN performs poorly on TT100K. One reason is that TT100K is not as large as ImageNet; another reason is that small traffic signs cannot be detected easily. However, it outperforms YOLO on TT100K.

The above experimental results show that the general object-detection models do not perform well in terms of small sign detection. Taking into account the difficulties of TT100K, the general object-detection models are not applicable for this benchmark. In the second part, we propose several improvements to address these problems.

For the feature extraction network, our intuitive idea is to replace the feature extraction network with the VGG-16 net [27] and ResNet-50 [15] while retaining the three branches. We use the model pre-trained on ImageNet to fine-tune the two networks on TT100K. The VGG-16 network is trained over 80,000 iterations, and the ResNet-50 network is trained over 100,000 iterations. We propose a shallow network similar to VGG net with smaller (3 * 3) and fewer convolution filters in most layers to achieve a 75% decrease in the number of model parameters. This network is regarded as a baseline in our experiment. The detection results are shown in Table 4. From the table, we can see that our model significantly improves the accuracy compared to before.

To verify the effectiveness of the feature fusion strategy, we branch multi-task learning on feature maps of different sizes. The results are shown in Table 5. In the "Our-conv3" model, the multi-task learning network is connected to convolution conv3. The feature fusion strategy is added to the "Our-conv34" model. From the results, we can see that the feature fusion strategy can increase recall and accuracy at the same time. Based on the "Our-conv34" model, we further add the hierarchical multi-task learning strategy to our multi-task learning network. The results are shown in Table 6. The model "Ours" is the proposed model. Based on the strategy, we further increase the recall rate, especially the recall rate of small traffic signs.

Table 3. Detection results of different universal object detection models (%)

Model	YOLO	R-FCN
mAP	33	43

Table 4. Comparison of the simultaneous detection and classification results of different feature extraction networks on TT100K. (R): Recall, (A): Accuracy

Object size	(0, 32]	(32, 96]	(96, 400]	(0, 400]
Zhu et al. [1] (R)	0.87	0.94	0.88	0.91
Zhu et al. [1] (A)	0.82	0.91	0.91	0.88
VGG-16 [41] (R)	0.88	0.92	0.87	0.90
VGG-16 [41] (A)	0.73	0.88	0.87	0.82
ResNet-50 [18] (R)	0.59	0.65	0.57	0.62
ResNet-50 [18] (A)	0.55	0.61	0.59	0.58
Ours-baseline (R)	0.86	0.96	0.90	0.92
Ours-baseline (A)	0.86	0.94	0.94	0.91

Table 5. Comparison of the simultaneous detection and classification results of the feature fusion strategy on TT100K. (R): Recall, (A): Accuracy

Object size	(0, 32]	(32, 96]	(96, 400]	(0, 400]
Ours-baseline (R)	0.86	0.96	0.90	0.92
Ours-baseline (A)	0.86	0.94	0.94	0.91
Ours-conv3 (R)	0.89	0.96	0.93	0.93
Ours-conv3 (A)	0.85	0.94	0.93	0.90
Ours-conv34 (R)	0.88	0.97	0.92	0.93
Ours-conv34 (A)	0.86	0.95	0.94	0.91

Table 6. Comparison of the simultaneous detection and classification results of the hierarchical multi-task learning strategy on TT100K. (R): Recall, (A): Accuracy

Object size	(0, 32]	(32, 96]	(96, 400]	(0, 400]
Ours-baseline (R)	0.86	0.96	0.90	0.92
Ours-baseline (A)	0.86	0.94	0.94	0.91
Ours-conv34 (R)	0.88	0.97	0.92	0.93
Ours-conv34 (A)	0.86	0.95	0.94	0.91
Ours (R)	0.90	0.97	0.93	0.94
Ours (A)	0.86	0.94	0.95	0.91

Table 7. Comparison of the detection performance of the latest published literature on TT100K. (R): Recall, (A): Accuracy

Object size	(0, 32]	(32, 96]	(96, 400]	(0, 400]
Fast R-CNN [16] (R)	0.24	0.74	0.96	-
Fast R-CNN [16] (A)	0.45	0.51	0.55	-
Faster R-CNN [40] (R)	0.50	0.84	0.91	-

(continued)

Table 7. (*continued*)

Object size	(0, 32]	(32, 96]	(96, 400]	(0, 400]
Faster R-CNN [40] (A)	0.24	0.66	0.81	-
Zhu et al. [16] (R)	0.87	0.94	0.88	0.91
Zhu et al. [16] (A)	0.82	0.91	0.91	0.88
Zhu et al.-fast [16] (R)	0.74	0.91	0.86	0.74
Zhu et al.-fast [16] (A)	0.79	0.90	0.91	0.87
Perceptual GAN [40] (R)	0.89	0.96	0.89	0.93
Perceptual GAN [40] (A)	0.84	0.91	0.91	0.88
SOS-CNN [39] (R)	-	-	-	0.93
SOS-CNN [39] (A)	-	-	-	0.90
Ours-fast (R)	0.82	0.97	0.94	0.91
Ours-fast (A)	0.85	0.94	0.93	0.90
Ours (R)	**0.90**	**0.97**	**0.93**	**0.94**
Ours (A)	**0.86**	**0.94**	**0.95**	**0.91**

Table 8. Comparison of the detection performance on CTSD. (R): Recall, (A): Accuracy (%)

Model	Recall	Accuracy
Yang et al. [17]	-	**98.77**
Zhu et al. [16]	91.38	95.21
Ours	**95.40**	97.46

4.3 Performance Comparison

The newest detection results on TT100K are reported in Table 7. In the testing phase, the default testing scales are $1\times$, $2\times$ and $4\times$ the source image. The fast version is tested on only two scales, i.e., $1\times$ and $2\times$, and the fast version is 4 times faster than the normal model. The results show that our proposed method achieves a recall rate of 94% and an accuracy of 91%, which are better than the results reported in [1–3]. Therefore, our proposed method achieves state-of-the-art results on TT100K. The precision-recall curves for different traffic sign sizes are shown in Fig. 7. Clearly, the performance of our approach on the three subsets has largely improved compared to before. The accuracy and the recall rate for each category for a Jaccard similarity coefficient of 0.5 are shown in Table 4, Table 5 and Table 3. We achieve nearly perfect results in several categories, such as "il100", "pl100" and "pl120". Some of the detection results for the TT100K testing set are shown in Fig. 9. Small traffic signs under different road conditions can be effectively detected by our proposed method, and our model can successfully detect the traffic signs that Zhu et al. [1] missed or detected incorrectly.

4.4   Generalization Experiments

We evaluate our method using the CTSD benchmark to verify the generalization. The images in the dataset have different sizes (typical sizes are 1024 * 768 and 1280 * 720); therefore, we resize the images to a fixed resolution (1024 * 1024) in the training and testing phases. We retrain the model in [1] and the proposed model on the CTSD. The model pre-trained on TT100K is used to initialize the network. We train both models over 50,000 iterations, and the results are shown in Table 8. From the results, we can see that our model also performs better than before on the CTSD. There are only 700 images available for training and 48 categories of traffic signs that need to be classified; thus, it is not suitable to train a CNN-based network on these data. Nevertheless, we still obtain results comparable with those of [11]. Our model achieves a recall rate of 95% and an accuracy of 97%. The precision-recall curves of the detection performance are shown in Fig. 8, and the detection results are shown in Fig. 9. In addition, we also collected some images in the field, the detection results for which are shown in Fig. 9. The results show the robustness of our model.

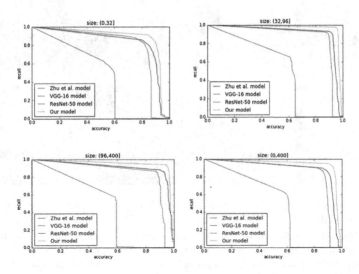

Fig. 7. Comparison of the overall detection performances on Tsinghua-Tencent 100K for small, medium and large traffic signs

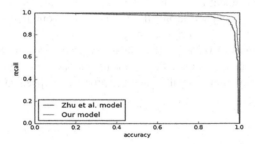

Fig. 8. The precision-recall curves of the detection performance on the CTSD

Fig. 9. The detection results on TT100K and the CTSD. The first row shows the detection results of Zhu et al. [1] on TT100K. The second row shows the detection results of our model on TT100K. The third row shows the detection results for our collected images. The fourth row shows the detection results of our model on the CTSD. The green, red and blue rectangles denote true positives, false positives and false negatives, respectively. (Color figure online)

4.5   Time Performance Analysis

The limitation of our model is its time performance. Because of the use of multi-scale and sliding window strategies during the testing phase, our model cannot meet the realtime requirements. For an original image with a resolution of 2048 * 2048, the processing speed can reach 0.25 fps. In this case, we can almost detect traffic signs at a distance of 100 m, which is important under the urban road environment. For the images of the CTSD, the resolution is smaller, and the processing speed can reach 1 fps.

5   Conclusions

In this paper, we aim to address the problem of small traffic sign detection and recognition in high-resolution images. To achieve this goal, we choose a multi-task learning model and make an improvement. First, we propose a feature extraction network with fewer parameters that is better than before. Second, we propose the feature fusion strategy to solve the problem of traffic sign detection for different sizes. Third, we propose a hierarchical multi-task learning strategy to improve the recall and accuracy. Our proposed model performs well in terms of small sign detection. To evaluate the performance of our model, we choose a challenging benchmark, TT100K, which contains high-resolution images with many small traffic signs. It is difficult for CNNs to process large images with a resolution of 2048 * 2048. To address this problem, the entire image is cropped into patches of fixed size. Our method generates relatively large feature maps that contain more contextual information and a larger receptive field. A multi-scale training and testing strategy is also applied. To verify the generalization of the model, we evaluate it on another benchmark.

The shortcoming of our proposed method is that it cannot be used for real-time applications. In the future, we will make the method more efficient.

Acknowledgment. This research was supported in part by the Shenzhen Science and Technology Innovation Commission research project JCYJ20170307151831260.

Ke Yu is the co-first author and contributed equally with You Lei. Wang Hongpeng is the corresponding author, his email is wanghp@hit.edu.cn.

References

1. Gudigar, A., Chokkadi, S., Raghavendra, U.: A review on automatic detection and recognition of traffic sign. Multimedia Tools Appl. **75**(1), 333 (2016)
2. Sermanet, P., LeCun, Y.: Traffic sign recognition with multi-scale convolutional networks. In: The 2011 International Joint Conference on Neural Networks (IJCNN), pp. 2809–2813. IEEE (2011)
3. Ciresan, D., Meier, U., Masci, J., et al.: A committee of neural networks for traffic sign classification. In: The 2011 International Joint Conference on Neural Networks (IJCNN), pp. 1918–1921. IEEE (2011)
4. Ciresan, D., Meier, U., Masci, J., et al.: Multi-column deep neural network for traffic sign classification. Neural Netw. **32**, 333–338 (2012)
5. Jin, J., Fu, K., Zhang, C.: Traffic sign recognition with hinge loss trained convolutional neural network. IEEE Trans. Intell. Transp. Syst. **15**(5), 1991–2000 (2014)
6. Houben, S., Stallkamp, J., Salmen, J., et al.: Detection of traffic signs in realworld images: the German Traffic Sign Detection Benchmark. In: The 2013 International Joint Conference on Neural Networks (IJCNN), pp. 1–8. IEEE (2013)
7. Stallkamp, J., Schlipsing, M., Salmen, J., et al.: Man vs. computer: benchmarking machine learning algorithms for traffic sign recognition. Neural Netw. **32**, 323–332 (2012)
8. Ellahyani, A., El Ansari, M., El Jaafari, I.: Traffic sign detection and recognition based on random forests. Appl. Soft Comput. **46**, 805–815 (2016)

9. Lillo-Castellano, J.M., Mora-Jimnez, I., Figuera-Pozuelo, C., et al.: Traffic sign segmentation and classification using statistical learning methods. Neurocomputing **153**, 286–299 (2015)
10. Mogelmose, A., Trivedi, M.M., Moeslund, T.B.: Vision-based traffic sign detection and analysis for intelligent driver assistance systems: perspectives and survey. IEEE Trans. Intell. Transp. Syst. **13**(4), 1484–1497 (2012)
11. Barnes, N., Zelinsky, A., Fletcher, L.S.: Real-time speed sign detection using the radial symmetry detector. IEEE Trans. Intell. Transp. Syst. **9**(2), 322–332 (2008)
12. Loy, G., Barnes, N.: Fast shape-based road sign detection for a driver assistance system. In: Proceedings 2004 IEEE/RSJ International Conference on Intelligent Robots and Systems (IROS 2004), vol. 1, pp. 70–75. IEEE (2004)
13. Liu, Wei, et al.: SSD: single shot multibox detector. In: Leibe, Bastian, Matas, Jiri, Sebe, Nicu, Welling, Max (eds.) ECCV 2016. LNCS, vol. 9905, pp. 21–37. Springer, Cham (2016). https://doi.org/10.1007/978-3-319-46448-0_2
14. Li, Y., He, K., Sun, J.: R-FCN: object detection via region-based fully convolutional networks. In: Advances in Neural Information Processing Systems, pp. 379–387 (2016)
15. Ren, S., He, K., Girshick, R., et al.: Faster R-CNN: towards real-time object detection with region proposal networks. In: Advances in Neural Information Processing Systems, pp. 91–99 (2015)
16. Zhu, Z., Liang, D., Zhang, S., et al.: Traffic-sign detection and classification in the wild. In: Proceedings of the IEEE Conference on Computer Vision and Pattern Recognition, pp. 2110–2118 (2016)
17. Yang, Y., Luo, H., Xu, H., et al.: Towards real-time traffic sign detection and classification. IEEE Trans. Intell. Transp. Syst. **17**(7), 2022–2031 (2016)
18. He, K., Zhang, X., Ren, S., et al.: Deep residual learning for image recognition. In: Proceedings of the IEEE Conference on Computer Vision and Pattern Recognition, pp. 770–778 (2016)
19. Han, Y., Virupakshappa, K., Oruklu, E.: Robust traffic sign recognition with feature extraction and k-NN classification methods. In: 2015 IEEE International Conference on Electro/Information Technology (EIT), pp. 484–488. IEEE (2015)
20. Salti, S., Petrelli, A., Tombari, F., et al.: Traffic sign detection via interest region extraction. Pattern Recogn. **48**(4), 1039–1049 (2015)
21. Ruta, A., Li, Y., Liu, X.: Real-time traffic sign recognition from video by class-specific discriminative features. Pattern Recogn. **43**(1), 416–430 (2010)
22. Ellahyani, A., El Ansari, M.: Mean shift and log-polar transform for road sign detection. Multimed. Tools Appl. **76**, 1–19 (2016)
23. Maldonado-Bascon, S., Lafuente-Arroyo, S., Gil-Jimenez, P., et al.: Roadsign detection and recognition based on support vector machines. IEEE Trans. Intell. Transp. Syst. **8**(2), 264–278 (2007)
24. Chen, T., Lu, S.: Accurate and efficient traffic sign detection using discriminative adaboost and support vector regression. IEEE Trans. Veh. Technol. **65**(6), 4006–4015 (2016)
25. Wang, G., Ren, G., Wu, Z., et al.: A robust, coarse-to-fine traffic sign detection method. In: The 2013 International Joint Conference on Neural Networks (IJCNN), pp. 1–5. IEEE (2013)
26. Zaklouta, F., Stanciulescu, B.: Real-time traffic sign recognition in three stages. Rob. Auton. Syst. **62**(1), 16–24 (2014)
27. Greenhalgh, J., Mirmehdi, M.: Real-time detection and recognition of road traffic signs. IEEE Trans. Intell. Transp. Syst. **13**(4), 1498–1506 (2012)
28. Berkaya, S.K., Gunduz, H., Ozsen, O., et al.: On circular traffic sign detection and recognition. Expert Syst. Appl. **48**, 67–75 (2016)

29. Wang, G., Ren, G., Wu, Z., et al.: A hierarchical method for traffic sign classification with support vector machines. In: The 2013 International Joint Conference on Neural Networks (IJCNN), pp. 1–6. IEEE (2013)
30. Huang, Z., Yu, Y., Gu, J., et al.: An efficient method for traffic sign recognition based on extreme learning machine. IEEE Trans. Cybern. **47**(4), 920–933 (2017)
31. Liu, C., Chang, F., Chen, Z., et al.: Fast traffic sign recognition via high contrast region extraction and extended sparse representation. IEEE Trans. Intell. Transp. Syst. **17**(1), 79–92 (2016)
32. Mathias, M., Timofte, R., Benenson, R., et al.: Traffic sign recognition - how far are we from the solution? In: The 2013 International Joint Conference on Neural Networks (IJCNN), pp. 1–8. IEEE (2013)
33. Girshick, R.: Fast R-CNN. In: Proceedings of the IEEE International Conference on Computer Vision, pp. 1440–1448 (2015)
34. Redmon, J., Divvala, S., Girshick, R., et al.: You only look once: unified, real-time object detection. In: Proceedings of the IEEE Conference on Computer Vision and Pattern Recognition, pp. 779–788 (2016)
35. Huval, B., Wang, T., Tandon, S., et al.: An empirical evaluation of deep learning on highway driving. arXiv preprint. arXiv:1504.01716 (2015)
36. Sermanet, P., Eigen, D., Zhang, X., et al.: OverFeat: integrated recognition, localization and detection using convolutional networks. Eprint arXiv (2013)
37. Zhu, Y., Zhang, C., Zhou, D.: Traffic sign detection and recognition using fully convolutional network guided proposals. Neurocomputing **214**, 758–766 (2016)
38. Hu, P., Ramanan, D.: Finding tiny faces. In: 2017 IEEE Conference on Computer Vision and Pattern Recognition (CVPR), pp. 1522–1530. IEEE (2017)
39. Meng, Z., Fan, X., Chen, X., et al.: Detecting small signs from large images. arXiv preprint. arXiv:1706.08574 (2017)
40. Li, J., Liang, X., Wei, Y., et al.: Perceptual generative adversarial networks for small object detection. In: IEEE CVPR (2017)
41. Simonyan, K., Zisserman, A.: Very deep convolutional networks for largescale image recognition. arXiv preprint. arXiv:1409.1556 (2014)
42. Liu, C., Chang, F., Chen, Z.: Rapid multiclass traffic sign detection in high resolution images. IEEE Trans. Intell. Transp. Syst. **15**(6), 2394–2403 (2014)

A Feature Extraction Algorithm for the Detection of "Five-Distances" in Hazardous Chemical Storage and Stacking in Night Vision Environment

Xuejun Liu[1], Yuchen Wei[1(⊠)], Jiandong Zhang[1], Bo Li[1], Jin Wang[1], Bo Dai[1], and Cuiqing Li[2]

[1] College of Information Engineering, Beijing Institute of Petrochemical Technology (BIPT), Beijing 102617, China
[2] College of Chemistry Engineering, Beijing Institute of Petrochemical Technology (BIPT), Beijing 102617, China

Abstract. The In recent years, safety distance monitoring of hazardous chemical stacking has become an increasingly important problem to be solved. It is a promising solution to build "Five-Distances" of binocular camera detection system based on cloud platform for intelligent safety distance warning. Aiming at the problem of feature extraction in "Five-Distances" detection of stacking in night vision environment, this paper proposes the construction of two-dimensional OSTU average gray function window and the average algorithm of threshold data results. The threshold value of feature extraction is calculated by combining the probability density distribution of foreground and background. Experiments on standard data sets and simulated experimental scene images show that this algorithm significantly reduces the number of noise points and improves the accuracy of subsequent edge detection and corner point detection compared with the gray straight square homogenization algorithm.

Keywords: Night vision · Two-dimensional OSTU · Function window · Feature extraction · "Five-Distances" detection · Hazardous chemical stacking

1 The Introduction

In recent years, the safety accidents of hazardous chemical stacking happen frequently, and there were many casualties, Such as Tianjin port incident, Shenghua chemical of Hebei Zhangjiakou incident [1, 2]. Therefore, more and more attention should be paid to the supervision of hazardous chemicals. However, the intelligent supervision measures are more important and effective scientific means in the new age [3]. At present, the research on safety Supervision and management of hazardous chemical stacking is developing gradually. There are laser scanning system, UWB positioning system and so on [4, 5]. In this paper, binocular cameras are used to build a "Five-Distance" measuring platform for hazardous chemical stacking, and use cloud services as a communication platform to supervise. In the measurement of binocular "Five-Distances", it is divided into camera calibration, corner point matching, depth information and other steps. The picture is shown in Fig. 1.

© Springer Nature Switzerland AG 2019
R. Xu et al. (Eds.): ICCC 2019, LNCS 11518, pp. 54–66, 2019.
https://doi.org/10.1007/978-3-030-23407-2_5

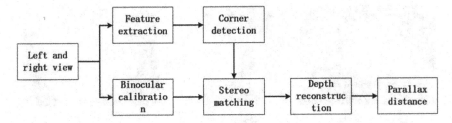

Fig. 1. Flow chart of binocular "Five-Distance" test system.

Feature extraction is related to the subsequent algorithm modules and greatly affects the accuracy of distance measurement results. Especially in the environment of night vision, pixel gray value is close to each other. In this paper, the two-dimensional OSTU average gray function window construction and threshold averaging algorithm are proposed to achieve the stacking feature extraction and corner point detection in the night vision environment, providing information for the subsequent "five distances" measurement.

2 Feature Extraction Algorithm for Stacking in Night Vision Environment

In the night vision environment, we use the binocular camera model 1920*1080 resolution. The configuration parameters of the computer are Inter Core i5-4200, 2G DDR3 independent graphics card, 8G memory and 500G hard disk. The pictures taken in the night vision environment are shown in Fig. 2.

Among them, the stacking was simulated with cube wood blocks. Figure 3 is the corner detection diagram of the image Fig. 2 in the night vision environment.

Therefore, binary ideas are selected to extract object information. However, the traditional one-dimensional OSTU cannot retrieve the information around the point, which may lead to inaccurate threshold and include noise [6]. The two-dimensional OSTU can avoid such problems. But construction of the average grayscale function window and two-dimensional threshold is always the core problem of this kind of algorithm [7, 8]. Therefore, this paper analyzes this problem and gives construction of the average grayscale function window and two-dimensional threshold averaging. After the foreground and background are extracted, Sobel algorithm is used to extract the edge of gradient dimensionality reduction, so as to carry out subsequent steps such as corner detection. Figure 4 shows the improved two-dimensional OSTU and edge extraction algorithm flow chart.

According to the steps in Fig. 4, the first step is to establish a two-dimensional gray scale array, where the first dimension is the gray value of a point, and the second

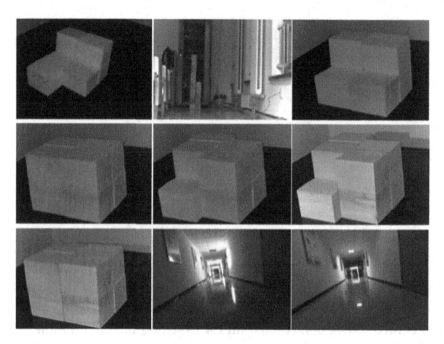

Fig. 2. The image of night vision environment.

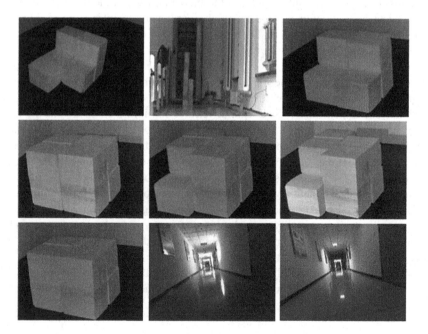

Fig. 3. The image of corner detection environment in the night vision

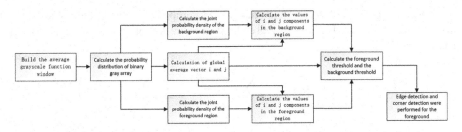

Fig. 4. Flow chart of improved two-dimensional OSTU and edge extraction algorithm

dimension data is centered on the point, and the average value of all points in a window is taken, as shown in formula (1).

$$
\begin{cases}
\left(\sum_{i=0}^{height} \sum_{j=0}^{wide} \sum_{m=i-1}^{i+1} \sum_{n=j-1}^{j+1} D''_{m*T+n} \right) \Big/ (x*y) \\
\underbrace{\sum_{i=0}^{height} \sum_{j=0}^{width} D'_{i*T+j}}
\end{cases}
, [m \geq 0, m < height, n \geq 0, n < width]
$$

(1)

In formula (1), I and j are iteration times respectively, Wide and height are the number of pixels in the image, m and n are the position of the length and width of the function window deviating from the pixel dot at a certain point, T is the actual memory length of the image, x and y are the length and width of the function window respectively, Its size is the value of the difference between the starting point and the ending point of m and n respectively, D''_{m*T+n} is the grayscale value of a point in the function window, D'_{i*T+j} is the grayscale value of each pixel of the picture. After that, the joint probability distribution of this two-dimensional array is calculated [6, 7]. As shown in formula (2).

$$
P_{ij} = \sum_{i=0}^{L} \sum_{j=0}^{L} \left(G_{ij} \big/ height * width \right)
$$

(2)

In formula (2), P_{ij} is the probability distribution, L is the maximum value of grayscale, its value is 256, G_{ij} is the number of occurrences of the same binary group. Then the joint probability density of the background region and the joint probability density of the foreground region are calculated respectively [6, 7]. As shown in formulas (3), (4).

$$
\omega_1 = \sum_{i=0}^{s} \sum_{j=0}^{t} P_{ij}
$$

(3)

$$
\omega_2 = \sum_{i=s+1}^{L-1} \sum_{j=t+1}^{L-1} P_{ij}
$$

(4)

ω_1 is the joint probability density of the foreground, ω_2 is the joint probability density of the backgrounds, s, t is the binary group threshold. The value of the foreground component i and j, the value of the background component i and j, the value of the average vector i and j. It is respectively obtained from the following formulas (5), (6) and (7) [6, 7].

$$\mu_1 = (\mu_{1i}, \mu_{1j})^T = \left(\sum_{i=0}^{s} \sum_{j=0}^{t} \frac{i * P_{ij}}{\omega_1}, \sum_{i=0}^{s} \sum_{j=0}^{t} \frac{j * P_{ij}}{\omega_1} \right)^T \qquad (5)$$

$$\mu_2 = (\mu_{2i}, \mu_{2j})^T = \left(\sum_{i=s+1}^{L-1} \sum_{j=t+1}^{L-1} \frac{i * P_{ij}}{\omega_2}, \sum_{i=0}^{s} \sum_{j=0}^{t} \frac{j * P_{ij}}{\omega_2} \right)^T \qquad (6)$$

$$\mu_T = (\mu_{Ti}, \mu_{Tj})^T = \left(\sum_{i=0}^{L-1} \sum_{j=0}^{L-1} i * P_{ij}, \sum_{i=0}^{L-1} \sum_{j=0}^{L-1} i * P_{ij} \right)^T \qquad (7)$$

μ_1 is the values of the foreground component i and j, Among them, μ_{1i} the value of the foreground component i, μ_{1j} is the value of the foreground component j. μ_T are the values of global region components i and j. Among them, μ_{Ti} is the value of global region component i, and μ_{Tj} is the value of global region component j [6, 7]. The two-dimensional maximum peak difference is shown in formula (8).

$$\text{Max}\{\text{TrMax}\} = \text{Max}\{[(\omega_1 * \mu_{Ti} - \mu_{1i}) * (\omega_1 * \mu_{Ti} - \mu_{1i}) + (\omega_1 * \mu_{Tj} - \mu_{1j}) \\ * (\omega_1 * \mu_{Tj} - \mu_{1j})]/(\omega_1 * \omega_2)\} \qquad (8)$$

In formula (8), Max{TrMax} is the maximum peak difference after iteration. The point where the maximum two-dimensional peak difference occurs is the demarcation point between foreground and background. But two dimensional points contain the values of i and j. One is the current gray value of the demarcation point. The other one is the gray value of the window function of this gray point. The final binary demarcation point formula is shown in (9).

$$\sqrt{i * j}\big/_1 = (0.99999 \sim 1.00000) \begin{cases} Y \to i \\ N \to (i + j)\big/_2 \end{cases} \qquad (9)$$

In formula (10), I and j are respectively the position coordinates of the maximum peak difference Max{TrMax}. In other words, this is the binary gray threshold, If the binary group threshold is processed by $\sqrt{i * j}\big/_i$, its value is close to 1, Then the threshold of the foreground and background is i, otherwise its value is $(i+j)\big/_2$, That's the average value of the binary group.

3   Analysis of Experimental Results

According to the above two - dimensional OSTU window function setting algorithm and two - dimensional threshold averaging algorithm, The next step is to test the standard data set and the simulated experimental scene data set respectively.

3.1   The Test Results of Standard Data Sets

Figure 5 is screenshot of some randomly selected images from the standard data set downloaded from GitHub.

Fig. 5. The screenshots of some randomly selected images from the standard data set.

For the data set picture shown in Fig. 5, Construction of the average grayscale function window and the average of two-dimensional threshold were carried out. Figure 6 is the binary image corresponding to Fig. 5.

Fig. 6. Binary images corresponding to some images randomly selected from the standard data set.

According to whether the constructed grayscale distribution is on the negative diagonal, the data-oriented evaluation algorithm is excellent [7, 8]. As shown in Fig. 7, the gray distribution corresponding to Fig. 6 is on the negative diagonal.

As show in Fig. 7, the randomly selected standard data set distributed on the negative diagonal, only art11.png is abnormal, but the binarization effect in Fig. 6 is acceptable.

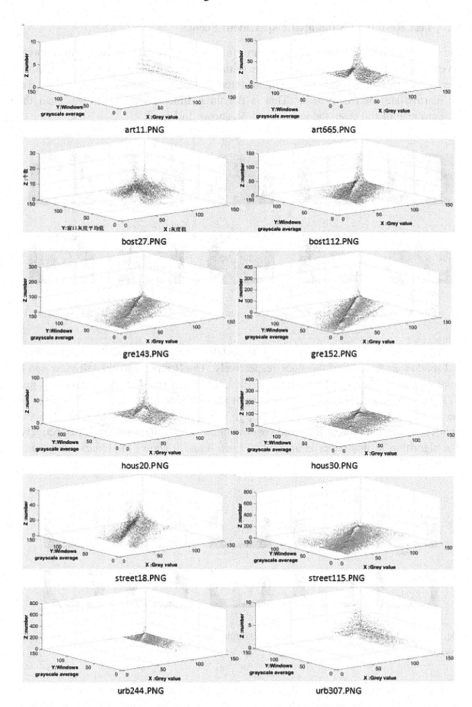

Fig. 7. The three-dimensional point distribution diagram corresponding to some images randomly selected from the standard data set.

3.2   Test Results of Simulated Experiment Scenes

The experimental simulation scenes are full-stack (That is the maximum three-dimensional standard size of the case, the critical point of the "Five -Distance" alarm), over-stack (That is beyond the maximum three-dimensional standard size of the case, the alarm state) and owe-stack (That is the three-dimensional size is less than the standard size of the case, the safe state). As shown in Fig. 8.

Fig. 8. The experiment simulation scene graph of full-stack, over-stack, owe-stack.

Y1R.jpg, Y5L.jpg, Y5R.jpg in Fig. 8 are left and right views under different light and shadow in the case of the stack respectively. The R represents the left view and L represents the right view (the following picture naming rules are the same). Y2l.jpg, Y2R.jpg, Y5L.jpg, Y5R.jpg are left and right views under different light and shadow in the case of full stack respectively. Y2l.jpg, Y3L.jpg, Y3R.jpg, Y4R.jpg are left and right views under different light and shadow in the case of the over-stack respectively. The algorithm in this paper is applied to Figs. 8 and 9 shows the binary image processed in Fig. 8.

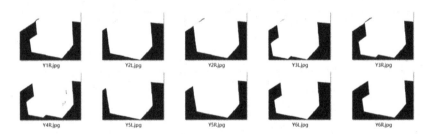

Fig. 9. The binarization diagram of the simulation scenes of full-stack, over-stack and owe-stack.

Figure 9 is numerically analyzed according to whether the constructed grayscale distribution is on the negative diagonal [7, 8]. As shown in Fig. 10, the gray scale distribution corresponding to Fig. 9 is on the negative diagonal.

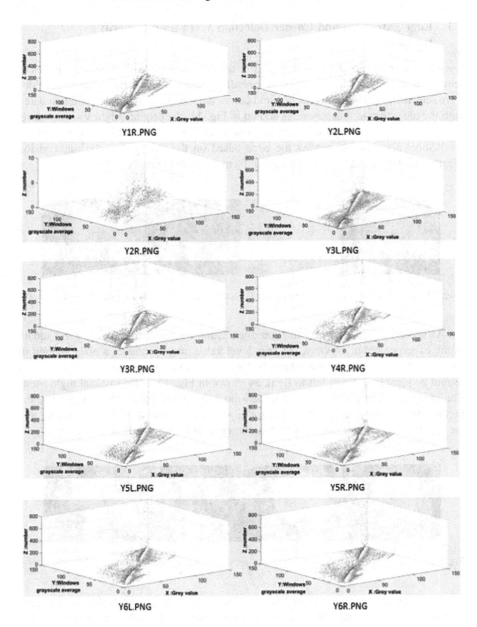

Fig. 10. The three-dimensional point distribution diagram of the simulated scenes of full-stack, over-stack and owe-stack.

It can be seen from Fig. 10 that the binarization 3d points in the experimental simulation scene can be roughly distributed on the negative diagonal to reach 100%.

3.3 Edge Extraction and Corner Detection Were Used to Verify the Results

Considering the low definition of Fig. 2 in the case of night vision, take measures to remove ambiguities, Gray histogram, one-dimensional OSTU and other algorithms were selected [9–11]. Edge detection and corner detection are performed and compared with the algorithm in this paper. As shown in Fig. 11, the original night vision picture, the night vision picture processed with gray level square homogenization, the picture used Sobel algorithm to extract the edge based on the left picture, the night vision picture that contain the corner position information are from left to right.

Fig. 11. Edge detection picture and corner detection picture after homogenization treatment.

As shown in Fig. 11, After the homogenization treatment of the gray level square of the experimental night view, the gray level value range produces a phenomenon of concentration, the edge is not relatively clear when extracting, and the corner points cannot be identified. From left to right, as shown in Fig. 12, is the original night view. The binomial picture after the one-dimensional OSTU based on the left picture, the pictures further using sobel algorithm for edge detection based on the left picture and the night vision picture that contain the corner position information.

Fig. 12. Edge detection and corner detection pictures after one-dimensional OSTU processing.

As shown in Fig. 12, although the edge and corner information of the object can be detected after the one-dimensional OSTU processing, the binarization image does not effectively extract the foreground information, As a result, the original night view contains a lot of noise information, that is, the upper left corner of pictures 2, 3 and 4 in Fig. 12. As shown in Fig. 13, from left to right are the original night view, the binomial view after two-dimensional OSTU processing based on the original image, the edge detection diagram of sobel algorithm after two-dimensional OSTU processing, and the night view after sobel algorithm corner point detection.

Fig. 13. Edge detection and corner detection pictures after two-dimensional OSTU processing.

As shown in Fig. 13, the two-dimension OSTU algorithm, which is averaged by two-dimensional threshold value, can fully extract the object foreground information in the night vision environment, as shown in Fig. 13, the second picture, and accurately detect the position of edges and corners according to the foreground information, as shown in Fig. 13, the third and fourth pictures.

4   The Conclusion

In the study of binocular "five-distance" measurement of hazardous chemicals, aiming at the problem of cargo feature extraction with fuzzy imaging or close gray value of binocular camera in night vision environment, an algorithm of two-dimensional otsu threshold function window design and two-dimensional threshold average is proposed. Experiments show that the algorithm can effectively remove noise and improve the accuracy of edge and corner extraction by combining foreground and background information.

Project Supporter. This paper is supported by the national key research and development project (2016YFC0801500). As well as the Innovation Ability Promotion Project of Municipal Colleges of Beijing Education Commission (2016014222000041).

References

1. Wenyu, J.: Major events and WeChat opinion - to "Tianjin port on August 12 extra-large fire explosion accident" as an example. China Newspaper Industry, 40–41 (2018)
2. Kai, Z.: How to prepare for the safety of the warehouse tank farm management - think of from zhangjiakou 11.28 accident. Chemical Enterp. Manage., 59–60 (2019)
3. Lichen, S., Rujun, W., Yingquan, D.: Problems and suggestions on safety supervision of dangerous chemicals in China. J. Saf. Sci. Technol., 161–166 (2014)
4. Bo, D., Zhichao, L., Xuejun, L., Xin, L., Guang, Y.: UWB location technology of hazardous chemicals stacking warehouse based on Thiessen polygon. J Chem. Ind. Eng. China, 878–884 (2016)
5. Xuejun, L., Yuchen, W., Bixian, Y.: For warehouse and laser ranging in adaptive hierarchical clustering denoising algorithm research. Comput. Sci., 208–211, 217 (2018)

6. Bing, F., Zhang, W., Jun, S..: Based on quantum particle swarm optimization (PSO) algorithm of Ostu threshold image segmentation. Comput. Eng. Des., 3429–3431, 3434 (2008)
7. Yang, Y., Lin, K., Chuang, Y.: Adaptive particle swarm optimization of two-dimensional image of OSTU threshold segmentation algorithm is proposed. J. Electron. Meas. Instrum., 827–832 (2017)
8. Zhibing, H., Tao, L., Kun, Y.: Based on the improved two-dimensional Ostu algorithm of SAR image segmentation method. J. Naval Aeronaut. Astronaut. Univ., 153–157 (2010)
9. Wei, W., Jin-jin, Z., Hong-jun, Z.: Segmenting, removing and ranking partial blur. SIViP 8(4), 647–655 (2014). https://doi.org/10.1007/s11760-013-0573-8
10. Tao, Z., Dequn, L., Xinnian, W.: Based on texture feature of reference image fuzzy degree evaluation method. Comput. Eng. Appl., 185–191 (2012)
11. Wei, W.: Fuzzy removal and quality evaluation research based on single image. University of Science and Technology of China, 133 (2014)

Structural-Based Graph Publishing Under Differential Privacy

Yiping Yin, Qing Liao, Yang Liu, and Ruifeng Xu[✉]

Harbin Institute of Technology (Shenzhen), Shenzhen, China
iron75951@gmail.com, {liaoqing,liu.yang,xuruifeng}@hit.edu.cn

Abstract. Mining data from social and communication network have been attracting recent attention from various research fields. However, these data represented by large-scale graphs are often sensitive and private. It is a necessity of developing algorithms to publish large-scale graph while not revealing sensitive information. As a standard for data privacy preservation, differential privacy based algorithm are also widely used in publishing graph-based dataset. However, previous differential privacy based methods often bring huge computational cost and lack the capability of modeling complicated graph structure. To address these challenge, we propose a novel graph publishing algorithm which combines community detection with differential privacy method. By segmenting the graph into several sub-graphs by community detection, differential privacy methods is able to handle large-scale graphs with complex structure. Experimental results on several datasets demonstrates the promising performance of the proposed algorithm compared with original differential privacy methods.

Keywords: Graph publishing · Partition · Differential privacy · Structural information

1 Introduction

Recent progress in information technology has led to impressive success in a wide range of applications, including recommendation system, medical services, tasks among Neutral Language Processing, etc. Such advances are enabled partly thanks to the availability of open large-scale graph based datasets. The graphs in such datasets are generally large and contain many sensitive information of users. Therefore, we need to explore methods that meet the demand of applications while offering principled and rigorous privacy guarantee.

Current methods in publishing private data could be partitioned into two aspects, including k-anonymity [1] and Differential Privacy [2]. The former is vulnerable to attackers with strong background knowledge, while the latter performs more robust for privacy preserving when facing strong attackers. Considering the specialization of abstract graphs, there are various of ways to convert them. The common procedure is to instantiate abstract graph as specific graph,

© Springer Nature Switzerland AG 2019
R. Xu et al. (Eds.): ICCC 2019, LNCS 11518, pp. 67–78, 2019.
https://doi.org/10.1007/978-3-030-23407-2_6

then to obtain the representation of graph, such as adjacency matrix [3], hierarchical random graph [4], quadtree [3,6], etc. These previous methods are often applicable in small-scale graph datasets. However, real graph are generally complex, which increases the difficulty on representation. Furthermore, the main limitation among the methods is that real graphs are generally large and sparse, leading to high computational expense.

In order to address these challenges, we propose a new algorithmic method for publishing graph dataset. To handle with the problem of high computational expense, we bring in a community detection algorithm to quickly partition the graph into several communities. To handle with the other problem of low utility, we explore a method by adding different degree of noises based on graph structural information. With the combination of Fast-unfolding community detection algorithm and the framework of differential privacy based on hierarchical representation, satisfactory performances are achieved on several large-scaled graph datasets.

2   Related Works

Differential privacy has been applied to a wide variety of scenes, including security of data publishing [8], machine learning [10], deep learning [9,10], etc. Data publishing is an essential step along the life circle of data. It can be divided into several branches by differing the type of objects, such as relational data, graph data, etc.

In order to publish graph data with privacy protection, we need to face the challenges on sanitizing graph with high-quality structural information. To address such problem, some proposed methods tried to add noises to edges within a graph, while others build an adjacency matrix first to store the information of a graph [3,5,11], or hierarchical structure [4], or use quadtree [6] to represent the graph, then do perturbation. However, most of the mentioned methods bring in large noises that threaten the utility of sanitized data. For instance, Wang et al. [11] propose to perturb the eigenvalues and eigenvectors of the corresponding adjacency matrix. It imposes noise of magnitude proportional to $\mathcal{O}\sqrt{n}$, where n is the number of nodes in the network. It also causes high computation expense.

Some methods have tried to partition a graph into many subgraphs [7], and then do perturbation. However, it seems to be lack of strict privacy guarantee and some interpretation on why partition them in those way. Meanwhile, same noises are added to edges with no differences, which affects the utility of sanitized data.

A key limitation to most of the mentioned methods is that the connection strength hidden in the graph is ignored (i.e., all the edges are added to the same noise). Thus, extra noises are brought into the weak connections. Furthermore, the size of real networks is generally so large that causes large computational expense.

3   Preliminaries

In this section, we briefly recall the relevant definition of Differential Privacy, introduce both Laplace mechanism and Exponential mechanism, also composition theorems. Furthermore, reveal the logical relationship between hierarchical and community structure.

3.1   Differential Privacy

Differential Privacy [2] provides a strong standard with privacy guarantees for algorithms on datasets. It is defined in terms of the concept of adjacent database. In our research, each training dataset is a set of node pairs representing edges. Two sets are adjacent if they differ in a single entry, that is, if one node pair (edge) is present in one set and absent in another.

Definition 1. *A randomized function $\mathcal{M}$ gives ε-differential privacy if for all data sets d and d' differing on at most one element, and all $S \subseteq Range(\mathcal{M})$,*

$$P_r[\mathcal{M}(d) \in S] \leq \exp(\varepsilon) \times P_r[\mathcal{M}(d') \in S]$$

A mechanism $\mathcal{M}$ satisfying this definition promises that even if the data of one participant is removed from the dataset, no outputs would become significantly more or less likely. ε is called privacy budget.

3.2   Laplace Mechanism

Before calling Laplace mechanism, we need to recall the definition of Sensitivity first.

Definition 2. *The sensitivity of a function $f : D \rightarrow \mathbb{R}^k$, which is a numeric query function that maps datasets to k real numbers, is:*

$$\Delta f = \max_{d,d' \in D} |f(d) - f(d')|, \|d - d'\| = 1$$

Where D is the dataset, d and d' are the arbitrary neighboring subsets belonging to D [14].

The sensitivity (global sensitivity) of a function f captures the magnitude by which a single individual's data can change the function f in the worst case. Therefore, it gives an upper bound on how much we must perturb its output to preserve privacy. Laplace mechanism will simply compute f, and perturb each coordinate with noise drawn from the Laplace distribution. The scale of the noise will be calibrated to the sensitivity of f (divided by ε). Thus, given any function $f : D \rightarrow \mathbb{R}^k$, the Laplace mechanism is defined as:

$$\mathcal{M}(d, f(\cdot), \varepsilon) = f(d) + (Y_1, \ldots, Y_k)$$

Where Y_i are *i.i.d.* random variables drawn from $\text{Lap}(\Delta f / \varepsilon)$. The Laplace mechanism preserves ε-differential privacy.

3.3 Exponential Mechanism

The exponential mechanism is the natural building block for answering queries with arbitrary utilities, especially non-numeric utilities.

Definition 3. *Given arbitrary range $\mathcal{R}$, the exponential mechanism is defined with respect to some utility function $u : \mathcal{D} \times \mathcal{R} \to \mathbb{R}$, which maps output to utility scores. Then the sensitivity of u is:*

$$\Delta u \equiv \max_{r \in R} \max_{d,d':\|d-d'\| \leq 1} |u(d,r) - u(d',r)|$$

The exponential mechanism outputs each possible $r \in \mathcal{R}$ with probability proportional to $\exp\left(\frac{\varepsilon u(d,r)}{\Delta u}\right)$ and so the privacy loss is approximately:

$$\ln\left(\frac{\exp(\varepsilon u(d,r)/\Delta u)}{\exp(\varepsilon u(d',r)/\Delta u)}\right) = \varepsilon\left[u(d,r) - u(d',r)\right]/\Delta u \leq \varepsilon$$

An exponential mechanism is ε-differential privacy when it selects and outputs an $r \in \mathcal{R}$ with probability proportional to $\exp\left(\frac{\varepsilon u(d,r)}{2\Delta u}\right)$.

3.4 Composition Theorems

Definition 4. *Let $\mathcal{M}_1 : \mathcal{D} \to \mathcal{R}_1$ be an ε-differentially private algorithm, and let $\mathcal{M}_2 : \mathcal{D} \to \mathcal{R}_2$ be an ε-differentially private algorithm. Then their combination, defined to be $\mathcal{M}_{1,2} : \mathcal{D} \to \mathcal{R}_1 \times \mathcal{R}_2$ by the mapping: $\mathcal{M}_{1,2} = \mathcal{M}_1(d), \mathcal{M}_2(d)$ is ε-differentially private.*

3.5 The Relationship Between Hierarchical and Community Structure

Hierarchical structure, which is represented by a binary tree, persistently partitions a network into a set of smaller communities until to the level of single node. The leaves of the hierarchical structure are nodes in the network. The instance drawn on karate club dataset is shown in Fig. 1. We can see that nodes in the same community are more likely to be divided into the same subtree [12].

4 Our Method

In this section, we describe four components of our method in turn: Fast-unfolding community detection algorithm, differentially private representation for hierarchical structure, differentially private noise addition, sanitized subgraphs generation. The framework is shown in Fig. 2.

Unlike the mentioned methods in Sect. 2, we explore the fast community detection algorithm to partition an entire graph into two parts, and then to build hierarchical representations of these two parts to make them satisfy Differential Privacy. Finally, we perturb the edges to generate an entire sanitized graph. By setting different privacy budget, we achieved different extend privacy preserving for edges located in different parts of a graph.

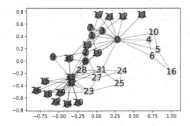

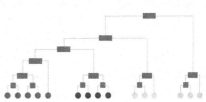

(a) Visualization of communities within karate club.

(b) Corresponding hierarchical structure.

Fig. 1. The abstract representation of communities within karate club partitioned by Fast-unfolding algorithm. Nodes in the same communities are of the same color, and the number marks id of a node.

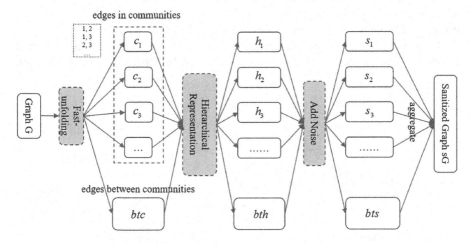

Fig. 2. The framework of our method.

4.1 Partition the Graph into Subgraphs by Using Fast-Unfolding Algorithm

Fast-Unfolding algorithm [13] is a heuristic community detection method based on modularity optimization, which extract the community structure of large networks. The main goal of the algorithm is to optimize the modularity of the entire network by continuously choosing the new nodes.

This algorithm is mainly divided into two phases that are repeated iteratively. One where modularity is optimized by allowing only local changed of communities; one where the found communities are aggregated in order to build a new network of communities. The phases are repeated iteratively until no increase of modularity is possible.

The reason why we choose the algorithm is that it performs high efficiency on large networks compared to other community detection algorithm [15].

Parts of the algorithm efficiency results from the fact that gain in modularity obtained by moving a node i into a community C can be easily computed by:

$$Q(G, s) = \frac{1}{4m} \sum_{i \in N} \sum_{j \in N} \left(A_{i,j} - \frac{k_i k_j}{2m} \right) s_i s_j$$

which unfolds a complete hierarchical community structure of a network.

4.2   Construct Differentially Private Representation for Hierarchical Structure

Intuitively, there is logical connection between the hierarchical structure and the results of partitioned communities.

A hierarchical structure shown in Fig. 1(b) can represent some structural information of network shown in Fig. 1(a). For instance, graph G consists of nodes and edges between the nodes. We use probability value to label the strength of links between nodes, which ranges from 0 to 1.

A specific form of the above expression is shown in Fig. 3. The strong links will be labeled a value close to 1, while weak links will be labeled a value close to 0.

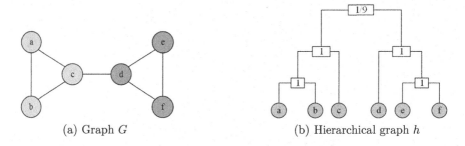

(a) Graph G (b) Hierarchical graph h

Fig. 3. The content of hierarchical graph h is corresponding to graph G. For instance, the value of link probability between subset $\{a, b, c, d\}$ and $\{e, f\}$ is close to 0. Thus means that there is a weak connection between them. On the contrary, the value of link probability between subset $\{a, b\}$ and node c is 1, which implies the very strong connection between them.

The leaves in h represents nodes in graph G, the internal nodes drawn by rectangle store the value of link probability P_r between nodes or node set.

$$P_r = |e_r| / (|n_{L_r}| \cdot |n_{R_r}|)$$

where r is corresponding to an internal node, e_r is the number of links between left and right node subset that have a common ancient r in h, n_{L_r} and n_{R_r} respectively are the number of nodes in the left and right node subsets.

We can construct a large set of h from the different view of a graph. A criterion known as Maximum Likelihood Estimation is used to measure how plausible an h is to represent G. The math equation is as follows.

$$L(h, \{P_r\}) = \prod_{r \in h} P_r^{e_r} (1 - P_r)^{n_{L_r} n_{R_r} - e_r}$$

where h is the hierarchical graph, $\{P_r\}$ is the set of link probabilities stored in the internal nodes of h.

Intuitively, the logarithmic form of the equation can be converted as follows.

$$\log L = \sum_{r \in h} n_{L_r} \cdot n_{R_r} \cdot h(P_r)$$

where $h(P_r) = P_r \log P_r + (1 - P_r) \log (1 - P_r)$ is Shannon Entropy. Essentially, an h with higher $logL$ is a better representation of the network structure than those with lower likelihoods.

Another problem occurs when we quantify "better h". There is an infinite space of h for a network with n nodes. Hence, directly computing the logL of each h is unfeasible.

Xiao et al. proposed a method [4] that uses MCMC to sample the best h. A detail in her algorithm is to transition operation along the Markov chain, then to use Monte Carlo sampling method to pick some "better h". But the network is so large that constructing a set of h leads to high computation expense.

A way to address this problem is to improve the computation efficiency within the algorithm. Changing nodes or subsets by first storing their paths from root to leaves into a list will help a lot. Furthermore, partitioning the entire graph G into two parts (edges stored in communities and between communities) and making different extend differential privacy for them will save the time of computation for very large networks.

4.3   Differentially Private Noise Addition

Having constructed the hierarchical structure, a next issue is computing the probabilities stored in internal nodes with applying Laplace noise. The ε-differential privacy allows us to add noise that obeys Laplace distribution with scale $\Delta f / \varepsilon$ to each internal node. Each internal node requires to be updated the new connection probability in a top-down direction, we are one step away from generating a sanitized graph.

4.4   Sanitized Subgraphs Generation

Regenerate edges of each subgraph by referring to the connection probabilities. In the end, aggregate these subgraphs to an entire graph for publishing.

5   Experimental Results and Discussion

In this section, we evaluate the utility of sanitized graph over three various real networks, which are online social networks, voting networks and collaboration networks. By measuring a group of statistic properties of the original and sanitized graphs, we demonstrate the robustness and generalization of our method.

5.1   Datasets

To approximate the real and various networks in the world, we use several different types of networks in this section as shown in Table 1.

Table 1. Large network datasets description.

Name	Type	#Nodes	#Edges	Description
ego-Facebook	Undirected, online social network	4039	88234	Social circles from Facebook
wiki-Vote	Directed, voting network	7115	103689	Wikipedia who-votes-on-whom network
ca-HepPh	Undirected, collaboration network	12008	118521	Collaboration network of Arxiv High Energy Physics

ego-Facebook is an online social network dataset, where nodes represent users in Facebook, and edges represent the friendship between them. wiki-Vote is a voting network that contain Wikipedia voting information for adminship elections. ca-HepPh is a collaboration network that covers scientific collaborations between authors submitted to High Energy Physics. All of the datasets are available in Stanford Network Analysis Projects.[1]

5.2   Evaluation Criteria

A set of graph evaluation criterias of statistic information about degree and path are used to measure the similarity between original graph and sanitized graph. Essentially, we consider an undirected network when compute these statistic properties [16].

Degree. Considering an undirected network, the degree of a node is defined as the number of its neighboring edges.

---

[1] http://snap.stanford.edu/data/index.html.

Average Degree (AD). For an undirected network, the average degree is defined as follows.

$$AD = \frac{1}{n_{i=1,n}} \deg(v_i)$$

Where n is the number of nodes in the network, v_i is a node from the set of nodes v of a network.

Maximum Degree (MD). The maximum degree of an undirected network is defined as follows.

$$MD = \max(\deg(v_i)), i = 1, \ldots, n$$

Degree Variance (DV). For an undirected network, degree variance is used to measure the dispersion of degree, which defined as follows.

$$DV = \frac{1}{n}\sum_{i=1,\ldots,n}(v_i - AD)^2$$

Clustering Coefficient (CC). Let node v_i has k_i neighbors, then at most $k_i(k_i - 1)/2$ edges can exist between them. CC denotes the fraction of these allowable edges that actually exist.

Degree Distribution (DD). The degree distribution denotes the histogram of degree of all nodes.

Path. Average path length is one of the three most robust measures of network topology, along with its clustering coefficient and its degree information.

Average Path Length (APL). The average path length is defined as the average number of steps along the shortest paths for all possible pairs of network nodes. For an undirected network with a set of vertices V, the APL is defined as follows.

$$APL = \frac{1}{n(n-1)} \cdot \sum_{i \neq j} d(v_i, v_j)$$

Where n is the number of vertices, $d(v_i, v_j)$ denotes the shortest distance between v_i and v_j, where $v_i, v_j \in v$.

Diameter (D). D is defined as the maximum distance among all possible pairs of network nodes.

$$D = \max(d(v_i, v_j))$$

Effective Diameter (ED). The effective diameter denotes 90% effective distance among all possible pairs of network nodes.

Connectivity Length (CL). The connectivity length is defined as the mean size of a smallest edge cut disconnecting v_i from v_j, which is an important measure of its resilience as a network.

Shortest Path Length Distribution (SPLD). The shortest path length distribution de-notes the histogram of shortest path length among all pairs of nodes.

5.3 Experimental Results

This section reports on our evaluation on three various type of datasets: Facebook, wiki-Vote and ca-HepPh. The following results show the utility of sanitized graph compared to the original graph and privHRG [4].

Statistics Information About Degree. Figure 4 shows a group of statistic information of degree mentioned in Sect. 4.2. It can be seen that, in all cases, our method better preserves information of original networks on the properties of degree, meaning that it preserves good degree feature within networks.

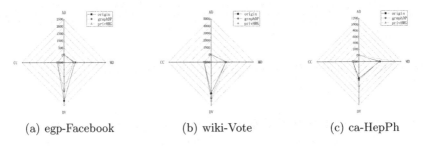

(a) egp-Facebook   (b) wiki-Vote   (c) ca-HepPh

Fig. 4. Results on statistics information about degree, including AD, CC, MD, DV mentioned in Sect. 4.1, on three real large network datasets. Each radar line in these charts corresponds to degree information of a network with different privacy protecting model (i.e. origin, graphDP, privHRG).

Statistics Information About Path. Figure 5 shows some statistic information of path mentioned in Sect. 4.2. It shows that, in all cases, our method preserves better skewness of the original networks than privHRG, meaning that it preserves good path feature within networks.

Shortest Path Length Distribution. Figure 6 depicts the shortest path length distribution of each network. We can observe that the sanitized networks preserve the shapes of the distributions with respect to those of the original networks than that of privHRG.

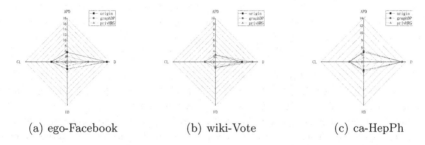

(a) ego-Facebook   (b) wiki-Vote   (c) ca-HepPh

Fig. 5. Results on statistics information about path, including APD, D, ED, CL mentioned in Sect. 4.1, on three real large network datasets.

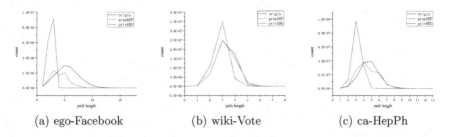

(a) ego-Facebook   (b) wiki-Vote   (c) ca-HepPh

Fig. 6. Results on shortest path length distribution on three real large network datasets. Each broken line corresponds to a graph with different privacy protecting model.

5.4   Discussion

We demonstrate the large network publishing under differential privacy, sanitizing the entire graph with different degree of protection, achieved by bringing in a community detection algorithm. In our experiments on ego-Facebook, wiki-Vote and ca-HepPh, the results are observed to have better performance on a group of statistic properties of degree and path, which reflect the utility of a network.

It is important to acknowledge that lots of real networks are much larger than those of ego-Facebook or wiki-Vote, and may have much more communities; except taking advantage of fast community detection algorithm, bounding the privacy budget also plays an important parts on sanitizing the large networks. That's will be the immediate focus of our future work.

Acknowledgement. This work was partly supported by National Key Research and Development Program of China (2017YFB0802204), National Natural Science Foundation of China U1636103, 61632011, and 61876053, Key Technologies Research and Development Program of Shenzhen JSGG20170817140856618, Shenzhen Foundational Research Funding JCYJ20170307150024907.

References

1. Sweeney, L.: k-anonymity. Int. J. Uncertainty Fuzziness Knowl. Based Syst. **10**(05), 557–570 (2008)
2. Dwork, C.: Differential privacy. Lect. Notes Comput. Sci. **26**(2), 1–12 (2006)
3. Chen, R., Fung, B.C.M., Yu, P.S., et al.: Correlated network data publication via differential privacy. VLDB J. **23**(4), 653–676 (2014)
4. Xiao, Q., Chen, R., Tan, K.L.: [ACM Press the 20th ACM SIGKDD international conference - New York, New York, USA (2014.08.24–2014.08.27)] Proceedings of the 20th ACM SIGKDD international conference on Knowledge discovery and data mining - Differentially private network data release via structural inference, pp. 911–920 (2014)
5. Ahmed, F., Jin, R., Liu, A.X.: A random matrix approach to differential privacy and structure preserved social network graph publishing. CoRRabs/1307.0475 (2013)
6. Cormode, G., Procopiuc, M., Shen, E., Srivastava, D., Yu, T.: Differentially private spatial decompositions. CoRRabs/1103.5170 (2011)
7. Bhagat, S., Cormode, G., Krishnamurthy, B., et al.: Class-based graph anonymization for social network data. Proc. VLDB Endow. **2**(1), 766–777 (2009)
8. Zhu, T., Li, G., Zhou, W., et al.: Differentially private data publishing and analysis: a survey. IEEE Trans. Knowl. Data Eng. **29**(8), 1619–1638 (2017)
9. Abadi, M., et al.: Deep learning with differential privacy. In: Proceedings of the 2016 ACM SIGSAC Conference on Computer and Communications Security, pp. 308–318 (2016)
10. Song, S., Chaudhuri, K., Sarwate, A.D.: Stochastic gradient descent with differentially private updates. In: 2013 IEEE Global Conference on Signal and Information Processing (Glob-alSIP). IEEE (2013)
11. Wang, Y., Wu, X., Wu, L.: Differential privacy preserving spectral graph analysis. In: Proceedings of 17th Pacific-Asia Conference on Knowledge Discovery and Data Mining, pp. 329–340 (2013)
12. Perotti, J.I., Tessone, C.J., Caldarelli, G.: Hierarchical mutual information for the comparison of hierarchical community structures in complex networks. Phys. Rev. E **92**(6), 062825 (2015)
13. Blondel, V.D., Guillaume, J.L., Lambiotte, R., et al.: Fast unfolding of communities in large networks. J. Stat. Mech. Theory Exp. **2008**(10), 0 (2008)
14. Dwork, C., Roth, A.: The algorithmic foundations of differential privacy. Found. Trends Theor. Comput. Sci. **9**(3–4), 211–407 (2013)
15. Lancichinetti, A., Fortunato, S.: Community detection algorithms: a comparative analysis. Phys. Rev. E **80**(5), 056117 (2009)
16. Leskovec, J., Faloutsos, C.: Sampling from large graphs. In: ACM SIGKDD International Conference on Knowledge Discovery & Data Mining (2006)

Face Detection Using Bionic Cascaded Framework

Jin Li$^{(\boxtimes)}$, Ziyue Chen, Shunxin Ouyang, Jingyu Xie,
Yue Hu, and Hui Lv

Hubei University of Technology,
Wuhan, Hubei, People's Republic of China
lijin@hbut.edu.cn

Abstract. Face interaction plays an irreplaceable role in the service robots human-robot interaction, while face detection in this kind of scenario are challenging due to restrictions on computing capabilities and power, the character of real-time and requirements of the interaction pattern. Recent studies show that deep learning approaches can achieve impressive performance on these kinds of tasks. Therefore, a bionic cascaded framework adopted a cascaded structure with two stages of carefully designed face detectors is proposed in this paper, which exploits saccade and attention mechanism of human eyes to balance the performance. In addition, in the working process of the service robots, a new online sampling strategy that can improve the performance of interaction patterns is presented. In this way, the real time face detection and more natural human-robot interaction pattern can be achieved in service robot systems.

Keywords: Face detection · Human-robot interaction ·
Bionic cascaded framework

1 Introduction

Face detection is essential to many applications, such as face recognition, facial expression analysis and human-robot interaction, while the large visual variations of faces, including occlusions, large pose variations and extreme lightings, impose great challenges for its applications. In some special scenario such as the service robots, some special requirements of computing capabilities, power limit, the character of real-time and the natural interaction pattern become new challenges.

Viola Jones Face Detector, a kind of cascade face detector, is first proposed by Viola and Jones [1], which utilizes Haar-Like features and AdaBoost to train cascaded classifiers. They have presented an approach for face detection to minimize the computation time and achieve high detection accuracy. The approach was used to construct a faster face detection system than the previous approach, which could be used to construct highly efficient detectors for other objects as well. Because its low computational complexity, good performance with real-time efficiency can be achieved, which is suitable for embedded system application such as service robots. However, although the Viola Jones Face Detector has excellent real-time capability, the detector may

R. Xu et al. (Eds.): ICCC 2019, LNCS 11518, pp. 79–90, 2019.
https://doi.org/10.1007/978-3-030-23407-2_7

degrade significantly in practical applications. In order to solve the problem mentioned above, many subsequent studies pay attentions to more powerful learning algorithms.

For example, Yang et al. [2] proposed that the feature representation used for face detection still cannot meet the demand for effectively and efficiently handling faces with large appearance variance in the wild. They borrow the concept of channel features to the face detection domain, which extends the image channel to diverse types such as gradient magnitude and oriented gradient histograms and therefore encodes rich information in a simple form. They adopt a novel variant called aggregate channel features, make a full exploration of feature design, and discover a multi-scale version of features with better performance. A multi-view detection approach is also proposed with consideration of featuring score re-ranking and detection adjustment to deal with facial poses in the wild. Pham et al. [3] present a method that extends the integral image to do fast integration over the interior of any polygon that is not necessarily rectilinear and apply the method to Viola and Jones' object detection framework. The polygonal Haar-like features are proposed to improve classical Haar-like features. Zhu et al. [4] integrate the cascade-of-rejectors approach with the Histograms of Oriented Gradients (HoG) features to achieve a fast and accurate human detection system.

Even with more advanced features and classifiers, the detection accuracy may also degrade significantly in the complex real environment. Thus, some works are done to improve the performance as well.

Mathias et al. [5] show a properly trained vanilla DPM that improves over commercial and research systems and a detector based on rigid templates-similar in structure to the Viola & Jones detector, which can reach similar performance. Yan et al. [6] solve the speed bottleneck of deformable part model (DPM), while maintaining the accuracy in detection on challenging datasets. A proximal gradient algorithm is adopted to progressively learn the low rank filter in a discriminative manner. For cascade part pruning, neighborhood aware cascade is proposed to capture the dependence in neighborhood regions for aggressive pruning. Look-up tables are constructed to replace expensive calculations of orientation partition and magnitude with simpler matrix index operations for HOG feature extraction. Zhu et al. [7] present a unified model for face detection, pose estimation, and landmark estimation in real-world, cluttered images. The model is based on a mixture of trees with a shared pool of parts and the results show that tree-structured models are surprisingly effective at capturing global elastic deformation, while being easy to optimize unlike dense graph structures.

Although the DPM for face detection achieve remarkable performance, they need high computational expense, which limits their application in service robots.

Recently, convolutional neural networks (CNNs) develop fast and are widely used in the computer vision tasks such as image classification [8], face detection and face recognition [9]. Recent researches proved that CNNs can achieve high performance in these kinds of tasks. Some CNNs based face detection approaches have been proposed in recent years.

Yang et al. [10] propose a novel deep convolutional network (DCN) that achieves outstanding performance on FDDB, PASCAL Face, and AFW. They consider finding faces from a new perspective through scoring facial parts responses by their spatial structure and arrangement. The scoring mechanism is carefully formulated considering challenging cases where faces are only partially visible. The network can detect faces under severe occlusion and unconstrained pose variation, which are the main difficulty and bottleneck of the face detection approaches above. Li et al. [11] propose a cascade architecture built on convolutional neural networks with very powerful discriminative capability, while maintaining high performance. The proposed CNN cascade operates at multiple resolutions, quickly rejects the background regions in the fast-low resolution stages, and carefully evaluates a small number of challenging candidates in the last high-resolution stage. To improve localization effectiveness, and reduce the number of candidates at later stages, a CNN-based calibration stage is introduced after each of the detection stages in the cascade. The proposed method achieves high detection performance on two public face detection benchmarks. CNN often need high computing resource, so some lighter and faster face detectors such as the MTCNN proposed in reference [12] and the LFFD proposed in reference [13] are developed. While general speaking, the computation load of CNN-based method is relatively high for an embedded system such like a service robot, so it's performances of real-time and energy consumption need to be improved.

In this paper, a bionic cascaded framework is proposed which exploits saccade and attention mechanism of human eyes to balance the performance. Our framework adopts a cascaded structure with one stage of vision attention and two stages of carefully designed cascaded detectors which can balance the performance and the costs. In addition, in the working process of the service robots, we propose a new online sampling strategy that can improve the performance of interaction patterns. Our method achieves real time face detection in service robot systems, and more natural human-robot interaction pattern.

2 Approach

In this section, we will describe our approach towards face detection and alignment by a bionic cascaded framework.

2.1 Overall Framework

The overall pipeline of our approach is shown in Fig. 1. Given an image as a frame the service robot has got, we initially send it into an attention captor to build an image pyramid in different scales, which is the input of the following two-stage cascaded detector.

Stage 1: Firstly, we introduce a unit named attention captor to deal with the frame. The attention captor focuses on parts of the image randomly, and generates a set of images including different parts of the original image, which forms an image pyramid. The pyramid contains different scales of the original image. The following detector modules will find patterns like face in this dynamic pyramid.

Stage 2: The second module is a Front Detector. Front Detector is a fast and light face detector. It is used to detect whether faces exist in the fragment the attention captor gets from the image in the field of view. Since the pyramid generated by the attention captor contains many sub-images, the Front Detector should have the capability of process pictures fast, and using limited computational power, which is important for an

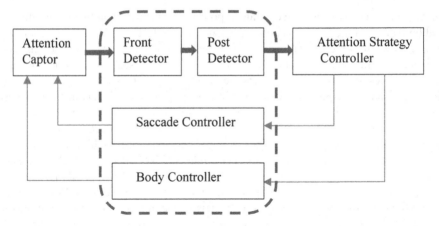

Fig. 1. The overall pipeline of the bionic cascaded framework.

embedded system to realize a real-time process. When the results of the Front Detector are given, the robot should choose one of the faces to establish eye contact at a particular moment.

Stage 3: The third module is a Post Detector. General speaking, a light and fast face detector has a relatively low accuracy. So, the result of the Front Detector should be confirmed by the Post Detector which has higher performance. The output of the Post Detector should be regards as faces. The Post Detector may need more computing resources and longer time, while the point is that it only deals with the sub-images generated by the Front Detector, which are more likely including faces. The number of this kind of sub-images is limited. In fact, the Motion Control Unit including Saccade Controller and Body Controller already moves to focus on one selected face when the Front Detector gives the results, which make the robot seem agile. The Post Detector and the eye contact process at the same time, and when the face is confirmed, the eye contact will continue, if it is proved that the sub-image does not contain a face, the robot may move its attention to another zone of the image.

Stage 4: The results of the cascaded detector is sent to the module of the Attention Strategy Controller. The Attention Strategy Controller control the behavior of the human-robot interaction, according to the information of faces detected by the detector. The Attention Strategy Controller may control the robot focus on one face, switch to another face, or move to a new area to search something new. When the action is decided, the Attention Strategy Controller will send control information to the execution units including the Saccade Controller and Body Controller. The small amplitude motion may be executed by the Saccade Controller and the greater amplitude motion may be executed by the Body Controller.

Stage 5: The decision of the Attention Strategy Controller may be executed by the Saccade Controller and Body Controller. The Saccade Controller controls the rapid and jerky movement of the eyes between positions of rest, which realized by driving the eyeballs of the robot. Saccade is a characteristic pattern of human eye movements. This design makes a more human-like robot when it communicates with people. What's more, the saccade is related to the attention shift, so this mechanism may bring a more human-like information processing pattern at the same time. When the moving range of focus exceeds the saccade, the Body Controller will drive the head or body to move. The moving of the focus affects the images captured by Attention Captor in turn.

2.2 The Implementation of Modules

Attention Captor: Attention Captor captures segments from the whole image. The size and location of the sub-image is random, which ensures that every part of the image may be observed. There are two style of method to capture sub-image. One is uniform distribution method, which capture every part of the image in the same probability. The other is normal distribution method, namely, the area close to a particular position has the higher probability to be captured, which means that the attention is focusing on a particular part of the image, normally speaking the center of the picture.

The Front Detector: As mentioned above, the Front Detector should be fast and light, and the accuracy is not so important. It should be run on a embedded system efficiently. Considering the above factors, we choose Viola Jones Face Framework to design the Front Detector. The Viola Jones face detection [1] classifies images based on the value of three kinds of rectangle features as shown in Fig. 2.

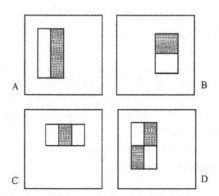

Fig. 2. Three kinds of rectangle features. Figure (A) and (B) show the two-rectangle features. Figure (C) shows a three-rectangle feature, and (D) shows a four-rectangle feature.

The rectangle features above can be computed very rapidly using an intermediate representation for the image which called the integral image [14]. The integral image at location x, y contains the sum of the pixels above and to the left of x, y.

A cascade of classifiers is constructed which achieves increased detection performance while radically reducing computation time. The key insight is that smaller, and therefore more efficient, boosted classifiers can be constructed which reject many of the negative sub-windows while detecting almost all positive instances. Simpler classifiers are used to reject the majority of sub-windows before more complex classifiers are called upon to achieve low false positive rates.

The Post Detector: As mentioned above, the Post Detector should have high performance and accuracy. So, in this paper, we choose the Multi-task Cascaded Convolutional Networks to build the post detector. This framework adopts a cascaded structure with three stages of carefully designed deep convolutional networks that predict face and landmark location in a coarse-to-fine manner. In addition, in the learning process, a new online hard sample mining strategy is proposed which can improve the performance automatically without manual sample selection. This method can achieve very fast speed in joint face detection and alignment and has relatively low computational complexity when performing inference.

Attention Strategy Controller: The Attention Strategy Controller determine the position of the focus on random time intervals. It makes the robots act like a human observing behavior. As we know, saccade is a specific behavior in human visual system. When we make a saccade, our visual system is blind during the flight of the saccade, so we can see at the beginning and we can see at the end but while the eye is moving, we cannot see. The Attention Strategy Controller controls the Saccade Controller, Body Controller and the Attention Captor to model this kind of human visual behavior and attention mechanism. The Attention Strategy Controller achieves similar features in average fixation duration, average saccade amplitude and fixation counts. Interest area locates in the faces with higher probability, which matches the visual instinct of human.

3   Experiments

In this section, we evaluate the effectiveness of the proposed Bionic Cascaded Framework, and test the system in three aspects: the random pyramids generating, the cascaded face detector and the attention distribution. The system is implemented by Python 3.5 in TensorFlow framework.

3.1   The Random Pyramids Generating

When a frame of image is obtained, the Attention Captor captures segments from the whole image. The size and location of the sub-image is random, and generate a set of sub-images including different parts of the original image, then an image pyramid is formed after normalization. A test image is shown in Fig. 3.

Fig. 3. A frame of image.

The sub-images captured by the Attention Captor and the random pyramid generated are shown in Figs. 4 and 5 respectively.

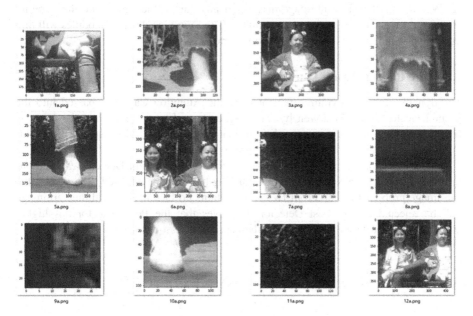

Fig. 4. The sub-images captured by the attention captor.

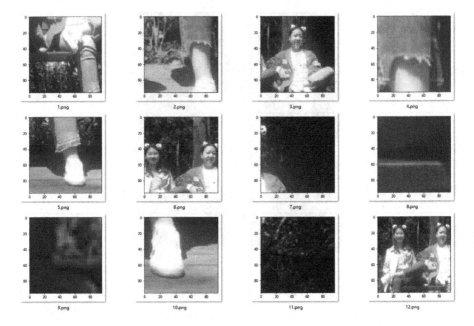

Fig. 5. The random pyramid.

We can see that the sub-image may cover any part of the frame, and the pyramid contains different scales of the original image. The following detector modules will find patterns like face in this dynamic random pyramid.

3.2   The Cascaded Face Detector

The dynamic random pyramid generated by the Attention Captor is passed into the Front Detector which is driven by Viola Jones Face Framework. Then the result is passed into the Post Detector which is driven by the Multi-task Cascaded Convolutional Networks to confirm. This procedure is shown in Fig. 6.

We can see that sometimes the faces proposed by the Front Detector can be confirmed by the Post Detector, while the bounding box may be adjusted. Sometimes, the sub-image proposed by the Front Detector contains no face in fact, and the sub-image will be rejected by the Post Detector. It proves that the Post Detector has higher accuracy than the Front Detector, and the cascade detector works.

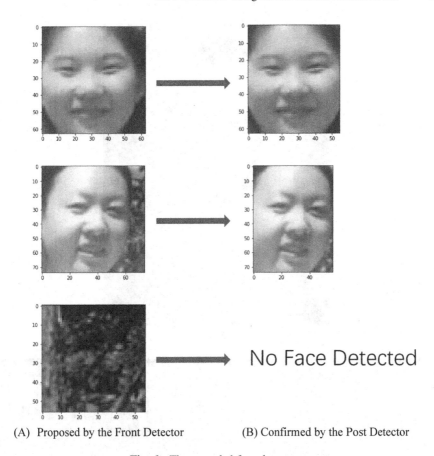

(A) Proposed by the Front Detector   (B) Confirmed by the Post Detector

Fig. 6. The cascaded face detector.

3.3 The Attention Distribution

Saccade is a specific behavior in human visual system. When we make a saccade, our visual system is blind during the flight of the saccade, so we can see at the beginning and we can see at the end but while the eye is moving, we cannot see. And saccade is considered to have relationship with attention shift. Eye tracking data can show the process of attention drifting when human observing, as shown in Fig. 7 [15].

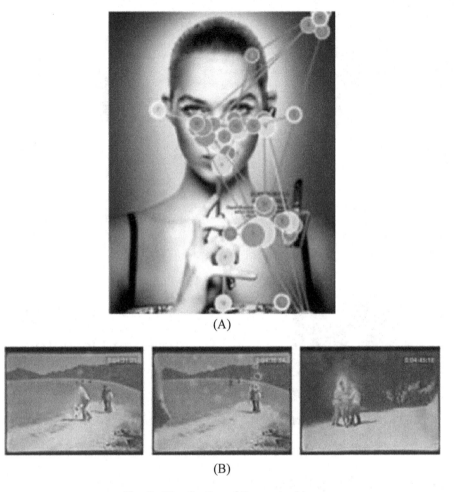

(A)

(B)

Fig. 7. Visualization of the eye tracking.

We can see that the areas containing faces are easy to attract the attention of the observers. We got similar results in our experiment using the Attention Strategy Controller, as shown in Fig. 8.

It's shown that the robot tends to focus on the faces just like humans do. This will help the service robots to act and observe in the similar way as human beings, which could improve the performance of interaction patterns.

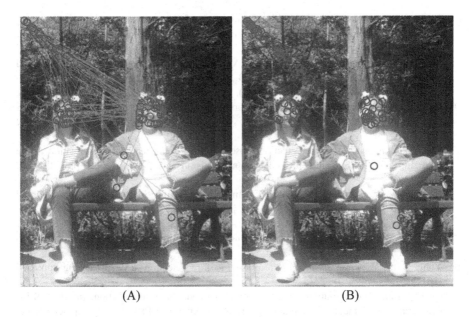

(A)   (B)

Fig. 8. The attention distribution generated by Attention Strategy Controller.

4 Conclusion

In this paper, we have proposed a bionic cascaded framework for face detection in service robots. Experimental results demonstrate that our methods are effective. The proposed algorithm is easy to run on an embedded system adopting the design of cascaded detector. The system can achieve real time face detection, and simulate the attention mechanism of human beings, which can improve the performance of interaction pattern. Combining the characteristic of service robot systems, the proposed design balance the power consumption, real-time performance, user experience etc. In the future, we will exploit more eye tracking data to train the system, to further improve the performance.

Acknowledgement. This research is supported by the Doctoral Scientific Research Fund of Hubei University of Technology (No. BSQD2017071).

References

1. Viola, P., Jones, M.: Robust real-time face detection. Int. J. Comput. Vis. **57**(2), 137–154 (2004)
2. Yang, B., et al.: Aggregate channel features for multi-view face detection, pp. 1–8 (2014)
3. Pham, M.T., et al.: Fast polygonal integration and its application in extending haar-like features to improve object detection. In: The Twenty-Third IEEE Conference on Computer Vision and Pattern Recognition, June 2010, CVPR 2010, pp. 13–18. IEEE, San Francisco (2010)

4. Zhu, Q., et al.: Fast human detection using a cascade of histograms of oriented gradients. In: 2006 IEEE Computer Society Conference on Computer Vision and Pattern Recognition. IEEE (2006)

5. Mathias, M., Benenson, R., Pedersoli, M., Van Gool, L.: Face detection without bells and whistles. In: Fleet, D., Pajdla, T., Schiele, B., Tuytelaars, T. (eds.) ECCV 2014. LNCS, vol. 8692, pp. 720–735. Springer, Cham (2014). https://doi.org/10.1007/978-3-319-10593-2_47

6. Yan, J., et al.: The fastest deformable part model for object detection. In: 2014 IEEE Conference on Computer Vision and Pattern Recognition (CVPR). IEEE Computer Society (2014)

7. Zhu, X., Ramanan, D.: Face detection, pose estimation, and landmark localization in the wild. In: 2012 IEEE Conference on Computer Vision and Pattern Recognition (CVPR). IEEE (2012)

8. Krizhevsky, A., Sutskever, I., Hinton, G.: ImageNet classification with deep convolutional neural networks. In: Advances in neural information processing systems, vol. 25, no. 2 (2012)

9. Sun, Y., Wang, X., Tang, X.: Deep learning face representation by joint identification-verification (2014)

10. Yang, S., et al.: From facial parts responses to face detection: a deep learning approach (2015)

11. Li, H., et al.: A convolutional neural network cascade for face detection. In: 2015 IEEE Conference on Computer Vision and Pattern Recognition (CVPR). IEEE Computer Society (2015)

12. Zhang, K., et al.: Joint face detection and alignment using multitask cascaded convolutional networks. IEEE Signal Process. Lett. **23**(10), 1499–1503 (2016)

13. Yonghao, H., Dezhong, X., Lifang, W., Meng, J., Shiming, X., Chunhong, P.: LFFD: a light and fast face detector for edge devices. https://arxiv.org/abs/1904.10633. Accessed 26 Apr 2019

14. Freeman, W.T., Adelson, E.H.: The design and use of steerable filters. IEEE Trans. Pattern Anal. Mach. Intell. **13**(9), 891–906 (2002)

15. Shiwei, C., Lingyun, S.: A survey on visualization for eye tracking data. J. Comput.-Aided Design Comput. Graphics **26**(5), 698–707 (2014). (In Chinese)

A Neural Rumor Detection Framework by Incorporating Uncertainty Attention on Social Media Texts

Yan Gao[1], Xu Han[2], and Binyang Li[1(✉)]

[1] School of Information Science and Technology,
University of International Relations, Beijing, China
`{ygao,byli}@uir.edu.cn`
[2] College of Information Engineering, Capital Normal University,
Beijing, China
`hanxu@cnu.edu.cn`

Abstract. Automatic rumor detection technology has become a very urgent need, as rumors can arise and spread dauntingly fast in social media, which bring unforeseeable and devastating impacts. However, current approaches mainly capture the event semantics or user-based features for rumor detection, but neglect the uncertainty expressions that strongly indicate the unverified nature of a rumor. As a result, these methods perform suboptimal when the topics of being verified rumors are changing wildly. In this paper, we present a neural rumor detection framework, namely NERUD. In NERUD, both uncertainty semantics and the event semantics of a word are represented by the attention mechanisms to generate a rumor representation for rumor detection. Experiments were conducted on the benchmark dataset and the Chinese Rumor Corpus (CRC), and the results showed that our NERUD outperformed state-of-the-art approaches on CRC dataset, and the uncertainty semantics was proven effective on rumor detection task.

Keywords: Rumor detection · Deep learning · Neural network · Attention

1 Introduction

The concept of rumor has a long history, and there are various definitions from different research communities [1]. In this paper, we follow a widely accepted definition of rumor, that is, "an **unverified** statement towards an **object, event**, or **issue of public concern**, circulating from person to person with a **context of uncertainty**. This unverified statement is circulating without known authority for its truthfulness at the current time, but may turn out to be true, or partly or entirely false; alternatively, it may also remain unresolved" [16]. For simplicity, this paper will use "rumor" to refer to "false rumor", i.e., rumor that eventually is verified to be false. Since the false rumors are often related to events of public concern that are widely circulated among the public, the widespread of rumors will always cause public disturbed and threat social stability.

© Springer Nature Switzerland AG 2019
R. Xu et al. (Eds.): ICCC 2019, LNCS 11518, pp. 91–101, 2019.
https://doi.org/10.1007/978-3-030-23407-2_8

Figure 1 illustrates two rumors generated from Sina Weibo and Twitter. As to Rumor 1, it was towards the earthquake occurred in Japan in 2011 that finally resulted in the nuclear crisis in Fukushima. This incident arouse the public anxiety and uncertainty about the nuclear radiation, and rumors were posted in both Twitter and Chinese Microblog platforms, which is spiking the demand in the U.S. and China for a cheap drug that can protect against the radiation damage, and leading to huge society chaos. Similarly, Rumor 2 was posted in Twitter in 2013 which caused severe social panic, and lead to great economic damage in the stock market.

Rumor 1: **食用含碘盐很可能预防辐射。**

**Salt** could probably prevent people from nuclear radiation.

Rumor 2: _**Someone witnessed** that Barack Obama was injured in an explosion in the White House._

Fig. 1. Two examples of rumors. (Those words in bold express uncertain semantics, while those words underlined express the semantics of rumor-related events.)

So, there is an urgent need to automatically identify rumors in social media, so that the diffusion of harmful rumors can be stopped to minimize the negative impact.

To address this problem, existing research on rumor detection mainly used a wide variety of features incorporated into machine learning algorithms to identify rumors [12]. These features involve tweets statistics [13], topic-based features [15], user-based features [6], and location-based features [15], etc. Furthermore, propagation information was also taken into consideration [4, 9, 14]. More recently, some studies employ deep learning approaches into rumor detection by integrating the semantics representation of the topic or event [7, 8, 11].

However, from the rumor definition, two aspect information should be accounted for rumor detection: (1) the representation of event of public concern; and (2) the context of uncertainty. The above approaches mainly focused on the information of event semantics, but ignore the uncertainty expressions that strongly indicate the unverified nature of a rumor. In fact, when producing a rumor, users often use uncertain descriptive information, such as it is said that..., likely, and etc. In Fig. 1, both rumors use uncertainty expressions, e.g. probably and witnessed. Different from event semantics that mainly represented by topical words, the uncertainty semantics are expressed more consistent, even if the topics of being verified events are changing wildly and frequently. So, we argue that current approaches only accounting for event semantics perform suboptimal for rumor detection in social media.

In this paper, we present a neural rumor detection framework, namely NERUD. In NERUD, both the event semantics and uncertainty semantics are represented by attention mechanisms to generate a rumor representation that facilitate the NERUD to identify rumors. Particularly, to the best of our knowledge, we are the first to exploits uncertainty semantics for rumor detection in social media texts. Furthermore, various sentence encoders are used in our model, including RNN, LSTM, and Bi-GRU, which are proven useful in text representation. Experiments were conducted on the benchmark dataset provided in [8] and the Chinese Rumor Corpus (CRC) constructed by ourselves, and the results showed that our NERUD outperformed state-of-the-art approaches on CRC dataset, and the uncertainty semantics was proven effective on rumor detection task. In addition, we also tested conventional machine learning models with and without uncertainty semantics, and the results confirmed that uncertain semantics could boost rumor detection of conventional models.

2   Neural Rumor Detection Framework

In this section, we will describe our neural rumor detection framework, namely NERUD. NERUD is consructed by twto parts: (1) Rumor detector, and (2) Uncertainty identifier. The rumor detector attempts to detect the rumor from the posts, while the uncertainty identifier aims to detect uncertainty expressions, which will be further integrated into rumor representation. The overall framework is illustrated in Fig. 2.

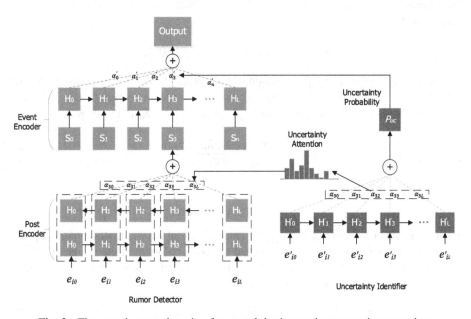

Fig. 2. The neural rumor detection framework by integrating uncertainty attention.

2.1   Rumor Detector

Without the loss of generality, an event can be defined as E, which consists of all the related posts $P_i \in E$, $i \in [0, T]$. A post can be formulated as a word sequence $P_i = \{x_{ij}\}, j \in [0, L]$ where L denotes the length of P_i. The objective of rumor detection is produce y for each E, and $y \in \{rumor, non\_rumor\}$, that is to identify if the event is a rumor.

More specifically, our rumor detector consists of 3 layers, i.e., a word embedding layer, a post encoder layer, and an event encoder layer.

In the word embedding layer, the pre-trained word vectors are used to transform each word x_{ij} into a vector, and then all the word vectors are connected together to generate a tensor of word embeddings vector e_{ij}. In addition, all sentences are segmented into words with the stop words being removed, and we set the words out of vocabulary as zero-vectors.

Then, we will encode each single post and the corresponding event, respectively. We will firstly use bidirectional GRU network to encode the post. Because the rumourous content is often mixed in the normal texts, the position where the rumorous content exactly starting cannot be determined. One-layer GRU network cannot capture all the information of the rumorous texts. So we use bidirectional GRU, Bi-GRU [2] network as a basic model to learn the features of rumors. After that, we will encode the event based on the corresponding posts by using GRU network.

Post encoder: a bidirectional GRU network [2] is applied to obtain post information. We follow the classic bidirectional GRU settings and obtain the concatenation of the utterance embedding $h_{ij} = [\overrightarrow{h_{ij}}, \overleftarrow{h_{ij}}]$. Thus the final utterance of a post h_{ij} can be calculated by:

$$h_{i0} : h_{ij} = BiGRU(e_{i0}...e_{ij}) j \in [0, L] \tag{1}$$

where e_{ij} is the vectorised representation of each word. In the post encoder layer, the attention mechanism is used to find the words that are important to the post, the attention distribution α_{ij} represents the importance of jth word in the ith post:

$$\alpha_{ij} = \frac{\exp(tanh(W_w h_{ij} + b_w))}{\sum_j \exp(tanh(W_w h_{ij} + b_w))} \tag{2}$$

$$s_i = \sum_{j=0}^{L} \alpha_{ij} h_{ij} \tag{3}$$

where s_i is the embedding of ith post that summarizes all the information of each post.

Event encoder: To encode the event, all the posts belonging to the same event are all used. Given an event E, each post $P_i \in E$ is represented by a vector s_i, and the event utterance $h = \{h_i : h_T\}$ can be computed by:

$$h_i : h_T = GRU(s_0...s_i) i \in [0, T] \tag{4}$$

Through the GRU encoder network, the event semantics can be represented by the attention vector α_i that measures the importance of each post vector.

$$\alpha_i = \frac{\exp(tanh(W_s h_i + b_s))}{\sum_i \exp(tanh(W_s h_i + b_s))} \tag{5}$$

$$d = \sum_{i=0}^{T} \alpha_i h_i \tag{6}$$

where d is the representation of an event. Then, a softmax function is used for rumor classification, and the training loss is calculated by cross entropy.

$$p_r = softmax(Wd + b) \tag{7}$$

In this way, we can obtain the event semantics representation, which will be further used in rumor detection. In order to the uncertainty expression, NERUD also incorporates uncertainty semantics into rumor detector, and well introduce in the following subsection.

2.2 Uncertainty Identifier

In order to represent the uncertainty semantics, we follow the work of [5], and integrate attention mechanism into sentence encoders for uncertainty detection. The purpose of this model is to learn the representation of uncertainty expression. To do this, we feed the vectorized representation of each word w_i in a sentence sequentially to an encoder network, and produce the post encoder hidden state h'_{ij} by RNN-based encoders. During this procedure, the attention distribution α'_{ij} is calculated by the following equations.

$$\alpha'_{ij} = \frac{exp(tanh(W_h h'_{ij} + b_h))}{\sum_L exp(tanh(W_h h'_{ij} + b_h))} \tag{8}$$

The uncertainty attention α'_{ij} indicates the importance of each word in uncertainty identifier. As a result, more attentions are paid to the words with uncertainty semantics, assigned with a higher weight. Then, the attention distribution will be used to generate the weighted sum of the hidden states of the encoder h'_i.

$$h'_i = \sum_{j=0}^{L} \alpha'_{ij} h'_{ij} \tag{9}$$

where h'_i is a vectorized representation of a post, which is fed through a softmax function to produce the uncertainty possibility distribution, and further to detect if the post is a rumor.

$$p_{ui} = softmax(W_u h'_i + b_u) \tag{10}$$

In this paper, RNN-based encoders have four variants, namely, RNN, LSTM, and Bi-GRU. Particularly, as Bi-GRU has two opposite directions, its uncertainty representation takes the concatenation of the last states from both directions, which come from two ends of a given context.

2.3 Rumor Detection by Exploiting Uncertainty Semantics

By now, we have acquired the semantics representation by using the uncertainty identifier. We will then employ the uncertainty attention into rumor detector. Rather than output the label of uncertainty identifier module, we employ the uncertainty distribution α'_{ij} and the uncertainty representation h'_i into rumor detector. In NERUD, we integrate the uncertainty semantics into both post encoder layer and event encoder layer.

First of all, we will obtain the post representation with uncertainty attention by the following equations:

$$\alpha_{s_{ij}} = \frac{exp(f(\alpha'_{ij}, \alpha_{ij}))}{\sum_{j=1}^{L} exp(f(\alpha'_{ij}, \alpha_{ij}))} \tag{11}$$

$$f\left(\alpha'_{ij}, \alpha_{ij}\right) = tanh(W_U \alpha'_{ij} + W_R \alpha_{ij} + b_s) \tag{12}$$

where $f()$ is used to calculate the important words for representing the sentence, while W_U, W_R and b_s are the weights.

Therefore, in rumor detector, we use the attention distribution $\alpha_{s_{ij}}$ that incorporating uncertainty attention to replace the α_{ij} in Eq. (3). The final post representation s_i can be expressed with the attention weight as $\alpha_{s_{ij}}$.

For the event encoder layer, the uncertainty probability distribution p_{ui} is used to combine the event representation and the uncertainty representation to form a rumor representation as follows:

$$\alpha_{d_i} = \frac{exp(f(s_i, p_{ui}))}{\sum_{i=1}^{T} exp(f(s_i, p_{ui}))} \tag{13}$$

$$f(s_i, p_{ui}) = tanh(W_S s_i + W_P p_{ui} + b_d) \tag{14}$$

Similar with the post layer encoder, α_i in Eq. (5) is replaced by α_{d_i} which represent the combination of the event and the uncertainty semantics. Finally, the rumor representation with both event semantics and uncertainty semantics is used for rumor detection.

3   Experiment

In this section, we design several experiments to evaluate the performance of our model. We will firstly introduce the experiment setup, including the dataset, the approaches for comparison, and parameter tuning. Then we will evaluate the effectiveness of NERUD, and discuss the experimental results in details.

3.1   Experiment Setup

Our experiments are conducted on three datasets. The first one was created by [8] and widely used by many studies on Chinese rumor detection tasks. The second one was constructed by ourselves, namely Chinese Rumor Corpus (CRC). CRC contains 2,542 rumors that are officially reported by Sina community management center. We also collected the same number of non-rumors from Sina Weibo to construct the corpus.

The details of the two datasets are shown in Table 1. Since we need to train our uncertainty identifier, we also use the Chinese benchmark dataset for uncertainty identification provided by [5].

In our experiment, precision, recall and F1-measure were used as the effectiveness evaluation metrics.

We utilized word2vec [10] to train Chinese word embeddings based on the experimental datasets. We set the dimensionality of the word vector as 150, and the window length of max pooling as the maximum word length. To build up the vocabulary, we retain the word appearing more than three times and the word not in the vocabulary will be replaced with an unknown token.

Table 1. Statistics on two experimental datasets.

Statistic	Ma's dataset	CRC dataset
Posts	3,805,656	4,017,365
Rumors	2,313	2,542
Non-Rumors	2,351	2,542

During the training of the uncertainty attention model, we set the dimension of hidden size as 500 for RNN and LSTM. For the Bi-GRU encoder, which has two directions, we set the state size as 250 for each direction. We following the work by [3] with learning rate 0.01 for training. Since several sentence encoders are utilized in uncertainty attention module, we will firstly compare the performance of different sentence encoders on uncertainty identification task based on the benchmark dataset provided by [5].

From Table 2, we can see that the uncertainty identifier with Bi-GRU encoder achieves the best performance, so we will use Bi-GRU encoder in the following experiments.

For the rumor detector model, we use a Bi-LSTM network with 250 hidden states for each direction. The learning rate is set as 0.001 and the dropout rate is set 0.5, both empirically. We only utilize 10% of Ma's dataset for parameter tuning, and the rest of the dataset were split with a ratio of 3:1 for training and test. Note that since NERUD exploits the uncertainty attention that will perform consistency based on different events, we also follow the same parameter setting for testing our CRC dataset.

Table 2. Comparison between different encoders.

Encoders	Precision	Recall	F1
RNN	0.712	0.680	0.696
LSTM	0.778	0.785	0.781
Bi-GRU	**0.792**	**0.789**	**0.790**

3.2   Approaches for Comparison

The effectiveness of our model is evaluated by comparing with the state-of-the-art methods. The contrastive methods include traditional machine learning model e.g. SVM and the neural network methods as follows:

- SVM: is the basic classification model which uses n-gram and tf-idf features for rumor detection. We set it as the baseline in our experiment;
- SVM-UN: is the SVM model with uncertainty feature for rumor detection;
- ML-GRU [8]: uses deep recurrent neural networks to represent the semantics for rumor detection. This model is considered as a neural network baseline without accounting for uncertainty semantics;
- CSI [11]: is the state-of-the-art approach;
- NERUD: is our proposed model which exploits uncertainty attention mechanism to capture the uncertainty expression for rumor detection.
- NERUD*: NERUD without uncertainty identifier.

3.3   Result and Discussion

We firstly compare the effectiveness of NERUD with other approaches on two datasets shown in Tables 3 and 4, and then showcase attention mechanism.

NERUD can effectively detect the rumor on social media texts. On Ma's dataset, although NERUD does not always outperform the others, its performance is close to the best one. On CRC dataset, NERUD achieves the best F1 score. Note that in our experiments, all the neural networks for rumor detection are trained based on Ma's dataset, but only NERUD achieves comparable performance on CRC dataset. It is because that the event semantics are hardly maintained on a new dataset, while the uncertainty semantics will be consistent with the changes of topics.

Table 3. Performance on Ma's dataset.

Method	Precision	Recall	F1
SVM	0.673	0.746	0.707
SVM-UN	0.703	0.766	0.733
ML-GRU	0.871	**0.958**	0.913
CSI	–	–	**0.954**
NERUD*	0.898	0.932	0.914
NERUD	**0.913**	0.941	0.926

Uncertainty feature is useful for rumor detection. By integrating the uncertainty feature into rumor detection, the F1 scores are better than those basic versions without uncertainty ones. It confirms that uncertainty expressions help in detecting rumors in social media texts.

We also visualize rumor representation with different attentions generated by NERUD in a heatmap shown in Fig. 3. It is observed that NERUD highlights different

Table 4. Performance on CRC dataset.

Method	Precision	Recall	F1
SVM	0.603	0.705	0.650
SVM-UN	0.687	0.731	0.708
ML-GRU	0.819	0.880	0.848
CSI	0.831	0.906	0.867
NERUD*	0.825	0.894	0.858
NERUD	**0.872**	**0.921**	**0.896**

types of words for rumor attention and uncertainty attention. For rumor attention, NERUD highlights topical words such as salt and nuclear. For uncertainty attention, NERUD highlights non-topic words, e.g., probably and could that express uncertainty semantics. Therefore, features learned for topical semantics and uncertainty semantics can thus benefit rumor detection.

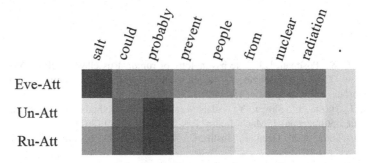

Fig. 3. The heatmap of the rumor attention(Ru Att), uncertainty attention(Un Att), and their combination generated by NERUD. Darker colors indicate higher weights.

4 Related Works

Traditionally, research on rumor detection has mainly focused on developing handcrafted features for machine learning algorithms [12]. [13] proposed a method for rumor detection on Twitter using cue words and tweets statistics. [17] applied two new types of features - client-based and location-based features - to rumor detection on Sina Weibo. Beyond this, user-based [6] and topic-based [15] features have also been explored. [4] demonstrated that there were structural differences in the propagation of rumors and non-rumors, and [14] and [9] experiment with using these propagation patterns extensively to improve detection.

More recently, deep learning models are explored for the task. Compared to traditional machine learning approaches, these deep learning models tended to rely less on sophisticated handcrafted features. [8] introduced a rumor detection model for microblogs based on recurrent networks. The input to their model was simple *tf-idf* features but it outperforms models leveraging handcrafted features. [18] showed that implicit linkages between conversation fragments improve detection accuracy. [7] presented a deep attention model that learns a hidden temporal representation for each sequential posts to represent the hypothesis. [11] integrated textual, user response, and source information into their neural models and achieved better performance.

5 Conclusions

In this paper, we present a neural rumor detection framework, namely NERUD. NERUD incorporates the uncertainty semantics into rumor representation through attention mechanism. Experiments were conducted on two Sina Weibo datasets, and the results showed that our NERUD outperformed state-of-the-art approaches on CRC dataset, and the uncertainty semantics is proven effective on rumor detection task.

Acknowledgement. This work is partially funded by the National Natural Science Foundation of China (61602326, U1636103, 61672361, and U1536207) and the Fundamental Research Fund for the Central Universities (3262019T29 and 3262019T54).

References

1. Allport, G.W., Postman, L.J.: The psychology of rumor. Russell&Russell (1965)
2. Bahdanau, D., Cho, K., Bengio, Y.: Neural machine translation by jointly learning to align and translate. arXiv preprint arXiv:1409.0473 (2014)
3. Duchi, J., Hazan, E., Singer, Y.: Adaptive subgradient methods for online learning and stochastic optimization. J. Mach. Learn. Res. **12**, 2121–2159 (2011)
4. Drien, F., Lada, A.A., Dean, E., Justin, C.: Rumor cascades. In: Proceedings of ICWSM (2014)
5. Li, B., Zhou, K., Gao, W., Han, X., Zhou, L.: Attention-based LSTM-CNNs for uncertainty identification on Chinese social media texts. In: Proceedings of ICSPAC (2017)
6. Liang, G., He, W., Chun, X., Chen, L., Zeng, J.: Rumor identification in microblogging systems based on users' behavior. IEEE Trans. Comput. Soc. Syst. **2**(3), 99–108 (2015)
7. Long, Y., Lu, Q., Xiang, R., Li, M., Huang, C.-R.: Fake news detection through multi-perspective speaker profiles. In: Proceedings of the Eighth International Joint Conference on Natural Language Processing (Volume 2: Short Papers), vol. 2 (2017)
8. Ma, J., et al.: Detecting rumors from microblogs with recurrent neural networks. In: Proceedings of IJCAI (2016)
9. Ma, J., Gao, W., Wong, K.-F.: Detect rumors in microblog posts using propagation structure via Kernel learning. In: Proceedings of the 55th Annual Meeting of the ACL (2017)
10. Mikolov, T., Sutskever, I., Chen, K., Corrado, G., Dean, J.: Distributed representations of words and phrases and their compositionality. In: Proceedings of NIPS 2013 (2013)
11. Natali, R., Seo, S., Liu, Y.: CSI: a hybrid deep model for fake news detection. In: Proceedings of the 2017 ACM on Conference on Information and Knowledge Management. ACM (2017)
12. Qazvinian, V., Rosengren, E., Radev, D.R., Mei, Q.: Rumor has it: identifying misinformation in microblogs. In: Proceedings of EMNLP, pp. 1589–1599 (2011)

13. Takahashi, T., Nobuyuki, I.: Rumor detection on twitter. In: 2012 Joint 6th International Conference on Soft Computing and Intelligent Systems (SCIS) and 13th International Symposium on Advanced Intelligent Systems (ISIS). IEEE (2012)
14. Wu, K., Yang, S., Zhu, K.Q.: False rumors detection on sina weibo by propagation structures. In: 2015 IEEE 31st International Conference on Data Engineering, pp. 651–662 (2015)
15. Yang, F., Liu, Y., Yu, X., Yang, M.: Automatic detection of rumor on sina weibo. In: Proceedings of the ACM SIGKDD Workshop on Mining Data Semantics (2012)
16. Zubiaga, A., Aker, A., Bontcheva, K., Liakata, M., Procter, R.: Detection and resolution of rumours in social media: a survey. arXiv preprint arXiv:1704.00656 (2017)
17. Yang, F., Liu, Y., Yu, X., Yang, M.: Automatic detection of rumor on sina weibo. In: Proceedings of the ACM SIGKDD Workshop on Mining Data Semantics, p. 13. ACM (2012)
18. Sampson, J., Morstatter, F., Wu, L., Liu, H.: Leveraging the implicit structure within social media for emergent rumor detection. In: Proceedings of the 25th ACM International on Conference on Information and Knowledge Management, pp. 2377–2382. ACM (2016)

Using GAN to Generate Sport News from Live Game Stats

Changliang Li[1]([✉]), Yixin Su[2], Ji Qi[3], and Min Xiao[4]

[1] Kingsoft AI Lab, Beijing, China
lichangliang@kingsoft.com
[2] University of Melbourne, Parkville, Australia
yixins1@student.unimelb.edu.au
[3] Kingsoft WPS AI, Wuhu, Anhui, China
qiji1@wps.cn
[4] Beijing University of Posts and Telecommunications, Beijing, China
xiaomincloud@gmail.com

Abstract. One goal in artificial intelligence field is to create well-formed and human-like natural language text given data input and a specific goal. Some data-to-text solutions have been proposed and successfully used in real applied domains. Our work focuses on a new domain, Automatic Sport News Generating, which aims to produce sport news immediately after each match is over so that both time and labor can be saved on writing the news articles. We propose to use Generative Adversarial Networks (GAN) architecture for generating sport news based on game stats. Our model can automatically determine what is worth reporting and generate various appropriate descriptions about the game. We apply our approach to generate NBA (National Basketball Association) game news. Especially, This paper focuses on reporting the summary of game result and performance of players. Our model achieves good results on both tasks. To our best knowledge, this is the first work based on GAN to generate sports news using game statistics.

Keywords: GANs · Text generation · Natural language processing

1 Introduction

Natural Language Generation (NLG) and data-to-text approaches have gained increasing attention in recent years due to the applicability and challenge. By automatically generating high quality texts based on extracted relevant information from the source data, these approaches can eliminate the gap between raw data and human users.

There are some data-to-text solutions have been proposed for specific domains. There are some examples, generation of weather reports from meteorological data in several languages [23,24], the creation of custom letters which answer customers' questions [25], the generation of reports about the state of

© Springer Nature Switzerland AG 2019
R. Xu et al. (Eds.): ICCC 2019, LNCS 11518, pp. 102–116, 2019.
https://doi.org/10.1007/978-3-030-23407-2_9

neonatal babies from intensive care data [26], and the generation of project management [27] and air quality reports [28].

With the development of sports (such as football and basketball), there are thousands of games concerned by billions of people every year. In this paper, we propose an Automatic Sport News Generating System, which aims to produce sport news immediately after each match is over so that saves both time and labor on writing the news articles. However, there are few researches in this area by now, especially using machine learning models, which leaves space in generating articles with better quality. One of the latest research in this area simplifies it into learning to rank problem. This method just pieces together past news sentences based on live comments instead of actually generating sentences using the match data [3]. In this paper, our system generates National Basketball Association (NBA) game news directly from stats. NBA games news usually consists of three parts: the first part summarizes the overall game result; the second part describes player's performance; the last part describes the situation and events occurred during each of four sections. This paper focuses on first two parts, which are closely related to the game stats.

Recently, Generative Adversarial Networks (GAN) [1] have been introduced as a novel way to train a generative model. It has significantly improved several machine learning research fields, such as image generation [13], video prediction [7] and other domains [6,8,14]. The newly proposed WGAN, which solved the convergence problem, has enable the GAN to be utilized on fields based on discrete data, such as Natural Language Procession (NLP).

In this work, our Automatic Sport News Generating System is based on WGAN. There are two models that fulfil different generating tasks in the system. First we leverage a WGAN model to generate most important and variable phrases that can accurately describe the match or player's performances. Then, by putting these phrases together with other constant information into template-based sentence generator, fluent sentences can be generated. This procedure ensures that the generated sentences are well-written and brings clarity to the reader, which is important in sports news. Concatenating outputs from Summary Sentence Generating Model (SSGM), and Player Performance Generating Model (PPGM), the system finally generates the most important parts in NBA sport news.

The main contribution of our system is that it can generate proper phrases to describe different matches, without the intervene of experts (news writers in sport news) or rules. For example, the system can judge which player plays good in a match and generates corresponding phrases to describe him. This process is automatically performed by WGAN according to real news and stats. Furthermore, we define a series of rules for sentence generator so that the generated sentences will be various, and are more close to idiomatic expression. As our best knowledge, this is the first framework that successfully generates sport news with the participating of GAN model based on game stats. It proves the potential of GAN model on NLP applications.

The rest of our paper is structured as follows: Sect. 2 describes related works; Sect. 3 gives a detailed description of our model; Sect. 4 analyzed experiment results and Sect. 5 summarizes this work and the future direction.

2   Related Work

Automatic Sports News Generating is a promising task that aims to generate sports news short after each game finishes. Then readers can receive the news quickly and saves human labor. Currently, there are not many researches on this area. A research recently [3] attempt to generate football news from live comments and use learning to rank method to extract most probable sentence appeared previously to fit a new live comment. Basically, the author reduced the problem into a ranking problem.

GAN has drawn significant attention as a new machine learning model recently [1]. The task of GAN is to produce a generator by a minimax game. In last few years, many variations have been invented to improve the original GAN, such as f-GAN [15], Energy based GAN [20], info GAN [17], and WGAN [21], which proves that GAN is a promising model.

Currently, A work that combines deep convolutional neural networks and GAN (DCGAN) [8] has been proposed, which proves that GAN has great potential in image generating area. Inspired by DCGAN, researchers have made much progress on image generating aspect. A model that utilize DCGAN within Laplacian pyramid framework [6] has been proved that it can produce higher quality images than original DCGAN. Meanwhile, DCGAN has been used to generate photo-realistic natural images by mainly updating the loss function cite.

Besides image generating, NLP is another important task in machine learning area. However, GAN is considered to be difficult to apply on NLP [1] since the update of GAN is based on continued space, but languages are discrete.

Though application of GAN on NLP is tough, there are several attempts on it. An effort that tries to learn words representation from documents [9] has bypass the problem of handling natural language sentences directly. In addition, researchers try to solve the discrete problem by modelling the generator as Reinforcement Learning (RL) called SeqGAN [18]. This model avoids the differentiate problem caused by gradient policy in generator. On the other hand, the discrete problem can be solved by mapping discrete natural languages into continuous vector spaces as well. Combining LSTM and CNN with generated vectors to do text generating [19], researchers successfully generated some realistic sentences. Another work, moreover, established a model that directly researches generating sentences from a continuous space using GAN [5], which is also a progress for GAN on NLP.

Traditional GAN and its applications only receive noise as input and produce output we expected in generator. We cannot decide which class to output if the expected output contains many categories. As solution, Convolutional Generative Adversarial Networks (CGAN) [4], are designed. It adds conditions as part of input both in generator and discriminator. Therefore, GAN can map conditions with expected output, and we are able to generate more accurate output when we feed conditions while testing. [13] is a typical application of CGAN that takes descriptions as conditions and corresponding images as output. Then generator can generate figures according to the descriptive words we input.

WGAN, and its refined version WGAN with gradient policy, is improved forms of GAN that aim to solve the problem that traditional GAN is hard to train. The author analyzed the reason why GAN usually not converge while training, and makes some specific modifies. The modification is very successful. WGAN even works on discrete embedding such as one-hot vectors.

In our research, we attempt to utilize WGAN in sports news generating tasks. Due to the limited usage of GAN on NLP, we reduced the aim of WGAN from generating a whole sentence to generate several phrases whose expression may be different between news. This idea is applicable and reasonable. In sports news, there are many similar sentences. Therefore, we can safely ignore these repeated words and just aiming at the variational words, which are mostly the judgemental words that contain mostly concerned information. Through combining the output words and other constant information, such as team name and player name, our model can generate summary sentences and player performance sentences very similar to what will appear in a real sports news.

3   Method

In this section, we will illustrate the method to generate NBA news. There are two models to fulfil different tasks. One is Summary Sentence Generating Model (SSGM), and another is Player Performance Generating Model (PPGM).

3.1   Summary Sentence Generating Model (SSGM)

SSGM is designed to summarize the overall game situation. It tends to get overall basic information (date, teams and score) as input, and output the summary sentence for the whole match.

The summary sentences contain the most abstract but important information in a match. The structure of summary sentence is relatively stable and simple. However, the phrases are various according to how one team beats another. For example, if Houston Rockets beats Dallas Mavericks with 131-102, the summary sentence in news may likely be "Rockets in home curt whup Mavericks with 131-102". "whup" is used here that is better than normal word "beat" so as to show that Rockets played an excellent game. These differences among words are often decided by news writers, or precisely, experts who can judge the expression by experience.

In our work, we would like SSGM to learn these expressions automatically, which will generate appropriate sentences without importing experts. Therefore, instead of producing the whole sentence using algorithm directly, which will be inefficient and unnecessary, we focus on generating the subjective phrases, such as "whup" in this instance. Then, combining the phrases and other constant information together into template, the SSMG finally output the generated summary sentence.

To fulfil this task, we need to design a generator that can generate phrases suitable for different situations. GAN, a powerful model that can train such a generator through confronting with a discriminator, is very popular in recent researches and produces impressive results. To overcome the problem that GAN is hard to converge while training, a conditional WGAN with gradient policy is used in SSGM.

Comparing to traditional GAN, which trains the discriminator to classify whether an input is real or fake, WGAN uses Wasserstein distance in discriminator to measure the difference between two kinds of inputs, which ensure the model will converge to a plausible result even for one-hot word embedding data. In addition, gradient policy method is utilized to stable the training process so that we can train the model without devoting energy on tuning the model for converging.

In SSGM, the most important factor that will influence the generated phrase is the score of each team. Therefore, a neural network is designed, with scores and noise as input and the phrase embedding as output. In discriminator, another neural network is designed to take scores and corresponding phrase vector as input and output a single value that refers how likely the input phrase and scores combination to be true.
Given:

- p_g: the probability distribution of generated phrase vector, calculated from generator function G, in SSGM, the function is represented as $G(s+z)$, where s is the score vector and z is the noise vector.
- p_r: the probability distribution of real phrase vector.
- $p_{\hat{x}}$: the probability distribution of randomly interpolation calculated by $\hat{x} = \epsilon x_r + (1 - \epsilon)x_g$, where $\hat{x} \sim p_{\hat{x}}$, $x_r \sim p_r$, $x_g \sim p_g$ and $\epsilon \sim Uniform[0,1]$.

The loss function of WGAN in SSGM is:

$$L_G = -E_{x \sim p_g}[D(x+s)] \tag{1}$$

$$L_D = -E_{x \sim p_r}[D(x+s)] + E_{x \sim p_g}[D(x+s)] \\ + \lambda E_{x \sim p_{\hat{x}}}[\|\nabla_x[D(x+s)]\|_p]^2 \tag{2}$$

Where L_G and L_D is the loss of generator and discriminator in WGAN with gradient policy, $D(x)$ is the function in discriminator.

While training WGAN, we try to minimize the two loss values alternatively until it reaches the equilibrium. Then the generator is expected to produce plausible result. After getting the phrases, we input them into Sentence Generator together with constant information to generate the final summary sentences. The constant information includes constant words include team name, score and home or away.

The Sentence Generator in SSGM is designed to combine constant information and generated sentences together according to some templates. For example, the template can be:

On [Date], [Team(A)] made a [Score(A)-Score[B] [SSGM phrase] [Team(B)].

Where [Team(K)] is the name of team K. [Score(K)] is the score that got by team K in the match, the [Date] is the date that the match happened and [Phrase] is the phrase that generated by WGAN. Figure 1 shows the flow chart of the SSGM.

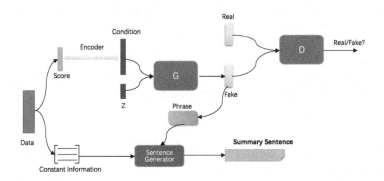

Fig. 1. Flow chart of SSGM

In the flow chart, Generator takes team scores as input and generate score vectors, which is called condition. Then, concatenating with noise, they form the input for neural networks. The output of generator is phrase representation as embeddings that try to imitate what subjective phrase that an expert would like to employ for given scores. In discriminator, the neural network combines the phrase vector (real or fake) and score vector together as input, then output whether the discriminator believes the phrase is real or generated from generator.

3.2 Player Performance Generating Model (PPGM)

Unlike the overall description of match that the sentence structure is relative stable and simple, players' performance is more variable. For instance, there are ten starting players and several alternates in each basketball game. However, not all players will be shown in the news. The news writer tends to report the players who are more eye-catching, such as star players and who acts surprisingly well in that game. In addition, which data of one player is going to be reported (scores, rebounds, assists, etc.) is also worth concerning.

In PPGM, as shown in Fig. 2, we considered all aspects above. The basic structure of PPGM is also a WGAN with gradient policy. In short, the goal of WGAN is to determine which data of a player in this match is worth reporting, and which phrases or words should be used to describe these data.

Firstly, each player will be represented as a vector called player embedding. Therefore, the model can learn the phrase distribution for different players with different data. For example, if an up-and-coming youngster hit 20 scores in his first match, we should report it as "delivered a sensational". However, if LeBron

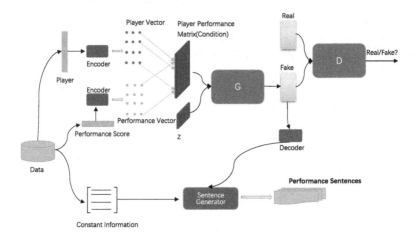

Fig. 2. Flow chart of PPGM

James (a super star in NBA) got 20 scores, it is a normal data for him, we would more likely to use "scored" rather than "delivered a sensational".

Furthermore, players' performance will be represented as performance matrix, which combines player embedding and corresponding performance data as follow:

$$PM_{ij} = py_i^T \times pf_{ij} \tag{3}$$

where PM_{ij} the Performance Matrix of the ith player in the jth match; py_i is the Player Vector of ith player and pf_{ij} is the Performance Vector of the ith player in the jth match.

Next, performance matrix will be used as condition in both generator and discriminator. The generator takes performance matrix and noise as input and outputs word/phrase embedding for each data. These phrases describe how the players perform in term of each data.

Additionally, there is a special embedding that represent "no report" for each data. If the model outputs this embedding with the highest probability, it means that this data of the player is not worth reporting in the news. Therefore, if all data of one player are outputted as "no report", this player's performance will not show in the news at all.

In discriminator, the input consists of performance matrix with real data or generated data together. The output of discriminator decides whether these phrases are in real news or just generated by the generator.

WGAN in PPGM is similar to that in SSGM, but with different conditions and generator output. The generator function is modified into $G(z + v_p^T v_s)$, where v_p is the player vector and v_s is the score vector got by corresponding players. Discriminator function is modified into $D([x + v]_p^T v_s)$, where x is either the output of generator or real phrase vector.

The loss function of WGAN in PPGM is:

$$L_G = -E_{x \sim p_g}[D(x + v_p^T v_s)] \tag{4}$$

$$L_D = -E_{x \sim p_r}[D(x + v_p^T v_s)] + E_{x \sim p_g}[D(x \\ + v_p^T v_s)] + \lambda E_{x \sim p_{\hat{x}}}[\|\nabla_x D(x + v_p^T v_s)\|_p]^2 \tag{5}$$

Since each player's performance phrases are generated separately, the function of Sentence Generator in PPGM is to generate the whole paragraph for all corresponding players combining some constant information. Specifically, constant information contains all constant information such as player names, which team they belongs to and monotonous presentation. The Sentence Generator in PPGM is designed to combine constant information and generated sentences together according to specific rules. Different rules map to different templates so that the expressions are diversified and more similar to a real news. For example:

If one player got outstanding performance on two indexes such as scores and assists, it should be reported as ([Player(i)] [PPGM phrase] points and [PPGM phrase] assists). The connection word "and" is utilized to make sentence smooth.

As a result, the outputs of SSGM and PPGM constitute the paragraphs of a NBA news, which is accomplished automatically.

4 Experiments

In this section, we tested the two models based on real game stats.

4.1 Dataset

The data is collected from NetEase NBA website, which is one of the most popular NBA website in China. It contains full data in each match, including reports and the detailed statistic data for the match and each player. For example, the detailed statistic data and corresponding new report details provided in supplementary material appendix A.

For example, there is a match between Cleveland Cavaliers and Oklahoma City Thunder, the detailed statistic data is as shown in Fig. 3. The corresponding news report is also available as shown in Fig. 4. The summary sentence is shown in green box and players' performance sentences are shown in red box. The translation:

> The Cavaliers scored 115-92 victory over Oklahoma City Thunder. Love scored 29 points, grabbed 11 rebounds and 4 assists, LeBron had 25 points, added 11 times Assists, 7 rebounds, 3 steals but had 5 turnovers, Jefferson got 15 points and 6 rebounds, Smith got 15 points, Thompson got 14 points and 14 rebounds, Mozgov got 11 points and 5 rebounds 15, rebounds and 3 assists, Westbrook gets 20 points, 11 assists and 9 rebounds, Durant finished 26 points, had 5 rebounds and 3 assists, Westbrook had 20 points, added 11 assists and 9 rebounds, Ibaka added 12 points.

The data will then be further processed for both two tasks in subsequent parts.

In the following subsections, to make non-Chinese readers easier to understand the news reports, we translate them into English for illustration.

克里夫兰骑士球员详细

首发球员	时间	投篮	三分	罚球	前场篮板	总篮板	助攻	犯规	抢断	失误	封盖	得分
勒布朗-詹姆斯	40:02	9-20	2-6	8-12	3	15	8	4	0	8	2	28
JR-史密斯	28:12	1-4	1-2	0-0	0	0	0	1	0	2	0	3
凯文-勒夫	34:13	4-13	3-6	4-4	5	21	1	4	0	1	3	15
凯瑞-厄文	34:53	10-22	3-4	1-1	3	3	2	3	0	4	1	24
特里斯坦-汤普森	22:25	0-3	0-0	0-0	3	4	2	2	0	1	0	0
替补球员	时间	投篮	三分	罚球	前场篮板	总篮板	助攻	犯规	抢断	失误	封盖	得分
理查德-杰弗森	14:48	3-6	0-2	3-4	1	4	0	5	0	2	0	9
Dahntay Jones	04:06	1-2	1-2	4-4	0	0	0	0	0	0	0	7
凯尔-科沃尔	19:43	0-3	0-3	0-0	0	4	1	0	0	0	0	0
詹姆斯-琼斯	02:16	0-1	0-1	0-0	0	0	0	0	0	0	0	0
钱宁-弗莱	00:00	0-0	0-0	0-0	0	0	0	0	0	0	0	0
德隆-威廉姆斯	18:30	0-4	0-2	0-0	0	3	1	3	0	2	0	0
艾曼-舒伯特	16:46	2-6	1-3	0-0	0	5	0	1	0	0	0	5
德里克-威廉姆斯	04:06	0-2	0-0	0-0	0	0	0	0	0	0	0	0
凯-费尔德	00:00	0-0	0-0	0-0	0	0	0	0	0	0	0	0
沃尔特-塔瓦雷斯	00:00	0-0	0-0	0-0	0	0	0	0	0	0	0	0
总计	-	30-86	11-31	20-25	15	59	15	23	0	20	6	91
命中率	-	34.9%	35.5%	80%	-	-	-	-	-	-	-	-

Fig. 3. Match stats

4.2   Experiment Settings and Results

In this subsection, we will describe experiment settings and analyze the results.

SSGM Settings. In SSGM, WGAN model takes scores as input, and generates the phrases that describe how one team beat another team. We extract the summary sentences from news reports and related data. Then we process and organize them into form as shown in Table 1.

In this experiment, two scores are both duplicated 10 times into 10 dimensionalities and normalized to guarantee that WGAN will fully use the score information. Then the scores vector are concatenated together to form the conditions. In generator, conditions are concatenated with 5 dimensionality noise vector as the input. Meanwhile, the output phrases are embedded using one-hot embedding method.

阿杜38+8勇士屠骑士1-0 库里28+10詹皇空砍28+15

来源: 网易体育 作者: 小柳 有 145472 人参与 手机看赛事

网易体育6月2日报道:

金州勇士队在总决赛中赢得开门红。虽然勒布朗得到28分、15个篮板和8次助攻,但杜兰特更为抢眼拿到38分、8个篮板和8次助攻,库里得到28分和10次助攻,他们率队第三节进攻发力确立大比分优势,勇士队在总决赛首战主场以113-91击败克里夫兰骑士。勇士队以1-0领先,总决赛的第二场将继续留在奥克兰进行。

17/98 勒布朗防守库里。

勇士队的杜兰特得到38分、8个篮板和8次助攻,库里得到28分、10次助攻、6个篮板和3次抢断,格林得到9分和11个篮板,汤普森16投3中,得到6分和4次助攻。骑士队的勒布朗得到28分、15个篮板、8次助攻和8次失误,厄文得到24分和4次失误,勒夫得到15分、21个篮板和3次盖帽。

Fig. 4. News report (Color figure online)

In discriminator, conditions vector are concatenated the phrase vector together to form the input, and get one value in $[0, 1]$ to indicate whether the discriminator believe the condition and phrase combination comes from real news.

After training, the generator can generate phrases given two scores. SSGM then put it together with other information into templates. Then we can get the summary sentence.

Table 1. SSGM training dataset

ID	Teams	Score	Phrase	Date
1	Boston-Los Angeles	119-113	beat	2.20
2	Miami-Oklahoma City	115-92	whup	2.22
3	Houston-San Antonio	114-117	lose by a neck	2.24
4	Golden State-Cleveland	121-118	edged out	2.28
...	...	...	...	...

SSGM Result. Given the data from NBA game in 2016-2-22, Cavaliers vs Thunder, Table 2 lists several results generated from our approach, compared to the news on website.

Table 2. SSGM generated result compared with real report

Score	Category	Sentence
115-92	Generated	Cleveland Cavaliers made a 115-92 beat the Golden State on February 22
		Cleveland Cavaliers made a 115-92 whup the Golden State on February 22
	Reported	Cleveland Cavaliers made a 115-92 beat the Golden State on February 22

From the result, it should be noticed that the generated summary sentence is amazingly similar as the real news. It is scarcely possible for people to distinguish whether the report is generated automatically or written by sports-writers. It shows that WGAN in SSGM learned the pattern that reports the summary result for different score combination, without an expert getting involved.

PPGM Settings. In PPGM, situations are more complicated than SSGM. The data is processed as shown in Table 3. First, we set each players' vector as length 50 with random value within $[-1, 1]$. Next, through statistic, only 5 kinds data are shown in the player performance sentence. They are "scores", "rebounds", "assists", "mistakes", "first start". Among the 5 data, the first 4 are all integers and will be normalized. On the other hand, the "first start" data is Boolean, which 1 represent first start and 0 otherwise. Therefore, the performance information is a vector of length 5.

For each kind of data, we employ one-hot embedding to represent corresponding frequently used phrases. We embedded each data output as a vector of length 5 with the last dimension representing "no report". Therefore, the output of generator in WGAN is a matrix of $5 * 5$, which phrases of all data generated at once. The discriminator form the input as the concatenation of Performance Matrix

Table 3. PPGM training dataset

Player ID	Rebound	Assist	Turnover	Points	Starter
1	11 (grabbed)	4	0	29 (scored)	1
2	7 (had)	11 (had)	5 (but had)	25 (had)	1
3	1	7 (added)	3	2	0
4	6 (got)	0	3	15 (got)	0 (sub)
5	5 (had)	3 (had)	3	26 (finished)	1
...	...	...	...	...	...

and phrase embedding matrix then output a single value representing whether it believes the Performance Matrix and phrase embedding matrix comes from real news.

After training, in each game, each player will be evaluated whether his performance is worth reporting and which phrases should be reported. Finally, adding all the results from WGAN together with corresponding name into template. PPGM will generate the player performance sentences using the rules for all reported players.

PPGM Result. Given the data from NBA game in 2016-2-22, Cavaliers vs Thunder, we finally got the generated paragraph shown in Table 2.

From the results, we can see that the player performance sentences are clear and plausible. Furthermore, the sentence generator leveraged various templates and rules to generate the whole paragraph. It fully utilizes the input data and prevent monotonous description for all players. This brings even better effect than the original news.

Among all the input data, PPGM chose what kind of data to report automatically. All the chosen data are prominent and worth reporting. For example, Tristan Thompson got 14 rebounds, which is amazing in NBA match. our model reported it as "Tristan Thompson grabbed 14 rebounds". For another example, Kyrie Irving only got 2 scores in the match. However, PPGM still reports him because our model can learn that he is NBA star concerned by many fans, based on his history performance as represented as Performance Matrix. And the corresponding report, "Kyrie Irving performed poorly, 5 hit 1, and only got 2 scores", gives the vivid description about his performance (Table 4).

In sum, PPGM takes all players' data in a match and capable of deciding which data worthy reporting and generating diverse description of players' performance.

Based on the both results of SSGM and PPGM, we are confident to extend our model to replace this part from human writer and save the time to generate NBA news.

Table 4. PPGM generated results compared with real reports

Category	Result
Generated	Cleveland Cavaliers blasted enemy in the game. Love and James Combined 54 points, Thompson grabbed 14 rebounds and scored 4 of 6 shooting. Smith finished with 15 points, with 5 of 12 shooting 5-12. Dellavedova was substituted and added 7 assists, shotted 1-3. Jefferson was substituted and scored 15 points on 4 of 5 shooting. Irving performed murky and only had 2 points on 1 of 5 shooting among the playing time of 9:16. Meanwhile, Oklahoma City Thunder fails to defend on their home curt. Durant and Westbrook combined 46 points. Ibaka scored 12 points on 6 of 14 shootings. Adams grabbed 9 rebounds and hit 4 out of 5. Cavaliers had blossom in the game and finished with six players in double figures. On the other hand, Thunder lose their hit rate from behind the arc and only had 22.7%
	Cleveland Cavaliers played a wonderful match. Headed by LeBron-James scored 25 points, 11 assists, 7 rebounds, but also 5 turnovers, Love got the team's highest 29 points and contributed 11 rebounds and 4 Assists, Tristan-Thompson grabbed 14 rebounds. Richard-Jefferson was Substituted and performed outstanding of having 15 points and 6 rebounds. Matthew-De La Vitoria off the bench sent 7 assists. Kerry-Erwin started but only 2 points. Oklahoma City Thunder fails to defend on their home court. Kevin-Durant finished a game-high of 26 points and sent 5 assists, Russell-Westbrook almost got three double and add 20 points, 11 assists and 9 rebounds. Cavaliers finished with six players in double figures
Reported	The Cleveland cavaliers won the game, Kevin love had 29 points and 11 rebounds, and lebron James scored 25 points, 11 assists 7 rebounds and 3 steals, but there are 5 turnovers, Tristan Thompson grabbed 14 rebounds. JR. Smith scored 15 points. Substitute Matthew delevedo sent out seven assists. Substitute Richard Jefferson scored 15 points. Kerry Ervin played nine minutes and 16 s and scored 1 of 5, just 2 points. The Oklahoma city thunder team lost home, Durant had a team-high 26 points and five rebounds and three assists, Westbrooke had 20 points and 11 assists and 9 rebounds, Serge Ibaka had 12 points. Stephen Adams picked up nine rebounds. The Cleveland cavaliers scored double with many people

5   Conclusion and Future Work

In this work, we propose an Automatic Sport News Generating System, which aims to produce sport news immediately after each match is over. We utilize WGAN combining with template to generate the summary sentences and player performance sentences in NBA match news. This is the first work that applied GAN on automatic sport news generation field. The system not only fulfil the task of generating sports news based on WGAN model, but also gives new angle of leverage GAN on NLP area.

As to future work, we will continue generating the remaining of NBA match news. For the abstract description of the whole match part, we will train WGAN model on sequence of data, which is a new attempt that combines GAN and sequence model together on NLP tasks.

References

1. Goodfellow, I., et al.: Generative adversarial nets. In: Advances in Neural Information Processing Systems (2014)
2. Mikolov, T., et al.: Efficient estimation of word representations in vector space. arXiv preprint arXiv:1301.3781 (2013)
3. Zhang, J., Yao, J.-g., Wan, X.: Towards constructing sports news from live text commentary. In: Proceedings of the 54th Annual Meeting of the Association for Computational Linguistics (Volume 1: Long Papers), vol. 1 (2016)
4. Mirza, M., Osindero, S.: Conditional generative adversarial nets. arXiv preprint arXiv:1411.1784 (2014)
5. Bowman, S.R., et al.: Generating sentences from a continuous space. arXiv preprint arXiv:1511.06349 (2015)
6. Denton, E.L., Chintala, S., Fergus, R.: Deep generative image models using a Laplacian pyramid of adversarial networks. In: Advances in Neural Information Processing Systems (2015)
7. Mathieu, M., Couprie, C., LeCun, Y.: Deep multi-scale video prediction beyond mean square error. arXiv preprint arXiv:1511.05440 (2015)
8. Radford, A., Metz, L., Chintala, S.: Unsupervised representation learning with deep convolutional generative adversarial networks. arXiv preprint arXiv:1511.06434 (2015)
9. Glover, J.: Modeling documents with generative adversarial networks. arXiv preprint arXiv:1612.09122 (2016)
10. Jang, E., Gu, S., Poole, B.: Categorical reparameterization with gumbel-softmax. arXiv preprint arXiv:1611.01144 (2016)
11. Ledig, C., et al.: Photo-realistic single image super-resolution using a generative adversarial network. In: CVPR, vol. 2, no. 3 (2017)
12. Maddison, C.J., Mnih, A., Teh, Y.W.: The concrete distribution: a continuous relaxation of discrete random variables. arXiv preprint arXiv:1611.00712 (2016)
13. Reed, S., et al.: Generative adversarial text to image synthesis. arXiv preprint arXiv:1605.05396 (2016)
14. Salimans, T., et al.: Improved techniques for training GANs. In: Advances in Neural Information Processing Systems (2016)
15. Nowozin, S., Cseke, B., Tomioka, R.: f-GAN: training generative neural samplers using variational divergence minimization. In: Advances in Neural Information Processing Systems (2016)
16. Tang, D., Qin, B., Liu, T.: Aspect level sentiment classification with deep memory network. arXiv preprint arXiv:1605.08900 (2016)
17. Chen, X., et al.: InfoGAN: interpretable representation learning by information maximizing generative adversarial nets. In: Advances in Neural Information Processing Systems (2016)
18. Yu, L., et al.: SeqGAN: sequence generative adversarial nets with policy gradient. In: AAAI (2017)

19. Zhang, Y., Gan, Z., Carin, L.: Generating text via adversarial training. In: NIPS Workshop on Adversarial Training, vol. 21 (2016)
20. Zhao, J., Mathieu, M., LeCun, Y.: Energy-based generative adversarial network. arXiv preprint arXiv:1609.03126 (2016)
21. Arjovsky, M., Chintala, S., Bottou, L.: Wasserstein GAN. arXiv preprint arXiv:1701.07875 (2017)
22. Williams, R.J.: Simple statistical gradient-following algorithms for connectionist reinforcement learning. Mach. Learn. **8**(3–4), 229–256 (1992)
23. Goldberg, E., Driedger, N., Kittredge, R.I.: Using natural-language processing to produce weather forecasts. IEEE Intell. Syst. **2**, 45–53 (1994)
24. Coch, J.: System demonstration interactive generation and knowledge administration in MultiMeteo. Natural Language Generation (1998)
25. Coch, J., David, R., Magnoler, J.: Quality tests for a mail generation system. In: IA 95. Journées internationales (1995)
26. Portet, F., et al.: Automatic generation of textual summaries from neonatal intensive care data. Artif. Intell. **173**(7–8), 789–816 (2009)
27. White, M., Caldwell, T.: EXEMPLARS: a practical, extensible framework for dynamic text generation. Natural Language Generation (1998)
28. Busemann, S., Horacek, H.: Generating air quality reports from environmental data. In: Proceedings of the DFKI Workshop on Natural Language Generation (1997)

Speech Emotion Recognition Using Multi-granularity Feature Fusion Through Auditory Cognitive Mechanism

Cong Xu[1(✉)], Haifeng Li[1,2(✉)], Hongjian Bo[2(✉)], and Lin Ma[1,2(✉)]

[1] Harbin Institute of Technology, 92, West Dazhi Street, Nan Gang District,
Harbin, People's Republic of China
xucong08@163.com, lihaifeng@hit.edu.cn,
malin_li@lhit.edu.cn
[2] Shen Zhen Academy of Aerospace Technology, 6, Keji South 10th Road,
Nan Shan District, Shen Zhen, People's Republic of China
bosaat@163.com

Abstract. In this paper, we focus on the problems of single granularity in feature extraction, loss of temporal information and inefficient use of frame features in discrete speech emotion recognition. Firstly, preliminary cognitive mechanism of auditory emotion is explored through cognitive experiments, and then a multi-granularity fusion feature extraction method inspired by the mechanism for discrete emotional speech signals is proposed. The method can extract 3 different granularity features, including short-term dynamic features of frame granularity, dynamic features of segment granularity and long-term static features of global granularity. Finally, we use the LSTM network model to classify emotions according to the long-term and short-term characteristics of the fusion features. We implement experiment on the discrete emotion datasets of CHEAVD (CASIA Chinese Emotional Audio-Visual Database) released by the Institute of automation, China Research Academy of Sciences, and achieved improvement in recognition rate, increasing the MAP by 6.48%.

Keywords: Speech emotion recognition · Auditory cognitive mechanism · Multi-granularity feature fusion · CNN-LSTM

1 Introduction

Speech emotion recognition is to judge the current emotional state by analyzing and processing the audio signals of human speech. The stimulation of the emotions is related to the cognitive response in the brain after the speech signal is acquired. Thus, the analysis and the estimation of speech emotion based on the auditory cognitive mechanism is the focal points and difficulty in the research of intelligent human-computer interaction, and is the important foundation for the realization of machine hearing [1, 2]. Because of the non-stationary and time-series characteristics of speech signals, the analysis and extraction of emotional information contained in speech signals has become the focus of speech emotion recognition task, and it is also a hotspot of current research.

© Springer Nature Switzerland AG 2019
R. Xu et al. (Eds.): ICCC 2019, LNCS 11518, pp. 117–131, 2019.
https://doi.org/10.1007/978-3-030-23407-2_10

Researchers usually use two kinds of acoustic features for the speech emotion recognition. One is the global statistical features based on sentences, including prosodic features [3–5], power spectrum features [6, 7] and voice quality features [8, 9]. Seppänen et al. [10] used 43-dimensional global prosodic features related to fundamental frequency, energy and duration to recognize the emotion of Finnish speech, and achieved 60% recognition rate in the case of speaker-independent. Li et al. [11] used frequency perturbation and amplitude perturbation as voice quality features to recognize speaker-independent emotions in SUAS database, increasing the recognition rate from 65.5% to 69.1%. He et al. [12] extracted the area under the envelope of glottic waveform energy spectrum and the area under the envelope of speech signal energy spectrum as voice quality features, and achieved good recognition performance. Sanchez et al. [13] achieved outstanding results in the fusion of different types of features. They applied 90-dimensional global statistical features, such as fundamental frequency, energy, resonance peak and spectral tilt, to detect the emotion of depression in WCGS database [14], and achieved 81.3% recognition rate. Haifeng et al. [15] realized the recognition of Activation, Dominance and Valence in dimensional speech emotion recognition by fusing different global granularity features. The other one is time sequential features based on speech frames. As the emotional speech features are unequal in length and unsteady in the audio signal [16, 17], Li et al. [18] proposed vowel temporal features based on global features and implemented four kinds of emotion recognition experiments, which achieved good recognition results.

In these studies, speech emotion features are mostly extracted by frame, but use the global static feature of a sentence or longer speech segment in the progress of recognition [19]. This kind of feature cannot reflect the dynamic change of speech emotion during the speaker's speaking. In order to extract better features that can describe the dynamic changes of emotion in speech, researchers have started exploring the emotion features contained in audio signals from the perspective of auditory cognition.

Thus, in this paper, we implemented a speech emotion cognitive experiment to explore the auditory cognitive mechanism of how the brain process the speech during the recognition of emotions. Inspired by the cognitive mechanism, we proposed a multi-granularity dynamic and static fusion feature and the method to extract it. This fusion feature can avoid the problem of unequal length of the dynamic features, and retains as much emotion information as possible at the same time. The framework of the work is shown in Fig. 1. We first calculated the prosodic features, spectrum features and voice quality features from the frames. Then the static global granularity features of the whole sentence are obtained by statistical calculation. At the same time, we use the Gauss window to convolute the adjacent frame features in time series, and get the multi-granularity time-varying dynamic features, which can not only depict the speaker's overall speech features, but also describe the change of speech emotion features over time.

For the classification part, we use Long-Short Term Memory (LSTM) network model. LSTM model can effectively model time series and make full use of time series information in speech. On the other hand, LSTM's long-term and short-term memory mechanism enables the network to selectively remember and recognize features at different time points. And at last, LSTM network model can deal with variable length input effectively, so as to solve the problem that different utterance has different number of frames.

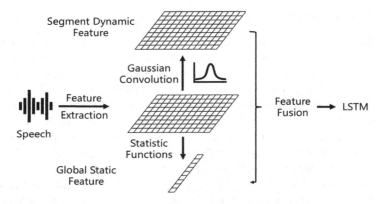

Fig. 1. The framework of speech emotion recognition

2 Exploration of Auditory Cognitive Mechanism

And that of human beings. A man can easily feel the speaker's emotions from a speech, even if he does not understand the language in the speech. This indicates semantics is not a key factor in the emotion recognition. Compared with human beings, the recognition rate of current speech emotion recognition methods is still at a relatively low level. Therefore, we intend to explore the mechanism of human brain in speech emotion recognition by analyzing the cognitive activities when hearing audios with different emotions, and use the mechanism to optimize the speech emotion features.

2.1 Exploratory Experiment on Auditory Cognitive Mechanism

There are many kinds of sound in this world, and different sound, such as the speech, music, noise etc., can evoke different emotions. In this work, we select sounds with low auditory attribute complexity and semantic complexity from 3 open database of emotional sounds: (1) IADS2 (2007); (2) Montreal Affective Voices (MAV, 2008); (3) Musical Emotional Bust (MEB, 2013). The sounds include living sound, non-living sound, wind sound, water sound, other natural environment sounds, and piano solos in different modes representing different emotions. With all these sound, we conducted a cognitive experiment of auditory emotion. We asked subjects to listen to different kinds of sounds, and recorded the EEG data of the subjects in the experiment using 64 electrodes, sampling with 1000 Hz. And then analyze the cognitive mechanism during the process of emotional change.

The subjects in the experiment are consist of 15 health college students aged between 19 and 22, including 7 women. And all subjects were right-handed. For each subject, we conduct 16 trials, the timing scheme of each trial is as follows:

(1) Record 15 s continuous EEG signal of the subject;
(2) Play a clip of one of the sounds, human voices, or music;
(3) Record another 15 s continuous EEG signal of the subject;
(4) Self assessment and scoring of the subject's emotional state.

2.2   Result and Analysis

We analyze the EEG signals collected under different emotions by time-related potential (ERP), and the results were shown in Fig. 2. Firstly, we compared the ERP of living sound and non-living sound, significant differences in N1-P2 components can be found at FZ, CZ and other electrodes. And Auditory-object Specific Response (ASR) components related to object category can be found at 350 ms, which is consistent with the results of Levy [20], Murray [21] and other researchers. This proves that the experiment is correctly conducted. Then we compared the ERP of different emotion sound. Similarly, significant differences in N1-P2 components can be found at FZ, CZ and other electrodes, while no ASR component can be found at 350 ms, but new emotional components can be found around 400 ms, which we call ESR (Emotion Specific Response). This indicates that the earliest response of human brain to emotion is about 150 ms in N1-P2 auditory components, and the most significant difference in ESR components occurs at 450 ms. In addition, the time of ESR component of emotion is about 100 ms later than that of ASR component of object category, which indicates that emotion has a higher level of information processing.

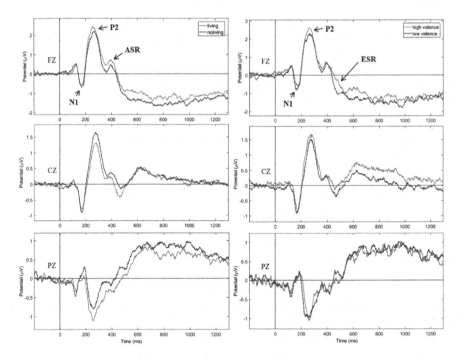

Fig. 2. ERP analysis of sound evoked emotions. ERP of living and non-living sounds (left); ERP of high and low valence sounds (right).

We also plotted the brain topographic map of EEG signals in timing series, as shown in Fig. 3. We can see that the activated brain regions of different emotion changed at 350–450 ms. That is different neural pathways is using for processing emotional information.

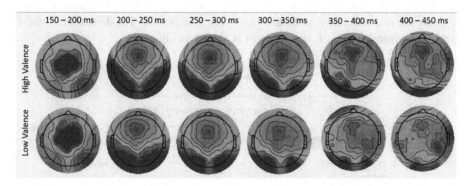

Fig. 3. Time series brain topographic maps of sound evoked emotions.

2.3   Enlightenment to Speech Emotion Features

Through the aforementioned analysis of EEG data of human brain in emotional cognitive activities, we have obtained some preliminary mechanism of emotional cognitive. These mechanism suggest that we should pay attention to the following points in speech emotion recognition:

Emotion is Based on Acoustic Features but More Than Acoustic Features. It takes more time for brain to respond to the living sound than to the non-living sound, and emotional components of the brain appear between 350 ms and 450 ms. This indicates that the brain obviously undergoes more advanced information processing mechanism when hearing a human speech. The evocation of emotion in human brain is not a simple stimulus-response process, but involves in the arrangement and combination of acoustic features. From this we can infer that emotional information is based on acoustic features, but more than acoustic features. It is not necessarily effective to extract features from simple acoustic attributes of speech signals.

The Response Time Varies from Different Emotion. The response time of the brain to different emotions is slightly different, therefore, multi-granularity features will play an important role in speech emotion and even sequence signals, facilitating the further extraction of emotional information. Moreover, the response time of human brain to emotion information is 350–450 ms, which provides a theoretical basis for the size of the granularity. In the later experiments, we set the length of the window to extract segment granularity feature to 350 ms.

3 Extraction Method for Multi-Granularity Fusion Feature

In view of the above-mentioned enlightenment, we propose a multi-granularity dynamic and static fusion feature extraction method. We divide features into three granularities: frame, segment and global. The first two correspond to dynamic features, and the last correspond to static features. In this way, the temporal information in audio is preserved, and the ability of feature expression is improved. The definition of multi-granularity dynamic-static fusion features is shown in Fig. 4.

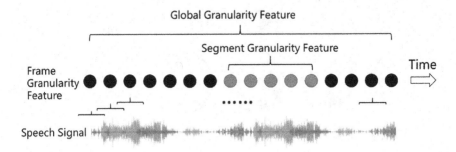

Fig. 4. The definition of multi-granularity dynamic-static fusion feature.

3.1 Dynamic Feature Extraction Method

Frame Granularity Dynamic Feature. Frame feature is the smallest granularity in speech signal analysis and processing. It represents the short-term features of speech. The frame feature sequence obtained from an utterance also retains most kinds of information about how the signal varies with time.

In this work, we divided the continuous speech signal into several approximate stationary speech frames. The frame length was 25 ms, the frame shift was 10 ms, window function was Hamming window. We extract 65-dimensional features including fundamental frequency, short-term energy, short-term average energy, zero-crossing rate, average amplitude difference, resonance peak and MFCC. The specific features are shown in Table 2.

Segment Granularity Dynamic Feature. When the human brain processes an utterance and extracts information, it does not recognize it one by one at the smallest granularity. It needs an advanced processing in a bigger granularity to extract emotional information. Therefore, based on the dynamic feature of frame granularity, we propose a dynamic feature extraction of segment granularity with 350 ms window length.

Segment feature is obtained by convoluting the frame features within a certain window length using a convolution function. This makes segment feature be able to reflect the temporal relationship between consecutive frames, which means that the dynamic changing process is depicted. We use $x_t = (a_{(t,1)}, a_{(t,2)}, \ldots, a_{(t,P)})$ to denote the frame feature vector at time t, where P is the dimension of the frame feature. An utterance of length T can be expressed by a frame feature matrix consist of frame feature vectors as follows:

$$X_T^T = (x_1, x_2, \ldots, x_T) \tag{1}$$

For each frame feature matrix of $P \times T$ size, we use pre-defined segment length L, here is 350 ms, and corresponding convolution function group $K(M, T)$ to convolute it, where M is the number of convolution functions in the convolution function group. Then the segment feature matrix $S_{M \times T}$ is obtained:

$$S_{(m,t)} = K_{(m,t)} * (x_{t-L+1}, x_{t-L+2}, \ldots, x_t)^T \tag{2}$$

As the emotion in an utterance usually rises at first and then degrade. The middle part usually carries the most emotional information, while the two ends are relatively less. So we use different Gaussian function $G(m,t)$, as shown in Fig. 5, as the convolution function to convolute frame features in different positions in the segment window.

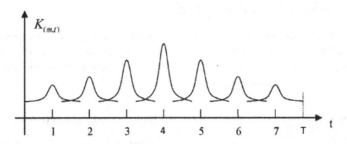

Fig. 5. Gaussian function group.

The Gaussian function we used can be expressed as:

$$G_{(m,t)} = \frac{1}{\sqrt{2\pi}\sigma_m} e^{-\frac{(t-mT_D)^2}{2\sigma_m^2}} \tag{3}$$

Where σ_m can be computed through:

$$\sigma_m^2 = \sigma_{\frac{M+1}{2}}^2 \left(m - \frac{M+1}{2} \right)^2 \tag{4}$$

After the above steps, we transform the frame feature matrix of $P \times T$ size into segment feature matrix of $M \times T$ size. Since the dimension of time is not changed, segment feature still retains the timing characteristics of the original utterance and the advanced information contained in it.

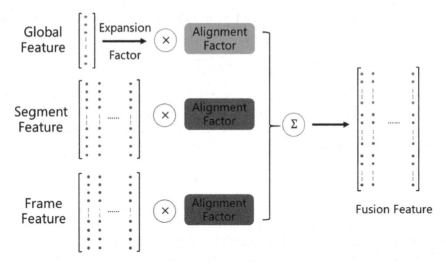

Fig. 6. Process of multi-granularity dynamic-static features fusion.

3.2 Static Feature Extraction Method

For static features, we use the current mainstream feature extraction method, which is to obtain global static features by calculating the corresponding frame feature statistics on the entire utterance. The statistics we calculate here include the maximum value, the minimum value, the average value, the variance, etc.

3.3 Fusion Method of Multi-Granularity Dynamic-Static Features

When the three features are fused, since the global static feature is calculated by the frame feature through the statistical function, then the frame feature with dimension P will be transformed into global statistical feature with dimension $P * R$, after the global statistical calculation is performed using R statistical functions. That means the dimension of global feature will be R times that of frame feature, which makes the global part of the fused feature account for the vast majority of the total. But in fact, dynamic information as time changes, corresponding to the frame feature and the segment feature, is relatively more important.

Therefore, in the feature fusion, we first use the PCA algorithm to select the feature of the calculated global static feature, keep the first P_g dimension, so that the dimension ratio of the dynamic feature and the static feature are balanced. And finally, the global static feature G_{P_g} becomes a vector of P_g dimension.

We set the alignment factor matrices A_x, A_s, A_g for the frame feature matrix $X_{P \times T}$, the segment feature matrix $S_{M \times T}$, and the global feature vector G_{P_g}, respectively. Then the fusion feature matrix F can be computed through the following equation:

$$F_{(P+M+P_g)\times T} = A_x X_{P\times T} + A_s S_{M\times T} + A_g G_{P_g} B_g \tag{5}$$

Where B_g is a T-dimensional vector consisting of T ones, we call it global feature vector expansion factor. The alignment factor matrices are set as follows:

$$A_x = \begin{pmatrix} \mathbf{0} \\ \mathbf{0} \\ I_p \end{pmatrix}_{(P+M+P_g)\times T} \tag{6}$$

$$A_s = \begin{pmatrix} \mathbf{0} \\ I_s \\ \mathbf{0} \end{pmatrix}_{(P+M+P_g)\times T} \tag{7}$$

$$A_g = \begin{pmatrix} I_{P_g} \\ \mathbf{0} \\ \mathbf{0} \end{pmatrix}_{(P+M+P_g)\times T} \tag{8}$$

Where I is unit array.

Thus each column in matrix F is a fused multi-granularity feature consisting of 3 parts: dynamic frame granularity features, segment granularity dynamic features obtained by convolution on frame features, and global statistical static feature based on all frames in the utterance. The feature fusion process is shown in Fig. 6.

4 Speech Emotion Recognition Experiment

4.1 Dataset

We used the CHEAVD (Chinese Natural Emotional Audio-Visual Database) dataset [22], which is constructed by the team of Institute of Automation, Chinese Academy of Sciences. The data are from the audio and video clips intercepted in the movies and TV shows. And in this experiment, we only use the audio clips data for the speech emotion recognition. There are total of 8 kinds of emotion in the dataset, and the distribution of the sample size for each emotion is shown in Table 1 below.

From the table we can see that, the sample numbers of different emotion are not balance. "Neutral" has 815 samples which is the most, while "Disgust" only has 50. Moreover, the data is collected from many different scenarios, including movies, TV plays, talk shows, etc. So it is very close to the emotional expression in real life. This makes it difficult and challenging to recognize emotion on the dataset.

4.2 Feature Set

We extract features on the original audio in CHEAVD using OpenSmile [23], an open source tool. We refer to the feature set in The INTERSPEECH 2016 Computational Paralinguistic Challenge [24], and select 65 of them as our frame feature, as is listed in Table 2.

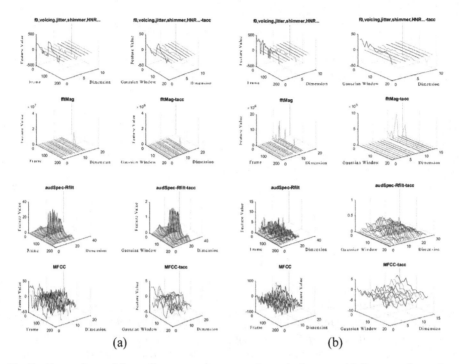

Fig. 7. Comparison of frame features and segment dynamic features. (a) features of emotion 'surprise': frame feature (left), segment feature (right); (b) features of emotion 'angry': frame feature (left), segment feature (right).

Table 1. Sample distribution of eight emotion classes.

Emotion	Train sample number	Test sample number	Total
Neutral	725	90	815
Angry	399	49	448
Happy	307	38	345
Sad	256	31	387
Worried	93	11	104
Anxious	89	11	100
Surprise	67	8	75
Disgust	45	5	50
Total	1981	243	2224

After getting the frame features, we calculate the segment features using the method mentioned above. Figure 7 show the feature comparison of the emotion "surprise" and "angry" respectively. In the figure, the left are the frame features, and the right are the segment features. And we can see that the curve of segmental granularity dynamic features obtained by convolution calculation is smoother and more regular.

Table 2. Frame feature set list.

Feature type	Feature abbr.	Dimension
Prosodic features	F0final	1
	voicingFinalUnclipped	1
	Zcr	1
Spectrum features	MFCC	14
	pcm RMSenergy	1
	audSpec Rfilt	28
	pcm fftMag	15
Voice quality features	jitterLocal	1
	jitterDDP	1
	shimmerLocal	1
	logHNR	1

In terms of global statistical static features, we selected 16 statistic functions as shown in Table 3. We would get 65 * 16 = 1040 dimensional global feature after applying 16 statistic function on 65-dimensional frame feature. To avoid the dimension imbalance of three different granularity, we use the PCA algorithm to reduce the global features dimension, and select the first 65 dimensions as the final global static feature.

Table 3. Statistic functions list.

Type	Statistics
Extremum	max/min, location of max/min
Mean value	geometric mean, arithmetic mean, square mean
Moment	variance, standard deviation, skewness, plainness
Regression coefficient	correlation coefficient of quadratic regression
Quantile	Quartile(0.25/0.5/0.75/0.9)

4.3 Experiment and Result Analysis

We conduct 4 different experiments on the dataset, using different features and classifiers. We use 88-dimensional global feature, which is the feature used in the baseline method, to compare the effects of different classifiers. We also only use 65-dimensional frame feature, which is the same as the frame granularity feature in the fusion feature, to verify the role of fusion features. For the classifiers, we use single layer LSTM and SVM. In LSTM, the number of hidden layer nodes is 128, the activation function is tanh function, and the output layer uses the *softmax* function.

Table 4 shows all the experimental results. The first line and the sixth line are the baseline method and winner's method for 2016 Multi-mode Speech Emotion Recognition Competition on the dataset. The accuracy and the macro average precision

(MAP) are calculated. MAP is widely used to measure the classification effect of classifier. Its calculation formula is as follows.

Table 4. Comparison of experiment result.

No.	Features - Method	Acc on Test set	MAP(%)
1	88-dimensional global feature - decision tree	41.98%	30.02
2	88-dimensional global feature - LSTM	41.56%	31.56
3	88-dimensional global feature - SVM	40.9%	28.94
4	65-dimensional frame feature - LSTM	41.98%	33.24
5	Multi-granularity fusion feature - LSTM	44.26%	36.5
6	DFFN based on GC	45.24%	20.81

$$MAP = \frac{1}{s} \times \sum_{i=1}^{s} \frac{TP_i}{TP_i + FP_i} \tag{9}$$

Where TP_i is the number of correct predict in class i, FP_i is the number of the samples of other classes identified as the class i.

From the table we can see that the method using multi-granularity fusion features has improved the recognition rate compared to the baseline method. Meanwhile, the effect of using fusion feature is better than using frame features alone or global features alone. This shows that multi-granularity feature extraction is helpful to improve the performance of the accuracy of the emotion recognition. On the other hand, the recognition result of using global features alone is lower than that of using frame features alone, which shows that the performance of frame features with more temporal information is better than that of global features in speech signals. We also compared the result with the method of the winner in the competition on the dataset [25]. In this method, the data are classified by sex first, and then uses deep feedforward neural network for classification. We can see from the results that although we have not classified the gender, our performance are still very close to its performance, and have achieved better results on the MAP value. Besides, all the above methods are better than traditional global statistical features and SVM classifiers.

We also calculated ROC curves for eight emotion classes, as shown in Fig. 7. The average area under the ROC curve (AUC) of the eight emotions reach 0.69, and the overall trend of the ROC curve of the eight emotions in the graph shows that the classifier using the multi-granularity dynamic-static fusion features has better performance, even for the emotion that is relatively difficult to recognize, such as 'anxious' and 'surprise' (Fig. 8).

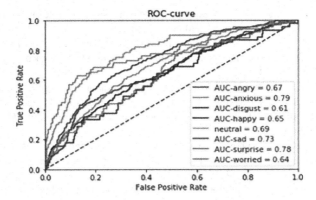

Fig. 8. ROC curve of 8 emotions.

5 Conclusion

In this paper, we aim at the problem of insufficient dynamic information processing mechanism in speech emotion recognition, and explores the auditory cognitive mechanism of speech emotion recognition by designing speech emotion recognition cognitive experiment. Based on the mechanism we get, a multi-granularity dynamic and static fusion feature extraction method is proposed. The frame feature, segment feature and global feature are extracted and fused to make full use of the frame feature and the temporal information contained in it. Meanwhile, the LSTM model is used to classify and recognize the long and short temporal information. Experiments show that multi-granularity fusion features can effectively improve the effect of speech emotion recognition. Finally, considering that there is no structural optimization of the LSTM network in this paper, there should be room for improvement in the recognition effect.

Acknowledgements. Our thanks to Gao Chang for the tremendous help provided in the experiment and supports from the National Key Research and Development Program of China (2018YFC0806800), National Natural Science Foundation of China (61671187), Shenzhen Foundational Research Funding (JCYJ20180507183608379, JCYJ20150929143955341), Shenzhen Key Laboratory of Innovation Environment Project (ZDSYS201707311437102), Open Funding of MOE-Microsoft Key Laboratory of Natural Language Processing and Speech (HIT. KLOF.20150xx, HIT.KLOF.20160xx), China Postdoctoral Science Foundation (2017M611187).

References

1. Ortony, A., Clore, G.L., Collins, A.: The Cognitive Structure of Emotions. Cambridge Univ Pr, Cambridge (1990)
2. Scherer, K.R.: Vocal communication of emotion: a review of research paradigms. Speech Commun. **40**(1), 227–256 (2003)
3. Arias, J.P.: Shape-based modeling of the fundamental frequency contour for emotion detection in speech. Comput. Speech Lang. **28**(1), 278–294 (2014)

4. Zao, L.: Time-Frequency feature and AMS-GMM mask for acoustic emotion classification. IEEE Signal Process. Lett. **21**(5), 620–624 (2014)
5. Mencatini, A., Martineli, E., Costantini, G., et al.: Speech emotion recognition using amplitude modulation parameters and a combined feature selection procedure. Knowl-Based Syst. **63**, 68–81 (2014)
6. Huang, Y., Zhang, G., Li, Y., Wu, A.: Improved emotion recognition with novel task-oriented wavelet packet features. In: Huang, D.-S., Bevilacqua, V., Premaratne, P. (eds.) ICIC 2014. LNCS, vol. 8588, pp. 706–714. Springer, Cham (2014). https://doi.org/10.1007/978-3-319-09333-8_77
7. Ziolko, M., Jaciow, P., Igras, M.: Combination of Fourier and wavelet transformations for detection of speech emotions. In: 7th International Conference on Human System Interactions (HSI), pp. 49–54. IEEE (2014)
8. Idris, I., Salam, M.S.H.: Emotion detection with hybrid voice quality and prosodic features using neural network. In: 2014 Fourth World Congress on Information and Communication Technologies (WICT), pp. 205–210. IEEE (2014)
9. Kachele, M., Zharkov, D., Meudt, S., et al.: Prosodic, spectral and voice quality features selection using a long-term stopping criterion for audio-based emotion recognition. In: 2nd International Conference on Pattern Recognition (ICPR), pp. 803–808. IEEE (2014)
10. Seppänen, T., Väyrynen, E., Toivanen, J.: Prosody-based classification of emotions in spoken finnish. In: Proceedings the 2003 European Conference on Speech Communication and Technology. EUROSPEECH, pp. 717–720. ISCA, Geneva (2003)
11. Li, X., Tao, J., Johnson, M.T., et al.: Stress and emotion classification using jitter and shimmer features. In: Proceedings the 2007 IEEE International Conference on Acoustics, Speech, and Signal Processing (ICASSP), IV, pp. 1081–1084. IEEE, Honolulu (2007)
12. He, L., Lechm, M., Allen, N.: On the importance of glottal flow spectral energy for the recognition of emotions in speech. In: Proceedings the 2010 INTERSPEECH, pp. 2346–2349. ISCA, Chiba (2010)
13. Sanchez, M.H., Vergyri, D., Ferrer, L., et al.: Using prosodic and spectral features in detecting depression in elderly males. In: Proceedings the 2011 INTERSPEECH, pp. 3001–3004. ISCA, Florence (2011)
14. Rosenman, R.H.: A predictive study of coronary heart disease: the western collaborative group study. JAMA **189**(1), 15–22 (1964)
15. Jing, C., Haifeng, L., Lin, Ma., et al.: Multi-granularity feature fusion for dimensional speech emotion recognition. J. Sig. Process. **33**(3), 374–382 (2017)
16. Cowie, R., Douglas-Cowie, E., Tsapatsoulis, N., et al.: Emotion recognition in human computer interaction. IEEE Signal Process. Mag. **18**(1), 32–80 (2001)
17. Murray, I., Arnott, J.: Toward a simulation of emotion in synthetic speech: a review of the literature on human vocal emotion. J. Acoust. Soc. Am. **93**(2), 1097–1108 (1993)
18. Li, Z., Zhiping, W., Wei, L., Cairong, Z., Zhenyang, W.: Speech emotional recognition using global and time sequence structure feature. Acta Automatica Sinica **30**(3), 423–429 (2004)
19. Wenjing, H., Haifeng, L., Huabin, R., et al.: Review on speech emotion recognition. J. Softw. **25**(1), 37–50 (2014)
20. Levy, D.A., Granot, R., Bentin, S.: Processing specificity for human voice stimuli: electrophysiological evidence. NeuroReport **12**(12), 2653–2657 (2001)
21. Murray, M.M., Camen, C., Gonzalez Andino, S.L., et al.: Rapid brain discrimination of sounds of objects. J. Neurosci. **26**(4), 1293–1302 (2006)
22. Li, Y., Tao, J., Schuller, B., Shan, S., Jiang, D., Jiam, J.: MEC 2016: the multimodal emotion recognition challenge of CCPR 2016. In: Chinese Conference on Pattern Recognition (CCPR), Chengdu (2016)

23. Eyben, F., Weninger, F., Gross, F., Schuller, B.: Recent developments in openSMILE, the Munich open-source multimedia feature extractor. In: Proceedings of the 21st ACM International Conference on Multimedia, pp. 835–838 (2013)
24. Schuller, B., et al.: The INTERSPEECH 2016 computational paralinguistics challenge: Deception, sincerity & native language. In: INTERSPEECH, pp. I–I. ISCA (2016)
25. Huang, Y., Hu, M., Yu, X., Wang, T., Yang, C.: Transfer learning of deep neural network for speech emotion recognition. In: Tan, T., Li, X., Chen, X., Zhou, J., Yang, J., Cheng, H. (eds.) CCPR 2016. CCIS, vol. 663, pp. 721–729. Springer, Singapore (2016). https://doi.org/10.1007/978-981-10-3005-5_59

Learning Contextual Features with Multi-head Self-attention for Fake News Detection

Yangqian Wang[1], Hao Han[1], Ye Ding[2], Xuan Wang[1], and Qing Liao[1,3(✉)]

[1] Harbin Institute of Technology (Shenzhen), Shenzhen 518055, China
1260893592wyq@gmail.com, hanhao@stu.hit.edu.cn, wangxuan@cs.hitsz.edu.cn,
liaoqing@hit.edu.cn
[2] Dongguan University of Technology, Dongguan, China
dingye@dgut.edu.cn
[3] Peng Cheng Laboratory, Shenzhen, China

Abstract. Automatic fake news detection has attracted great concern in recent years due to it's tremendous negative impacts on public. Since fake news is usually written to mislead readers, lexical features based methods have great limitations. Previous work has proven the effectiveness of contextual information for fake news detection. However, they ignore the influence of sequence order when extract features from contextual information. Inspired by transformer technique, we propose Contextual Features with Multi-head Self-attention model(CMS) to extract features from contextual information for fake news detection. CMS can automatic capture the dependencies between contextual information and learning a global representation from contextual information for fake news detection. Experimental results on the real-world data demonstrate the effectiveness of the proposed model.

Keywords: Fake news detection · Contextual information · Multi-head self-attention

1 Introduction

In recent years, social media has provided great convenience to the public because of it's more timely and more easier to share and discuss across various social media platforms. However, social media has become an ideal place for fake news propagating due to the lack of supervision mechanism. And the widespread of fake news on social media arise tremendous negative impacts on individual and public. For instances, many commentator believe that the result of the 2016 US presidential election was affected by fake news [1].

In order to mitigate the negative impact of fake news, several fact-checking organizations take enormous labour and times to identify fake news from massive Internet content. The automatic detection of fake news is a critical step in our fight against fake news. Early works for detect fake news often designed a

R. Xu et al. (Eds.): ICCC 2019, LNCS 11518, pp. 132–142, 2019.
https://doi.org/10.1007/978-3-030-23407-2_11

comprehensive sets of hand-crafted features, which is lack of generalization and almost impossible to design all-encompassing features since fake news are usually written across different types. Moreover, we don't have a comprehensive grasp of the linguistic characteristics of fake news yet. There are still great limitations to the methods that only based on text content alone.

On the other hand, news often accompanied with related contextual information, such as speaker of news and there historical data, etc. These contextual information provide more useful information beyond textual content for detecting fake news. In order to learn the high-level feature representation from contextual information, previous works mainly use deep learning methods to automatic capture the useful features. Specifically, contextual information has be seen as a sequence, then Convolutional Neural Network (CNN) based and Recurrent Neural Network (RNN) based methods are applied to capture the dependencies. However, these methods have their own shortcomings. For example, CNN-based methods only can learning local patterns while fails to capture the global feature representation. RNN-based methods usually take the input sequence as an ordered sequence and update the hidden states step by step. Based on this, it's natural for us to ask:

- Will different sequences order lead to quite different results?
- If the first hypothesis is true, then how did we determine the sequence order that can achieve a better performance?

To explore the influence of sequential of contextual information, we conduct a simple experiment based on LIAR dataset [2]. LIAR dataset contains a wealth of contextual information. We utilize a LSTM to encode the contextual information. Obviously, different order of sequence will affect the learning procedure of LSTM. We take followed sequence as examples:

- **S1**: credit history of speaker, context, speaker name, subject of statement, job title of speaker, home state of speaker, party affiliation of speaker.
- **S2**: context, credit history of speaker, speaker name, subject of statement, job title of speaker, home state of speaker, party affiliation of speaker.
- **S3**: subject of statement, speaker name, job title of speaker, party affiliation of speaker, credit history of speaker, home state of speaker, context.
- **S4**: credit history of speaker, context, party affiliation of speaker, speaker name, job title of speaker, home state of speaker, subject of statement.

Figure 1 shows the performance in different orders. As Fig. 1 shows, the performance is affected by the sequential. For example, the detection accuracy get 32.5% when input sequence take S3 while only get 25.7% when take S4. Given the fact that the number of all combinations of sequence order may be very large, it's not wise and inefficient to try all the possible combinations and then choose an optimal sequence manually.

To address above-mentioned challenges, in this paper, we proposed a novel hybrid model based on deep learning to automatic learning the features for fake news detection. Specifically, a Text-CNN [3] is applied to learn features

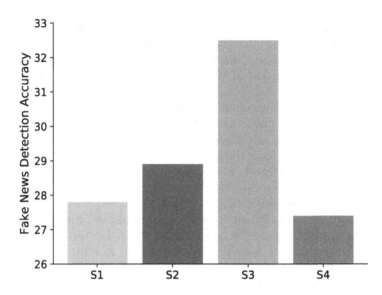

Fig. 1. Performance of LSTM on different order of contextual information.

from textual content. Inspired by transformer technique, we utilize multi-head self-attention to capture the dependencies between contextual information and learning a global feature representation of contextual information to assist in detecting fake news. Self-attention mechanism can ignore the influence of the relative position of each element in the sequence and capture the global representation of sequence. The contribution of this paper can be summarize as follows:

- Through experiments, we confirmed that performance of fake news detection is affected by the sequential of contextual information.
- We proposed a novel CMS model that can ignore the influence of sequential and learning a global representation from contextual information for fake news detection.
- Experiments on real-world fake news dataset demonstrate the effectiveness of the proposed CMS model.

The rest of the paper is organized as follows: Sect. 2 will briefly present the related work. The details of the proposed method will be introduced in Sect. 3. Experimental results are presented in Sects. 4 and 5 conclude this study.

2   Related Work

Fake news detection has attracted great concern in recent years due to it's tremendous negative impacts on public. With the help of big data technology [4–6] and machine learning, automatic fake news detection has made great advance. Early works on detecting fake news mainly focus on designing a complementary set of hand-crafted features based on linguistic features [7–11]. Unfortunately, we don't have a comprehensive grasp of the characteristics of fake news yet. And this procedure require large efforts to explore the effectiveness of manual features.

Recently, deep learning based methods were proposed to automatic learning the patterns to detect fake news. For example, Ma *et al.* [12] proposed a deep neural network based on RNN to capture the temporal and textual features from rumour posts. Liu and Wu [13] utilize CNN and GRU to capture the useful patterns from user profiles. Multi-Modal fake news detection that integrate the textual feature and visual feature get a certain improvements compared to textual feature only [14, 15].

Wang [2] presented a new publicly available dataset for fake news detection in 2017. It included 12.8k manually labeled short statements and each statements accompanied with rich contextual information, i.e., speaker name, job title, political party affiliation, etc. Wang also proposed a Hybrid CNN to detect fake news based this dataset. Based on LIAR dataset, some hybrid deep neural network methods were proposed to facilitate fake news detection. For instances, Long et al. [16] applied LSTM and attention mechanism to capture the patterns and Karimi et al. [17] proposed Multi-Source Multi-Class Fake News Detection (MMFD) models to discriminate different degrees of fakeness. However, above methods ignore the influence of sequence order of contextual information as we discussed in Sect. 1.

Different with above mentioned methods, we proposed a novel model CMS that can ignore the sequential order and capture the global representation from contextual information for fake news detection.

3 Methodology

3.1 Problem Definition

Let $X = \{x_1, x_2, ..., x_N\}$ be a set of news, and each news can be denoted as $x = \{s, c\}$, where s, c represent the statement and contextual information of the news item, respectively. Each statement is consisted of several words, which can be denoted as $s = \{w_1, w_2, ..., w_n\}$, where n is the length of statement. The representation of contextual information can be denoted as $c = \{c_1, c_2, ..., c_t\}$, where t is the number of features in contextual information, such as speaker name, subject of statement, etc. $Y = \{y_1, y_2, ..., y_N\}$ denotes the corresponding label. Our goal is using the news set X and the corresponding label set Y to learn a multi-classification model $\mathcal{F}$, which can predict the fakeness for unlabeled news.

3.2 Model Overview

Figure 2 depicts the architecture of CMS. CMS consists of two main components, a module for extracting the linguistic feature of news statement, and a module for capturing the contextual dependencies. Specifically, CMS is composed of three parts as followed:

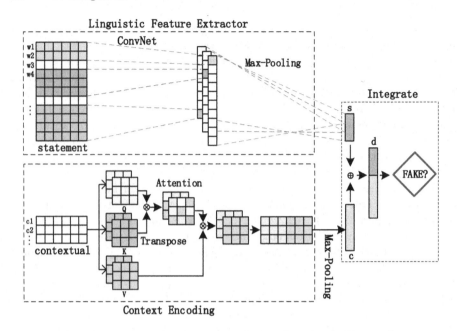

Fig. 2. The structure of CMS.

- Linguistic Feature Extractor: We use a Text-CNN to extract linguistic representation from statement. Statement is represented as word embedding matrix through word embedding layer and then Text-CNN is applied to learning an representation vector s.
- Context Encoding: To extract the global representation of contextual information and ignore the influence of the sequence order in contextual information, we use multi-head self-attention mechanism to encode the contextual information and outputs a high-level representation vector, denoted as c.
- Integrate: The outputs of the two above components are concatenated and finally obtain the hidden representation of news, denoted as d, which will fed into a fully connected layer for classification.

Linguistic Feature Extractor. We use Text-CNN [3] to extract linguistic features from statement. Statement is represented as a matrix of word embeddings denoted as $W \in \mathbb{R}^{n \times e}$, where e is the dimensions of the word embedding. Text-CNN usually applied multiple kernel with multiple filters to extract features with different granularities. A filter $f \in \mathbb{R}^{l \times e}$ is convolved with word embedding matrix and obtain a corresponding feature map $P \in \mathbb{R}^{n-l+1}$, where l is the length of the filter. For each $p_j \in P$, the filter operation can be formulated as follows:

$$p_j = \mathcal{C}(f \odot W_{j:j+l-1}) \tag{1}$$

where $W_{j:j+l-1}$ stand for l consecutive words starting with the j-th word in the statement, and $\mathcal{C}(\cdot)$ is a non-linear activation function, such as $ReLU$. We use max-pooling on each feature map to get the most important information:

$$v = \text{Max-Pooling}(P) \tag{2}$$

Now, we get the corresponding feature for one particular filter. The complementary feature for statement can be obtained by concatenating all pooling feature vectors:

$$s = [v_1, v_2, ..., v_k] \tag{3}$$

where k is the number of filters.

Context Encoding. In order to capture the global representation of contextual information without regard of the order of features, we employ a variant of transformer [18] as the core of the module.

Usually, the credibility of news is context-dependent, and the interactions between features in contextual information are important to fake news detection. Self-attention is used to capture the informative interactions between features in contextual information. In our case, the self-attention process is based on the assumption that all features in contextual information are closely related and disorder. The output of an attention function is a map of a query and a set of key-value pairs, where the query, keys, values, and output are all vectors. The weighted sum of values are the output, where the weight assigned to each value is computed by a compatibility function of the query with the corresponding key. In practice, a set of queries, keys and values are packed together into matrices $\boldsymbol{Q}$, $\boldsymbol{K}$, $\boldsymbol{V}$, respectively. Contextual information is represented as a matrix of word embedding denoted as $\boldsymbol{C} \in \mathbb{R}^{t \times e}$. $\boldsymbol{Q}$, $\boldsymbol{K}$, $\boldsymbol{V}$ are three different subspace matrix of $\boldsymbol{C}$, which is get by linear projection. So the process of self-attention with contextual information can be formulate as:

$$Attention\left(\boldsymbol{Q}, \boldsymbol{K}, \boldsymbol{V}\right) = softmax\left(\frac{\boldsymbol{Q}\boldsymbol{K}^T}{\sqrt{d_k}}\right)\boldsymbol{V} \tag{4}$$

where d_k is the dimension of vector in $\boldsymbol{Q}$. Now, a new representation of contextual information is got through a self-attention head. For the purpose of allowing the module to obtain high-quality representation of features, multi-head self-attention is used to drawing features interactions with different subspace of $\boldsymbol{C}$ jointly:

$$MultiHead\left(\boldsymbol{C}\right) = Concat\left(Attention_1, ..., Attention_H\right) \tag{5}$$

where H is the number of heads. After that, a fully connected layer is followed and the output size of the full connected network is equal to $\boldsymbol{C}$. In particular, the above compute process can be repeated K times, and the output of previous layer is the input of next layer. Taking a max-pooling operation on the output of last layer, denoted as $\boldsymbol{C}' \in \mathbb{R}^{t \times e}$, and obtain a global representation of contextual information:

$$c = \text{Max-Pooling}(\boldsymbol{r}_1, \boldsymbol{r}_2, ..., \boldsymbol{r}_e) \tag{6}$$

where $\boldsymbol{r}_i$ is the i-th columns in $\boldsymbol{C}'$. So the final representation of contextual information $\boldsymbol{c} \in \mathbb{R}^e$.

Integrate. The final feature representation of news, i.e., d, can be obtained by concatenating s and c. After that, d is fed into a fully connected layer followed by a *softmax* activation function to predict the label of news:

$$l = softmax(\boldsymbol{W}^T \boldsymbol{d} + b) \tag{7}$$

where $l \in \mathbb{R}^M$, M is the number of class. The loss function can be formulated as:

$$\mathcal{L} = -\frac{1}{N} \sum_{i=1}^{N} \boldsymbol{y}_i \log l_i + \frac{\lambda}{2} \|\Theta\|_2^2 \tag{8}$$

where $\boldsymbol{y}_i$ is the corresponding ground-truth, Θ denote the parameters of CMS, and λ is the trade-off coefficient of L_2 regularizer.

4   Experiment

4.1   Dataset

In order to evaluate the performance of CMS, we conducted a series of comparative experiments in a real-world dataset LIAR published in [2]. LIAR dataset contains a total of 12.8k manual labeled short statements, and each statement contains rich contextual information. Table 1 show the details of LIAR dataset.

Table 1. Details of *LIAR* dataset

Contextual information	speaker, speaker's job, state, party, context, credit history of speaker, subject of statement
Label	pants-fire, false, barely-true, half-true, mostly-true, true

4.2   Experimental Setting

We use pytorch[1] to implement the proposed model. We use 300-dimension pre-trained word2vec embedding [19] to initialize the word embeddings. We utilize batch size 64, and Adam optimizer [20] is adopted as the optimizer with learning rate 0.0001. L_2 regularization coefficient is $1e^{-4}$. In Linguistic Feature Extractor, we take (2,3,4) as kernel size and each kernel has 50 filters. As for Contextual Encoding component, the number of layers and heads is 3, 2, respectively. We use the average accuracy of 10 trials as the performance metric.

---

[1] https://pytorch.org/.

4.3   Performance Comparison

To demonstrate the effectiveness of CMS, we compare the following methods:

- **Random**: Randomly selecting the class of a test sample.
- **Majority**: Majority method choose a label that is the greater part of total dataset. In our experiment, we labeled each test sample as *half-true.*
- **Text-CNN**: Text-CNN model only use statement to classify news.
- **Hybrid-CNN**: Text-CNN is applied to learning textual feature from statements, and a CNN followed by a Bi-LSTM was applied to extract feature from contextual information.
- **LSTM-Attention**: Two LSTM was applied to extract features, one for textual context with attention, and another for contextual information.
- **MMFD**: CNN-LSTM was proposed to extract features from textual content and contextual information. Then the features were summed with weights by attention mechanism.

It is worth noting that the above-mentioned methods, Hybrid-CNN and LSTM-Attention use different combinations of contextual information and select a best performance manually, while our proposed model can be fully automated to achieve this goal. Table 2 shows the performance of all methods. As we can see, Text-CNN achieve worst performance since it only based on textual content of statement. Hybrid-CNN, LSTM-Attention and MMFD get a certain improvements compared to Text-CNN. Beyond the mentioned contextual information, MMFD also add the verdict reports generated by experts in *politifact.com* to further improve the detection accuracy. Even though, our proposed model still gets 6.5% improvements on detection accuracy compared to MMFD. Compared to LSTM-Attention and Hybrid-CNN, CMS can ignore the sequence order and capture the global features from contextual information and finally get 45.3% accuracy.

Table 2. Performance of detecting fake news.

Method	Accuracy(%)
Majority	20.8
Random	17.4
Text-CNN	21.7
Hybrid-CNN	27.4
MMFD	38.8
LSTM-Attention	41.5
CMS	45.3

4.4 Effectiveness of CMS

To evaluate the effectiveness of CMS, we conduct a comparison experiment to illustrate the superiority of CMS. We take several sequence orders and apply different methods to extract features from these sequence order. For the sake of fairness, we keep the textual features extractor as Text-CNN to all compared methods. Figure 3 shows the detailed results. The input sequence keeps consistent with Sect. 1. It is clearly show that the performance of Hybrid-CNN, LSTM-Attention and MMFD is severely constrained by the sequence order. For example, all compared methods achieve highest accuracy when adopt sequence S3 and get 32.5%, 40.0%, 41.5%, respectively. Such results may indicate that sequence S3 is a more appropriate order when extract features from contextual information. However, the performance can be very bad when those methods meets some not so appropriate sequence order. For example, LSTM-Attention only get 25.7% accuracy when the input sequence is S4.

In contrast, CMS always maintaining a better performance no matter how the sequence order is. Table 3 shows the detail results. As we can see, other methods

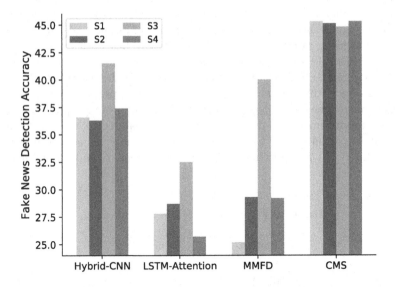

Fig. 3. The performance of CMS and compared methods on different sequence orders.

Table 3. Difference of sequence order.

Method	Best accuracy(%)	Worst accuracy(%)	Difference(%)
Hybrid-CNN	41.5	36.3	5.2
LSTM-Attention	32.5	25.7	6.8
MMFD	40.0	25.2	14.8
CMS	45.3	44.8	0.5

have a huge gap between the best sequence order and worst sequence order, while CMS only have 0.5% difference. Hence, our proposed model not only achieve better performance, but also keeps stable on accuracy. This further illustrate that CMS can neglect the order influence and capture the global patterns effectively.

5 Conclusion

In this paper, we proposed a novel hybrid model based on deep neural network to automatic learning the useful features from textual content and contextual information. Inspired by transformer technique, we applied multi-head self-attention to extract features from contextual information. Multi-head self-attention mechanism can ignore the distance and guarantee that each contextual information will be considered when capture the dependencies from contextual information. Experimental results further demonstrate the effectiveness of CMS method.

Acknowledgements. This work is partly supported by National Key Research and Development Program of China (2017YFB0802204) and National Natural Science Foundation of China (No.U1711261).

References

1. Allcott, H., Gentzkow, M.: Social media and fake news in the 2016 election. J. Econ. Perspect. **31**(2), 211–236 (2017)
2. Wang, W.Y.: "liar, liar pants on fire": a new benchmark dataset for fake news detection. In: Proceedings of the 55th Annual Meeting of the Association for Computational Linguistics (Volume 2: Short Papers), pp. 422–426 (2017)
3. Kim, Y.: Convolutional neural networks for sentence classification. In: Proceedings of the 2014 Conference on Empirical Methods in Natural Language Processing, EMNLP 2014, 25–29 October 2014, Doha, Qatar, A meeting of SIGDAT, A Special Interest Group of the ACL, pp. 1746–1751 (2014)
4. Kashlev, A., Lu, S., Mohan, A.: Big data workflows: a reference architecture and the dataview system. Serv. Trans. Big Data **4**, 1–19 (2017)
5. Zhang, L.J., Zeng, J.: 5c, a new model of defining big data. Serv. Trans. Big Data **4**, 48–61 (2017)
6. Sinanc, D., Demirezen, M., Sagiroglu, S.: Evaluations of big data processing. Serv. Trans. Big Data **3**, 44–54 (2016)
7. Castillo, C., Mendoza, M., Poblete, B.: Information credibility on twitter. In: Proceedings of the 20th International Conference on World Wide Web, pp. 675–684. ACM (2011)
8. Feng, S., Banerjee, R., Choi, Y.: Syntactic stylometry for deception detection. In: Proceedings of the 50th Annual Meeting of the Association for Computational Linguistics: Short Papers, vol. 2, pp. 171–175. Association for Computational Linguistics (2012)
9. Yang, F., Liu, Y., Yu, X., Yang, M.: Automatic detection of rumor on sina weibo. In: Proceedings of the ACM SIGKDD Workshop on Mining Data Semantics, vol. 13. ACM (2012)

10. Liao, Q., Wang, W., Han, Y., Zhang, Q.: Analyzing the influential people in sina weibo dataset. In: 2013 IEEE Global Communications Conference, GLOBECOM 2013, Atlanta, GA, USA, 9–13 December 2013, pp. 3066–3071 (2013)
11. Liao, Q., Guan, N., Zhang, Q.: Logdet divergence based sparse non-negative matrix factorization for stable representation. In: 2015 IEEE International Conference on Data Mining, ICDM 2015, Atlantic City, NJ, USA, 14–17 November 2015, pp. 871–876 (2015)
12. Ma, J., et al.: Detecting rumors from microblogs with recurrent neural networks. In: Proceedings of the Twenty-Fifth International Joint Conference on Artificial Intelligence, IJCAI 2016, USA, pp. 3818–3824 (2016)
13. Liu, Y., Wu, Y.F.B.: Early detection of fake news on social media through propagation path classification with recurrent and convolutional networks. In: Thirty-Second AAAI Conference on Artificial Intelligence (2018)
14. Wang, Y., et al.: EANN: event adversarial neural networks for multi-modal fake news detection. In: Proceedings of the 24th ACM SIGKDD International Conference on Knowledge Discovery & Data Mining, pp. 849–857. ACM (2018)
15. Jin, Z., Cao, J., Guo, H., Zhang, Y., Luo, J.: Multimodal fusion with recurrent neural networks for rumor detection on microblogs. In: Proceedings of the 25th ACM International Conference on Multimedia, pp. 795–816. ACM (2017)
16. Long, Y., Lu, Q., Xiang, R., Li, M., Huang, C.R.: Fake news detection through multi-perspective speaker profiles. In: Proceedings of the Eighth International Joint Conference on Natural Language Processing (Volume 2: Short Papers), pp. 252–256 (2017)
17. Karimi, H., Roy, P., Saba-Sadiya, S., Tang, J.: Multi-source multi-class fake news detection. In: Proceedings of the 27th International Conference on Computational Linguistics, COLING 2018, USA, 2018, pp. 1546–1557 (2018)
18. Vaswani, A., et al.: Attention is all you need. In: Advances in Neural Information Processing Systems 30: Annual Conference on Neural Information Processing Systems 2017, pp. 6000–6010 (2017)
19. Mikolov, T., Chen, K., Corrado, G., Dean, J.: Efficient estimation of word representations in vector space. In: 1st International Conference on Learning Representations, ICLR 2013, Scottsdale, Arizona, USA, 2–4 May 2013, Workshop Track Proceedings (2013)
20. Kingma, D.P., Ba, J.: Adam: a method for stochastic optimization. In: 3rd International Conference on Learning Representations, ICLR 2015, San Diego, CA, USA, 7–9 May 2015, Conference Track Proceedings (2015)

Reduce the Warfighters' Cognitive Burden

Matthew Maher[✉] and Rob Orlando

Processus Group Inc., Belair, MD 12014, USA
maherm@processusgroup.org

Abstract. As the DoD and Military acquisitions shift the paradigm from antiquated software capabilities to artificial intelligence (AI) and machine learning (ML) capabilities, they need to ensure key infrastructure (big data and knowledge artifacts) is also mature enough to handle the transition. Before any organizations or domains develop or adopt a strategy based on AI, ML, or any other form of intelligent system, they need to do a self-assessment that answers three key questions. How well does your organization/domain share knowledge? What is the state of your data? Do you understand the cognitive requirements? Answering and understanding these questions is the key to knowing where you are now (point A) so you can take actionable and progressive steps towards where you want to go (point B) to make your organization or domain AI-capable.

To provide the answers and/or a path to solving the questions above we execute a Mission Engineering (ME) process that analyzes the organization's or domain's state of readiness. The ME process is a detailed analysis that provides an assessment of how the people, systems, knowledge, data, and processes are aligned to the operational outcomes. ME adds a layer of operational viability to existing engineering processes with the goal of ensuring the program enhances knowledge sharing, reduces cognitive burdens, and increases semantic understanding.

Keywords: Mission Engineering · Semantic model · Cognitive Architecture · Knowledge Graph

1 Mission Engineering

This whitepaper describes the Mission Engineering process we use to create the Semantic Data Models, Cognitive Architectures and Knowledge Graphs, to provide the answer to the three questions listed above. Providing the blueprints for how an organization can enhance cognitive problem solving through machine learning or artificial intelligence. We provide is a focused mission engineering process to solve complex issues that occur when knowledge and understanding are fragmented. A fragmentation that increases the cognitive burden on the warfighters. We use mission engineering to provide a solution set that assess the state of the domain for implementing intelligent system or to execute efficiently in a Multi-Domain battlespace and develops knowledge artifacts.

The ME process has roots in tactical operations and arose out of an operational need. A need to combine data science with operational experience. The requirement for

© Springer Nature Switzerland AG 2019
R. Xu et al. (Eds.): ICCC 2019, LNCS 11518, pp. 143–152, 2019.
https://doi.org/10.1007/978-3-030-23407-2_12

this pairing first became obvious when far too many of our after-action reviews in Bosnia, Iraq and Afghanistan focused on the lack of information and proper analysis of the information to support decision making.

"Once while on a specific operation, with the 3rd Special Forces Group (A), we were told that the objective was supported by only light contingent of forces. However, as we approached the target area, we saw heavy equipment at the target site. During the debriefing we realized we had the information that a heavy force was possible, but because individuals responsible for informing us had too much data to analyze and not enough time it was never included in the planning."

The above example highlights the heavy cognitive burden based on the amount of data, information and intelligence places on the operators. They had to apply their own, innate knowledge and understanding to the problem without any system assistance to lessen the burden. From then on, this group started developing an ME process that would lessen the cognitive burden on the warfighter while still applying knowledge and understanding that comes with experience.

Over the years, the ME process has evolved. The output of the process is three key components: Semantic Data Model (SDM), Cognitive Architecture (CA), and Knowledge Graph (KG). The three components work together to enhance the cognitive development in the following ways:

- SDM informs the AI/ML solution on the critical structured and unstructured data that is required to access for intelligent systems. The SDM defines the semantic (machine readable) definition, provenance and relationship of the data to core operational processes to reduce the cognitive burden of a systems and warfighter.
- CAs to provide a blue print for AI/ML developers to understand the how they develop systems to a Mission Engineering standard. The CA defines the key Data, Information, Knowledge, Understanding, and Intelligence (DIKUI) knowledge resources that are required for cognitive problem solving for domain and multidomain operations.
- KGs to provide the level of detail for how the operations is executed and maps how each function, task, systems and personnel depend, create, change and access the distributed data required to make an operational decision.

Together these three deliverables will provide a proven and operationally accurate cognitive problem-solving technique, a predictive analytic capability that provides the semantics and patterns for confident decision making, and a cognitive model tool and will reduce the cognitive workload.

It is from our operational and data science experience that we developed the Process Driven Ontologies (PDOs) to create the Semantic Data Models (SDMs), Cognitive Architecture (CA) and Knowledge Graphs (KGs) as deliverables in the mission Engineering process (Fig. 1).

We model the organization or domain, based on doctrine, SOPs, training products and tasks lists. From this model we then define the state of data in the form of a Semantic Data Model (SDM), then extract from the model how knowledge is shared through systems and people in a Cognitive Architecture (CA), and develop a Knowledge Graph (KG) that shows how efficiently knowledge that is produced

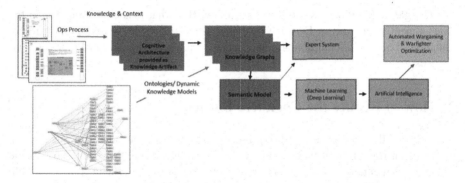

Fig. 1. Mission Engineering process

supports and is shared through the operational processes. The SDM, CA and KG are deliverables that result from the development of an operational representation of your domain in the form of a Process Driven Ontology (PDO). The PDO allows us to develop the SDM, CA and KG in a universal standard while also applying operational terminology and processes as properties within the model. The Ontology is a perfect pairing of engineering practices with operational context because it describes objects in an area of interest, the attributes of those objects, and the relationships between them. They function in the same manner as how organizations typically use a database but are unique in a couple of ways. Because our ontologies are both human and machine readable, they streamline the process of extracting knowledge from the minds of subject matter experts (SMEs) to integrating the model into a software application that can process the data (Fig. 2).

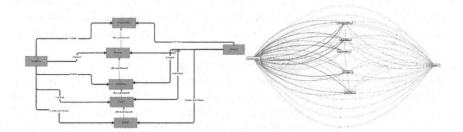

Fig. 2. Example human and machine-readable ontology outputs

Since most units operate in a dynamic organization with changing priorities and missions, the data systems need to be flexible and easily extensible. The flexibility and extensibility of ontologies allows for continuous extension without having to upgrade software applications dependent on previous versions ensuring. We are not unique in the use of ontologies to solve complex data issues and create knowledge artifacts for AI. Any company/industry that is data driven and expanding into intelligent systems uses ontologies to aid the representation of the data within their domain. Companies like Google, IBM, Pfizer, Kaiser to name a few. But what makes us unique is in the development of a Process Driven Ontologies (PDOs) that define the explicit representation of an operational domain. Ontologies form the foundation of Process Group services.

2   How to Reduce the Cognitive Burden

Execution of the Mission Engineering process will address the state of infrastructural pieces of an organization or domain by first providing the SDM, since most of the DoD's implementation of intelligent system are slowed by "poor data" our SDM help to organize and fix the data. Second, our cognitive architectures highlight the areas in the organization where a cognitive burden exists with blue prints for how to lessen the burden. Third we develop knowledge graphs that provides a detailed representation of how critical information and data relate to the systems and process. Not only will these three deliverables help to answer the questions if the organization/domain is ready for AI, but it will also deliver the knowledge artifacts to feed Artificial Intelligence, Machine Learning, Artificial Neural Networks and Robotic Process Automation (AI/ML, ANN & RPA).

2.1   Sematic Data Model

The function of the **Semantic Data Model (SDM)** is twofold. First it is used to analyze the structure of the organization's existing data and discern its suitability to support Machine Learning (ML) and Artificial intelligence (AI) technologies. Next the SDM is used to develop the most efficient and effective manner by which the data can be leveraged by the AI process. Put another way, the SDM creates a rule set (semantics), the existing data is then organized by this rule set, then the AI consumes this data based on the rule set, a.k.a. the Semantic Data Model. Trying to develop an Intelligent system without first addressing the data, cognitive relationships and knowledge will not be successful.

   The semantic models we create provide formal and explicit specifications of conceptualizations for an operational process or domain. Our SDM's play a crucial role in the representation of data in the form of knowledge to map them to the cognitive needs of the warfighter and intelligent systems. Across DoD we have been confronted with the "Garbage in Garbage out" (GIGO) when trying to leverage existing data sources. This is why we create the SDM, to extract data from a large diverse data sets, we create an ontology to formally and explicitly specify the concepts of a domain adding the semantics to describe how its data relates to each other. We can then structure the data based on operational dependencies. Especially if the large data sets are flawed, lacking in semantic and all together unorganized, the use of an ontology developed SDM brings meaning to the data, through the creation of semantic definitions and establishes better relationships to the existing data. Providing a cost-efficient solution for cleaning up large data sets by leveraging the ontology model as a semantic layer between existing databases and applications. Providing predictive analysis that can rapidly assess the data and its role in decision making.

2.2 Cognitive Architecture

The purpose of the **Cognitive Architecture (CA)** is to show how collected "Data", becomes actionable "Information" and is turned into disturbed "Knowledge" across the organization. Initially the CA explains how knowledge is shared across and outside the organization. It extends the SDM to label the knowledge as either data, information, knowledge, understanding or intelligence (DIKUI). It is through the DIKUI process that we architect how the raw **data**, from sensors or systems, is stored and organized. The data can be stored in a database or library. Next, the architecture maps how the data is turned into actionable **information**. This actionable information can be extracted in any of serval formats, including natural language chat or email messages. The CA then expands this concept to show how the combined information from internal and external sources creates **knowledge**. The CA enlarges the analysis to the **understanding** of data, information and knowledge by looking at the repetitiveness and how it is applied to a given task, function or capability. And then applies the implementation of **intelligence**, to any of the other forms (DIKU) that has been influenced by enemy data or from other domains. Our models, being based on operational processes, expand the semantic data models into a cognitive architecture that defines how the data, information, knowledge, understanding and intelligence from both personnel and artificial systems work together to yield intelligent behavior in diverse environments. The cognitive architecture provides a tool and technique for the assessment of reducing the cognitive burden of the warfighter (Fig. 3).

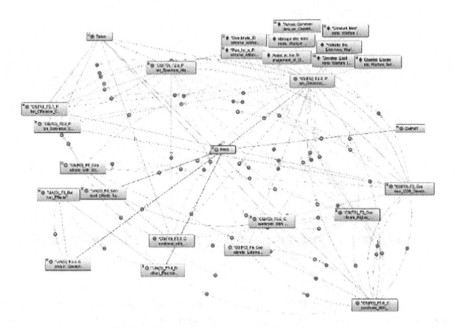

Fig. 3. Cognitive Arch of an EWO task mapping

2.3   Knowledge Graph

Knowledge Graphs (KG) are a representation of the unique relations between data elements within the data set. Organizational experience, whether gained from real world events, or training exercises, which reflect external influences (the enemy, weather etc.) becomes elements within the source data, which supports the development of action information, which then adds to the organization's shareable knowledge. As the data set grows so do the number of unique relations, expanding the KGs. This becomes a cyclical process, always expanding the origination's **Knowledge Base (KB)**. The KGs are the means by how an AI Technology recognizes which data elements are important. The AI is then trained by using a KG related to a Knowledge Base or data set. Over time as the KB and KG grow, the accuracy of the AI improves, soon reflecting on more variables in a moment than a team of humans could in hours. The more data fed into an AI technology; the more patterns it will identify in the data set by means of the Knowledge Graphs. The Knowledge Graphs we create have emerged as a critical starting point for AI/ML and RPA by generating knowledge resources.

As we expand these models to describe the interrelationships of multi domain dependencies we create the knowledge graph that leverages the semantics and metadata to provide an intelligent system a knowledge base that is operationally accurate (Fig. 4).

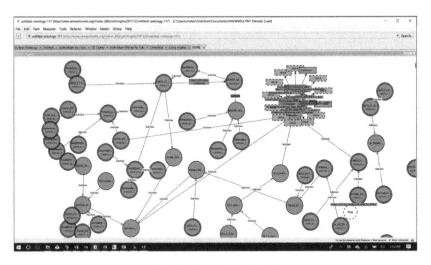

Fig. 4.   Knowledge Graph

Our knowledge graphs define the model "rule book" that provides the ability to learn military operations. This is critical and often the missing link in developing intelligent systems DoD.

It is from our operational and data science experience that we developed a unique method called Process Driven Ontologies (PDOs) to create the SDMs, KGs and CAs.

We use ontologies rather than typical architecture tools to give us greater flexibility while still providing E2E traceability all the way from SOPs to raw data. The PDOs connect multiple perspectives in one large model while defining the SDM, KG and CAs layers, rather than creating a new architecture for each perspective. Using an ontology is far more adaptable and extensible than a relational data model; if we need to add new perspectives or relationships, we don't need to change the model. Anything relying on the previous versions is unaffected by the extensions. Our PDOs can quickly form the foundation of an intelligent system by applying knowledge of multiple functions. Teaching the system to extract the most meaning from the data quickly and, on the fly, to come up with operationally based solutions. However, the data explosion of the last two decades and the sheer volume of data available has made it almost impossible for a human to identify which data is even relevant, let alone analyze it all to develop creative solutions that will achieve the maximum effect. Attempting to accomplish this goal with training alone would be futile. Rather, we must combine the resourcefulness and ingenuity of SOCOM soldiers with the advanced pattern recognition and processing power of software. However, the software must be properly trained. For the software to "learn", it needs a starting point describing how the world works so it can begin to learn and improve it's understanding to augment operations. A base built on SDMs, KGs, and CAs.

Intelligent systems will not have a basis to "learn" from without applying our mission engineering process to any intelligent systems development. The mission engineering flow that is represented in following images captures the explicate representation of a domain for CEMA Planning. This representation includes the SDM definition of the data and the model of how the data is created, modified, stored, and used in this process. It also represents the CA of how the "supporting staff" augment the planning process through the linkages of functions, tasks, system and personnel that have a role directly or indirectly of creating knowledge artifacts (DIKUI) to execute this process. An example of this would be the targeting and IPB working groups develop their own planning data and information that will correlate to information needed by the EWO to execute their internal processes.

3   Mission Engineering Example

Figure 5 shows a model representation of the tasks and data that is created across a staff process that does not have a defined relationship to the EWO effort. The image represents the universe of all possible variant…an endless sea of qualitative and quantitative values without a cognitive pattern. Through analysis and software reasoning (Fig. 6) our model is filtered and sampled to separate useful measurements (facts) and to form data. Data is created via our cognitive representation of the process and we start to see potential patterns that represents knowledge sharing through the inputs and outputs between systems or people in the form of Data, Information, Knowledge, Understanding or Intelligence.

As we inject a specific mission thread or function, in this case "Plan an EW effect". A more specific pattern evolves through providence of DIKUI that is shared to achieve the desired plan (Fig. 7).

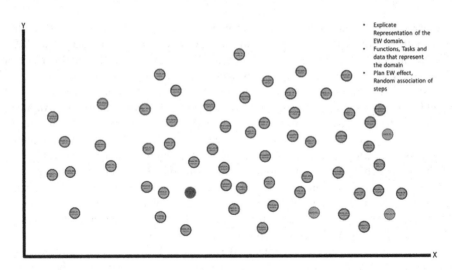

Fig. 5. Representative sematic data model view

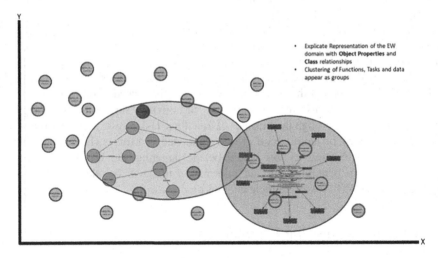

Fig. 6. Cognitive Architecture applied to the data

This is how we create a supervised "learning" capability for Artificial Intelligence, Machine Learning, Artificial Neural Networks and Robotic Process Automation. Providing the knowledge artifacts to implement an intelligent system. It is through this process that we can assess if an organization/domain has the infrastructural capability to reduce the cognitive burden or the warfighter.

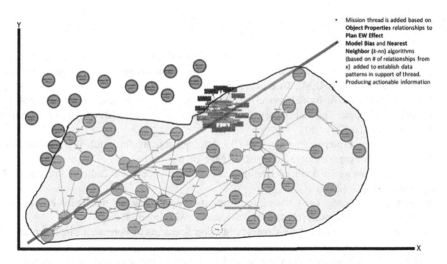

Mission thread is added based on **Object Properties** relationships to **Plan EW Effect**
Model Bias and **Nearest Neighbor** (*k-nn*) algorithms (based on # of relationships from *x*) added to establish data patterns in support of thread.
• Producing actionable information

Fig. 7. Knowledge Graph of a mission thread "Plan EW Effect"

4   Summary

We address the state of infrastructural pieces by using Semantic Data Models (SDMs), Knowledge Graphs (KGs), and Cognitive Architectures (CAs) to determine what needs to be modified to enact Artificial Intelligence, Machine Learning, Artificial Neural Networks and Robotic Process Automation (AI/ML, ANN & RPA). Capturing cognitive capabilities using PDOs is a critical step for Operational Forces. The Warfighter is most effective when they can decentralize decision making through SOPs. The explosion of IT and data has caused two problems for Commanders and Staffs: degraded ability to tailor processes and procedures using current fielded systems to the data and an increased cognitive burden related to processing and finding meaning in the vast amounts of data collected. Industry is using ontologies to enhance cognitive capabilities and so can DoD. However, these capabilities require an understanding of the domains data, knowledge/understanding of a domain's objective and creation of a knowledge base comprised of facts, beliefs, basic information, and relationships that can be used to develop patterns for learning. We create knowledge artifacts based on cognitive capabilities defined by the data, processes, intelligence and dependencies to generate meaningful recommendations - a knowledge base built in PDOs that delivers a Semantic Data Model, Cognitive Architecture and Knowledge Graphs.

Our process informs you if you are ready to move to AI by defining the state your organization. And if you are not ready then it provides the roadmap to change these areas to make you ready.

References

1. Fornara, N., Vigano, F., Colombetti, M.: An event driven approach to norms in artificial institutions. In: AAMAS05 Workshop: Agents, Norms and Institutions for Regulated Multi-agent Systems (ANI@REM), Utrecht (2005)
2. Nogueira, J.H.M.: A formal model of organisation in multi-agents systems based on mathematical logic and set theory. In: Proceedings of 58th SBPC Annual Meeting, Florianópolis (2006)
3. Protégé, The Protege Project (2007). http://protege.stanford.eduLNCS Homepage. http://www.springer.com/lncs. Accessed 21 Nov 2016
4. Russell, S., Norvig, P.: Artificial Intelligence: A Modern Approach, 2nd edn. Prentice Hall, Englewood Cliffs (2002)
5. Salas, E., Fiore, S.M.: Team Cognition. Understanding the Factors that Drive Process and Performance. American Psychological Association, Washington (2004)
6. Nogueira, J.H.M.: Ontology for Complex Mission Scenarios in Forensic Computing, Brazil (2009)
7. Broekstra, J., Kampman, A., van Harmelen, F.: Sesame: a generic architecture for storing and querying RDF and RDF Schema. In: Horrocks, I., Hendler, J. (eds.) ISWC 2002. LNCS, vol. 2342, pp. 54–68. Springer, Heidelberg (2002). https://doi.org/10.1007/3-540-48005-6_7
8. Dou, D., LePendu, P.: Ontology-based integration for relational databases. In: ACM Symposium on Applied Computing (SAC), pp. 461–466 (2006)
9. Motik, B., Horrocks, I., Sattler, U.: Bridging the gap between owl and relational databases. In: Proceedings of the 16th International Conference on World Wide Web (WWW), pp. 807–816 (2007)'

An Ensemble Method: Case-Based Reasoning and the Inverse Problems in Investigating Financial Bubbles

Francis Ekpenyong[1](✉), Georgios Samakovitis[2], Stelios Kapetanakis[1], and Miltos Petridis[3]

[1] University of Brighton, Brighton, UK
{F.Ekpenyong,S.Kapetanakis}@brighton.ac.uk
[2] University of Greenwich, London, UK
G.Samakovitis@gre.ac.uk
[3] Middlesex University, London, UK
M.Petridis@mdx.ac.uk

Abstract. This paper presents an ensemble approach and model; IPCBR, that leverages the capabilities of Case based Reasoning (CBR) and Inverse Problem Techniques (IPTs) to describe and model abnormal stock market fluctuations (often associated with asset bubbles) in time series datasets from historical stock market prices. The framework proposes to use a rich set of past observations and geometric pattern description and then applies a CBR to formulate the forward problem; Inverse Problem formulation is then applied to identify a set of parameters that can statistically be associated with the occurrence of the observed patterns.

The technique brings a novel perspective to the problem of asset bubbles predictability. Conventional research practice uses traditional forward approaches to predict abnormal fluctuations in financial time series; conversely, this work proposes a formative strategy aimed to determine the causes of behaviour, rather than predict future time series points. This suggests a deviation from the existing research trend.

Keywords: Case-based reasoning · Inverse problems · Asset bubble · Machine learning · Time series

1 Introduction

Asset value predictability has always been one of the thorny research issues in Finance. While real uses of Artificial Intelligence in the field are as old as the mid-80s, it has been the more topical technological developments that appear to impact direct real time implementation of machine learning in the field. Relevant researches have delivered statistical prediction models [1–3] which, though promising improved predictive capability, they are yet to receive wider acceptance in practice. The reasons for that may stem from the stochastic nature of asset fluctuations in the market which makes it difficult to build reliable models.

© Springer Nature Switzerland AG 2019
R. Xu et al. (Eds.): ICCC 2019, LNCS 11518, pp. 153–168, 2019.
https://doi.org/10.1007/978-3-030-23407-2_13

A major concern arises with the increase in complexity of the problem, so it becomes very difficult to mathematically formulate the problems, which often leads the choice of parameters to be set by heuristics. This in turn contributes to further deficiencies in reliability and explainability, specifically because it becomes very hard to identify which parameters need to be optimized and in what way, in order to improve the descriptive power of the model. The large scale impact of asset price bubble around many historic periods of economic downturn and instability, coupled with the difficulty of identifying a bubble and a general misunderstanding of bubbles, warrants further research study as evident from [4] who reported that econometric detection of asset price bubbles cannot be achieved with a satisfactory degree of certainty despite all the research advancements.

These and other reports demonstrate the need to enhance the explanatory capability of existing artificial intelligence models; to that end, we propose an ensemble IPCBR model that aims to

(i) use CBR to deliver a more robust representation of asset value fluctuation patterns (and their subsequest classification as asset bubbles) and;
(ii) implement an Inverse Problem formulation approach to identify the factors that are most likely causes of those patterns.

CBR has been successfully applied to various financial and management domains such as supply chain management and scheduling [5–8], stock selection [9], bond rating [10], bankruptcy prediction and credit analysis [11], and time series prediction [12,13]. The term "inverse problem" which first appeared in the late 1960s, has witnessed a great drift from its original use in geophysics to determine the unknown parameters through input/output or cause-effect experiments, to a contemporary "inverse problems" that designates the best possible reconstruction of missing information, in order to estimate either the identification of sources or of the cause, or the value of undetermined parameters [14].

Inverse Problem approaches have been successfully applied mainly in science and engineering fields, and provide a truly multidisciplinary platform where related problems from different disciplines can be studied under a common approach with comparable results [15]; these includes Pattern recognition [16], Civil engineering [14] soil hydraulics, [17] computer vision [16], Real-time decision support system [18] machine learning [19,20] and (big) data analysis in general, amongst others. To the small extent, used in financial applications [21] to provide early warning signalling. In spite of the occurrence frequencies of stock market bubbles, the inverse problem approach may contribute to identifying a defining sets of parameters that statistically cause these bubbles.

To tackle the inverse problem, the forward model needs to be first created; to do this, a knowledge mining model is created starting from developing a generic model which covers relevant information on historical stock transactions including the applied results.

The outcome of this will then be used as a case base for standard Case-based Reasoning process, and will be evaluated against a known episodic (real) data and human expert advice. The dataset is drawn from the world largest recorded stock market repository; New York Stock Exchange (NYSE). About 2,800 companies are listed on the NYSE. In this experiment, we'll look at the daily stock prices of six companies namely: IBM, General Electric (GE), SP500, Tesla, Microsoft and Oracle. The data used in this problem comes from one of the widely used repositories, Yahoo finance.

The remainder of this paper is organised as follows: Sect. 2 outlines the class of asset bubble problems to be addressed in this research, and outlines the proposed relevant features/qualities of CBR that make it suitable, as well as the overall IP formulation approach. A simple stochastic asset bubble model is then proposed in Sect. 3 with a brief review of the rational bubble model, which is the theoretical backbone of rational bubble tests, while Sect. 4 expands on a structural geometric representation of the model, which is proposed to act as a base description for our CBR training and subsequent implementation. Section 5 provides an articulation of the overall model to be used where also the Inverse Problem formulation component is discussed. The paper closes with a critical discussion of the major contributions this work intends to deliver, and a set of relevant concluding observations.

2   Prior Research

This section introduces the scope of our research in the well-documented area of stock market bubbles and also examines the general concept of CBR and the IP, with particular reference to previous research. That later provides the grounds for proposing the CBR/IP ensemble approach as a method for identifying the causative parameters in stock market bubbles.

2.1   Asset Bubbles

Various definitions are available in the Finance literature for asset bubbles [22–24], however, broadly described, asset bubbles are significant growths in the market that are not based on substantial change in market or industry performance, and usually escalate and equally dissipate with little or no warning.

Bubbles are often defined relative to the fundamental value of an asset [25, 26]. This can occur if investors hold the asset because they believe that they can sell it at an even higher price to some other investor even though the asset's price exceeds its fundamental value [21]. Detecting a bubble in real time is quite challenging because what attributes to the fundamental value is difficult to pin down. Although every bubble differs in their initiation and specific details, there is a trend in pattern in which informed assumption can be derived this trend makes is possible to recognise bubbles in advance because. Creating a more efficient and effective system that can analyse these fluctuations in patterns can give investors a competitive advantage over others as they can identify stocks with potentials of bubbles with minimum efforts.

A large and growing number of papers propose methods of detecting asset bubbles [21, 23, 27–29].

Many machine learning algorithms have been adopted over the years towards attempting to predict asset bubbles [9, 30]. However, while both academic and trade literature have long been examining their occurrence [23, 26, 31, 32], that extensive literature falls well beyond the scope of this work; for our purposes we adopt a relatively narrow definition of asset bubbles as patterns which can be described as, 'a short-term continuous, sustained, and extra-ordinary price growth of an asset or portfolio of assets that occurs in a short period of time, and which is followed by an equally extra-ordinary price decay in a comparably short period'.

The motivation for this relatively constrained focus is evident: due to the extremely convoluted nature of asset bubbles as these have been historically manifested and documented in Finance, Accounting and Economics literature, any attempt to address the phenomenon in its fullness in engineering terms would require a very large set of features and data points and involve infeasible computational complexity.

2.2   Case Based Reasoning

It is assumed that a decision-maker can only learn from experience, by evaluating an act based on its past performance in similar circumstances which informs the application of case-based Reasoning(CBR) Case-based reasoning [33] is an Artificial Intelligence (AI) technique that supports the capability of reasoning and learning in advanced Decision Support System (DSS)[34, 35]. It is a paradigm for combining problem solving and learning which is analogous to problem solving that compares new cases with previous indexes cases. CBR provides two main functions: storage of new cases in the database through indexation module and searching the indexes cases with the similarities of new cases in case retrieval module [36, 37]. The case-based reasoning methodology incorporates four main stages [33, 38]

- Retrieve: given a target problem, retrieve from the case memory, cases that are most relevant and promise to proffer solution to the target case.
- Reuse: the solutions of the best; map the solution from the previous case to the target situation, test the new solution in the real world or perform a simulation, and if necessary.
- Revise: the solution provided by the query case is evaluated and information about whether the solution has or has not provided a desired outcome is gathered.
- Retain: After the solution has been successfully adapted to the target problem, the new problem-solving experience can be stored or not stored in memory, depending on the revise outcomes and the CBR policy regarding case retention.

A CBR cycle is shown in Fig. 1

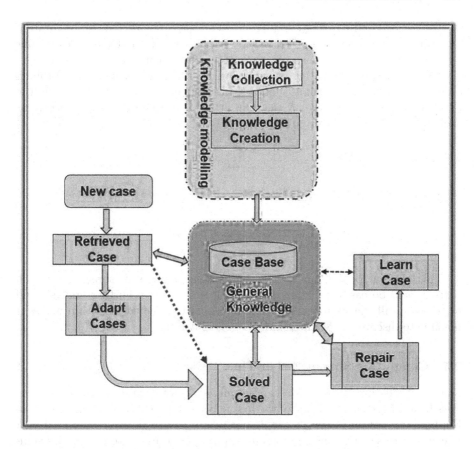

Fig. 1. A modified CBR cycle [33]

2.3   Case Representation

Case representation is a fundamental issue in a Case-based Reasoning methodology. Despite being a plausible and promising data mining methodology, CBR is seldom used in time series domains. This is because the use of case-based reasoning for time series processing introduces some unaccustomed features that do not exist in the processing of the traditional "attribute-value" data representation. Also, direct manipulation of continuous, high dimensional data which involves very long sequences with variable lengths is extremely difficult [39]. In order to make a good case representation, two approaches can be used, namely: the cases represented by succession of points and the cases represented by relations between temporal intervals. Our focus will be on the latter.

2.4   Definition of Cases in the Time Series Context

Case formation tends to be domain specific, and there seems to exist no hard and fast rule in case formation. In our case, we will consider forming a library pattern of observations and treating every group as a case category. Our representation will mimic the concept proposed in [40]. Where the entire Time series is split into smaller sequences of patterns, each of which is then treated as a case.

This could be achieved by decomposing the series into a sequence of rolling observation patterns or rolling windows. In which case, every observation in the pattern constitutes the case. A case can attain a predefined upward, steady or declining patterns as shown in Fig. 2

Fig. 2. Sample case patterns

This also infers that an interval comprising a series of three observation patterns can be easily recognized as constituting a case. Further analysis and matching of all the similar cases using appropriate selected algorithm makes it possible to discover a specific relation to the pattern.

2.5   Computing Similarities in Time Series

Similarity measure is the most essential ingredient of time series clustering and classification systems, and one of the first decisions to be made in order to establish how the distance between two independent vectors must be measured [41]. Because of this importance, numerous approaches to estimate time series similarity have been proposed. Among these, Longest common subsequence (LCS) [42,43] Histogram-based similarity measure [44] Cubic Spline [45], dynamic Time Wrapping [46,47] have been extensively used.

Similarity in real sense is subjective, highly dependent on the domain and application. It is often measured in the range 0 to 1 [0,1], where 1 indicates the maximum of similarity.

Similarity between two numbers x and y can be represented as:

$$nSim(X,Y) = 1 - \frac{|x - y|}{|x| + |y|} \tag{1}$$

When considering two time series $X = x1,.., xn, Y = y1,..., yn$, some similarity measures that could be used are:

mean similarity defined as:

$$MSim(X,Y) = \frac{1}{n} \sum_{i=1}^{n} nSim(x_i, y_i) \tag{2}$$

Root mean Square similarity defined as:

$$RMSim(X,Y) = \sqrt{\frac{1}{n}\sum_{i=1}^{n} nSim(x_i, y_i)^2} \tag{3}$$

Peak similarity defined as:

$$PSim(X,Y) = \frac{1}{n}\sum_{i=1}^{n}[\frac{|x_i - y_i|}{2max(|x_i|, |y_i|)}] \tag{4}$$

Despite the sporadic introduction of various methods of measuring similarity, the challenge of determining the best method for assignment of attributes' weight value in CBR still needs to be addressed [37].

Euclidean distance is by far the most popular distance measure in data mining, and it has the advantage of being a distance metric. However, a major demerit of Euclidean distance is that it requires that both input sequences be of the same length, and it is sensitive to distortions, e.g. shifting, along the time axis. Such a problem can generally be handled by elastic distance measures such as Dynamic Time Warping (DTW)

In this research, the dynamic time warping (DTW) distance was chosen owing to the fact that it overcomes some limitations of other distance metrics by using dynamic programming technique to determine the best alignment that will produce the optimal distance. It is an extensively used technique in speech recognition [48,49] and many other domains, including Time Series analysis [46,47].

2.6   Inverse Problem

Inverse problems (also called model inversion) arise in many fields, where one tries to find a model that typically approximates observational data. Any inverse theory requirement is to relate a physical parameter "u" that describes a model to acquire observations making up some set of data "f". Assuming there is a clear picture of the underlying concept of the model, then an operator can be assigned a relation or mapping u to f through the equation:

$$f = Ku \tag{5}$$

where f is an N- dimensional constant coefficients data vector and u is an M-dimensional model parameter, and K (the Kernel) is an N x M matrix containing only constant coefficients. It can be referred to as the Green's function because of the analogy with the continuous function case:

$$f(dx) = K(x,t)u(t)dx \tag{6}$$

In a case where the experiment is drawn from i observations and k model parameters will be:
data: f = $[f_1, f_2, ...f_i]^T$

and model parameters: $u = [u_1, u_2, ...u_j]^T$

with d and m representing I and J dimensional column vectors, respectively, and T denoting the transpose.

Most relevant application find it very difficult to invert the forward problem for some obvious reasons; either a (unique) inverse model simply does not exist, or a small perturbation of the system causes a relatively large change in the exact solution. In the sense of Hadamard the problem above is called well-posed under the conditions of:

- Existence: ∀ input data there exists a solution of the problem, i.e. for all $f \in$ there exists a $u \in U$ with $Ku = f$.
- Uniqueness: ∀ input data, this existing solution is unique meaning $u \neq v$ implies $Kv \neq f$
- Stability: the solution of the problem depends continuously on the input datum, i.e. $\forall U k_{k \in N}$ with $Ku_k \mapsto f$ we have $u_k \mapsto u$ u.

The well-posedness of a model highly depends on the stated conditions, Violation of any of the conditions results in ill posedness, or approximately ill-posed [50]. One way of finding the inverse of this in the use of Convolution [51], which is widely significant as a physical concept and offers an advantageous starting point for many theoretical developments.

A convolution operation describes the action of an observing instrument when it takes a weighted mean of a physical quantity over a narrow range of a variable. It is widely used in time series analysis as well to represent physical processes. The convolution of two functions f(x) and g(x) represented as f(x)*g(x) is

$$\int_{-\infty}^{\infty} f(u)g(x-u)du \qquad (7)$$

As such a more logical step is to take the forward problem in Eq. 5 and invert it for an estimate of the model parameters f^{est} as

$$f^{est} = K^{inverse}u$$

by performing a Deconvolution to it which could be represented as

$$f = K^{-1}u \qquad (8)$$

Alternatively, the equation can be reformulate the problem as

$$f^T K f = K^T u \qquad (9)$$

and find the solution as

$$f = [K^T K]^{-1}[K^T u] \qquad (10)$$

Considering the large number of reported asset bubbles in stock markets, there appears to exist a rich body of pattern occurrences to allow for applying the Inverse Problem approach to identify a defining set of parameters that statistically cause them.

3 Asset Bubble from Price Theory

This section gives a brief review of the rational bubble model, which is the theoretical backbone of rational bubble tests. A simple linear asset pricing model is employed that draws its arguments from the basic financial theory [26,52], which expresses asset price as a discount factor multiplied by the flows of all future payments relating to the asset [23].

Let P_t denote the price of an asset at time t, and return rate R_t at time t based on the work of [28] The return rate of the asset in the next period is denoted with R_Δ, and its equivalent change in price at a time t_Δ to be denoted with P_Δ. Then The return rate R_Δ of a stock can be expressed as the as the sum of the price change $(P_\Delta - P_t)$ and the dividend D_Δ, adjusted to the price of a stock in period t, given by

$$R_\Delta = \frac{P_\Delta - P_t + D_\Delta}{P_t} \tag{11}$$

The change in price and the dividends becomes apparent only in the period t_Δ as they realise, one can take mathematical expectation of Eq. 11 based on available information on period t, this being

$$E_t(R_\Delta) = \frac{E(P_\Delta - P_t + D_\Delta) - P_t}{P_t} = R \tag{12}$$

Where
$E_t(P_t) - P_t + D_\Delta) = RP_t$ Rearranging 12 results in

$$P_t = E_t\left(\frac{D_\Delta}{1+R}\right) + E_t\left(\frac{P_\Delta}{1+R}\right) \tag{13}$$

For periods more than singular denoted by k the forward solution could further be stated as

$$P_t = E_t\left[\sum_{i=1}^{k}\left(\frac{1}{1+R}\right)^i D_\Delta\right] + E_t\left[\sum_{i=1}^{k}\left(\frac{1}{1+R}\right)^j P_\Delta\right] \tag{14}$$

And again, applying the elements of uniqueness to solution for this equation, it is also assumed that the expected discounted value of a stock converges to zero in Eq. 14 under assumption on indefinite amount future periods [28].

$$Lim_{k\mapsto\infty}E_t\left[\left(\frac{1}{1+R_{t+k}}\right)^i P_{t+k}\right] = 0 \tag{15}$$

Hence, reducing the forward solution of the stocks fundamental price

$$(P_t^f) = E_t\left[\sum_{i=1}^{\infty}\left(\frac{1}{1+R_{t+i}}\right)^i D_{t+i}\right] \tag{16}$$

where (P_t^f) is the expected discounted value of future dividends. Failure of which would result in infinite number of solutions that can be represented as

$$P_t = (P_t^f) + B_t, \tag{17}$$

where $B_t = E_t \left[\frac{B_\Delta}{1+R_\Delta} \right]$

B_t in equation above would present the 'rational bubble' as this components value would consist of the expected path of stock price returns.

To promote the financial stability, an effective warning mechanism is always desirable to signal the formation of asset price misalignments. This research provides a methods to accomplish this task by the use of ensemble method, CBR/IP.

The study from [21] presented an early-warning signalling approach for financial bubbles by benefiting from the theory of optimization, of inverse problems and clustering method. The research reported a method which approaches the bubble concept geometrically by determining and evaluating ellipsoids and reported that when the bubble-burst time approaches, the volumes of the ellipsoids gradually decrease and, correspondingly, the figures obtained by Radon transform become more "brilliant" presenting more strongly warning.

The authors of [28] stated that although every bubble has its own unique features, there are some common early symptoms. He further showed that the conventional unit root tests in modified forms can be used to construct early warning indicators for bubbles in financial markets.

4   Structural Representation of the Model

Despite the fact that there are many opinions about bubbles in various literature, one thing is obvious, none of the authors seems to disagree about the theoretical determination of the fundamental asset price. An asset price bubble according to [32] is defined as the difference between two components: the observed market price of a given financial asset, which represents the amount that the marginal buyer is willing to pay, and the asset's intrinsic or fundamental value, which is defined as the expected sum of future discounted dividends. In trying to give meaning to what a bubble is, let us define what a fundamental value of an asset is. The representation is adopted from the concept given in [52] which starts with a case of an asset that yields a known and fixed stream of dividends. In which case, d_t denote the dividend income paid out by the asset at date t, where t runs from 0 to infinity, and q_t denote the current price of a bond that pays one dollar at date t. Its states the value any trader attaches to the dividend stream from this asset is given by

$$F_t = \sum_{i=0}^{\infty} q_t d_t \tag{18}$$

here, F denotes the fundamental value of a stock. A stock bubble deduces a stock whose price P is not equal to its fundamental value, meaning $P \neq F$. a bubble case would assume the market price to sell above its fundamental value, in which case $P > F$. Also, on the assumption dividends are uncertain, given a state of the world represented as states in a set Φ which denotes a set of all possible outcomes at a date t, and given that $\tau_t \in \Phi$ refers to a particular state of the world at date t which all dealers hope will occur with a probability say $Prob(\tau_t)$ which determines the value of a dividend at date t given by the fundamental values dealers allocates to the asset in this case is expectation

$$F_t = [\sum_{i=0}^{\infty} q(\tau_t)d(\tau_t)] \tag{19}$$

$$= [\sum_{i=0}^{\infty} \sum_{\tau_t \in \Phi} q(\tau_t)d(\tau_t)] \tag{20}$$

In this case, an asset would be considered a bubble if its price $P > F$. as defined in the equation. The $P <> F$ refers to an asset being "unfairly priced" in the sense of perhaps being valued at discount.

The equation above could be related to a descriptive bubble case adopted from the work of [53], which represents a growing asset prize with respect to time t. shown in Fig. 3. Time here is considered continuous and infinite with periods $t \subset R$.

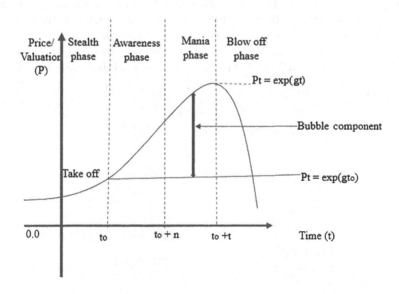

Fig. 3. A smoothed approximation representation of a bubble

The figure shows an initial constant steady growth in asset price based on the fundamental value at some random time t, At a point say t_o, (take off point or the Stealth phase) the price driven by bubble grows in time value with expectation

(gt_o), From t_o the asset price pt grows exponentially at $g > 0$, denoting evolving price with a growing expectation given by $p_t = exp(gt)$. Hence the bubble component is denoted by $exp(gt) - exp(go)$ where $t > to$. The assumption is that the starting point of a bubble is t_o is discrete as $t_o = 0, \delta, 2\delta, 3\delta, ...$, where $\delta > 0$ and that t_o is exponentially distributed on $[0, \infty)$ with cumulative distribution $\psi(t_o) = 1 - exp(-\beta t_o)$ [54]. Investors considered are risk neutral investors that have a discount rate of zero, whereby, as long as they hold the assets, the have two choices; either to sell of retain the assets. But when $\alpha \in (0, 1)$ of investors sell their assets, the bubble bursts and the asset price drops to the true value. If fewer than α of the investors sell their assets at time ρ after t_o, the bubble bursts automatically at $t_o + \rho$ but if she sells his assets at t i.e before the bubble bursts, he receives the price in the selling period otherwise he only receives true value $exp(gt_o)$ below the price at $t > t_o$.

5 Proposed Framework

Owing the complexity of the problem at hand, we will attempt to tackle the problem by defining and solving its simplified forward problem and then with a clear definition of this, the solution of which will then be an input to the inverse problem. As such, the ensemble in made up two sections: The Case Based Reasoning Model and the Inverse Problem Model. First of all, the CBR model evaluates the potential indicators of all the stocks and output with potentially high yielding stocks with respect to the predefined criteria as a preselected stock set. Secondly, input this stock set, together with its corresponding indicators into the inverse Problem Model. The holistic framework is detailed in Fig. 4.

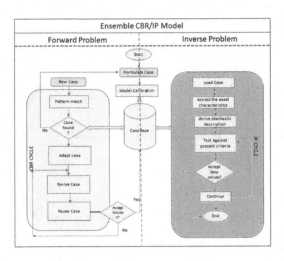

Fig. 4. CBR/IP Model framework

With all the afore stated assumptions that defines our descriptive model, we aim to arrive at a representative of the descriptive model by calibrating the model parameters of the seed model through Case Base knowledge, which will be used to initially populate our case base. This involves representing our bubble model in a case structure which is made of historical stock projections represented by a set of points, where each point was given with the time of measuring and the equivalent stock volume. It follows from this that these processes could be represented as curves.

Then follows a Pattern Matching phase which entails the process of automatically mapping an input representation for an entity or relationship to an output category.

This involves using the new model perform pattern recognition to identify new instances that fit into the model with the use of appropriate similarity metric.

For this investigation, the Dynamic Time Warping will be considered as it is proven to be effective in finding distances Time Series [42] and also because most classic data mining algorithms do not perform or scale well on time series data [55] If a perfect match is found, then the complete cycle of the CBR will be adopted and solutions adapted, otherwise, a new problem case will be reformulated. The output of this phase signifies the end of the forward problem and the solution then used as a seed for the Inverse Problem phase.

IP implementation requires taking the newly identified structure from the retrieved case and extract the asset characteristics around the time of the occurrence. It then requires that we identify any correlation between such characteristics and the forward problem model parameters in order to derive stochastic description of the factors that accompany the said bubbles. The output of this phase will as well be stored in the Knowledge base for easy recommendation.

6   Conclusion and Future Work

This paper proposes an approach that uses an AI ensemble of CBR and Inverse Problem formulation, to describe, identify and ultimately predict abnormal fluctuations in stock markets, widely known as bubbles. The proposed framework uses a flexible query engine based on historical time series data and seeks to identify price fluctuations in temporal constraints.

The ensemble is aimed to select representative candidate object which has specified 'bubble' characteristics from the time series dataset based on the objects' degree in their neighbour network through clustering. The neighbour network is built based on the similarity of time series objects which is measured by suitable similarity metrics.

Once the candidates are chosen, further investigation will be performed to extract the asset characteristics around the time of the occurrence in order to derive stochastic description of the factors that accompany the above 'bubbles'. The output of this phase will as well be stored in the Knowledge base for easy recommendation.

By capturing such experiences in a new ensemble model, investors can learn lessons about actual challenges to trading assumptions, adequate project preparedness and planned execution and be able to leverage that knowledge for efficient and effective management of future similar transactions.

For future work, the plan will be to create a knowledge pool of distinct types of stock patterns and apply CBR in computing the similarities and characteristics of the case using controlled experiment.

References

1. Ou, P., Wang, H.: Prediction of stock market index movement by ten data mining techniques. Mod. Appl. Sci. **3**(12), 28–42 (2009)
2. Milosevic, N.: Equity forecast: predicting long term stock price movement using machine learning. J. Econ. Libr. **3**(2), 8 (2016)
3. Xu, Y., Cohen, S.B.: Stock movement prediction from tweets and historical prices. In: ACL, pp. 1–10 (2018)
4. Gurkaynak, R.S.: Econometric Tests of Asset Price Bubbles: Taking Stock Econometric Tests of Asset Price Bubbles (2005)
5. Dalal, S., Athavale, V.: Analysing supply chain strategy using case-based reasoning. J. Supply Chain Manage. **1**, 40 (2012)
6. Kaur, M.: Inventory Cost Optimization in Supply Chain System Through Case-based Reasoning, vol. I, no. V, pp. 20–23 (2012)
7. Fu, J., Fu, Y.: Case-based reasoning and multi-agents for cost collaborative management in supply chain. Procedia Eng. **29**, 1088–1098 (2012)
8. Lim, S.H.: Case-based reasoning system for prediction of collaboration level using balanced scorecard: a dyadic approach form distributing and manufacturing companies. J. Comput. Sci. **6**(9), 9–12 (2006)
9. Ince, H.: Short term stock selection with case-based reasoning technique. Appl. Soft Comput. J. **22**, 205–212 (2014)
10. Shin, K.S., Han, I.: A case-based approach using inductive indexing for corporate bond rating. Decis. Support Syst. **32**(1), 41–52 (2001)
11. Bryant, S.M.: A case-based reasoning approach to bankruptcy prediction modeling. Intell. Syst. Account. Finance Manage. **6**(3), 195–214 (1997)
12. Kurbalija, V., Budimac, Z.: Case-based reasoning framework for generating decision support systems. Novi Sad J. Math. **38**(3), 219–226 (2008)
13. Elsayed, A., Hijazi, M.H.A., Coenen, F., Garcıa-Finana, M., Sluming, V., Zheng, Y.: Time series case based reasoning for image categorisation. In: Case-Based Peasoning Research and Development, pp. 423–436 (2011)
14. Argoul, P.: Overview of Inverse Problems, Parameter Identification in Civil Engineering, pp. 1–13 (2012)
15. Gomez-ramirez, J.: Inverse thinking in economic theory: a radical approach to economic thinking. Four problems in classical economic modeling (2003)
16. Sever, A.: An inverse problem approach to pattern recognition in industry. Appl. Comput. Inf. **11**(1), 1–12 (2015)
17. Ritter, A., Hupet, F., Mun, R., Lambot, S., Vanclooster, M.: Using inverse methods for estimating soil hydraulic properties from ®; eld data as an alternative to direct methods. Agric. Water Manag. **59**, 77–96 (2003)

18. Gundersen, O.E., Srmo, F., Aamot, A., Skalle, P.: A real-time decision support system for high cost oil-well drilling operations. In: Proceedings of the Twenty-Fourth Innovative Applications of Artificial Intelligence Conference A, pp. 2209–2216 (2012)

19. Sever, A.: A machine learning algorithm based on inverse problems for software requirements selection. J. Adv. Math. Comput. Sci. **23**(2), 1–16 (2017)

20. Search, H., Journals, C., Contact, A., Iopscience, M., Address, I.P.: Inverse problems Problems in in machine learning: machine learning: an an application Interpretation application to activity interpretation. Theory Pract. **135**, 012085 (2008)

21. Kürüm, E., Weber, G.W., Iyigun, C.: Early warning on stock market bubbles via methods of optimization, clustering and inverse problems. Ann. Oper. Res. **260**(1–2), 293–320 (2018)

22. Herzog, B.: An econophysics model of financial bubbles. Nat. Sci. **7**(7), 55–63 (2007)

23. Kubicová, I., Komárek, L.: The classification and identification. Finance a úvěr-Czech J. Econ. Finan. **61**, 1(403), 34–48 (2011)

24. Martin, A., Ventura, J.: Economic growth with bubbles. Am. Econ. Rev. **102**(6), 3033–3058 (2012)

25. Barberis, N., Greenwood, R., Jin, L., Shleifer, A.: Extrapolation and Bubbles (2017)

26. Sornette, D., Cauwels, P.: Financial Bubbles: Mechanisms and Diagnostics, pp. 1–24, January 2014

27. Jiang, Z.Q., Zhou, W.X., Sornette, D., Woodard, R., Bastiaensen, K., Cauwels, P.: Bubble diagnosis and prediction of the 2005–2007 and 2008–2009 Chinese stock market bubbles. J. Econ. Behav. Organ. **74**(3), 149–162 (2010)

28. Taipalus, K.: Detecting Asset Price Bubbles with Time-series Methods (2012)

29. Dvhg, D.V.H., et al.: A case-based reasoning-decision tree hybrid system for stock selection. Int. J. Comput. Inf. Eng. **10**(6), 1181–1187 (2016)

30. Zhou, W.X.: Should Monetary Policy Target Asset Bubbles? (2007)

31. Press, P., Profit, T.: Bursting Bubbles: Finance, Crisis and the Efficient Market Hypothesis. The Profit Doctrine, pp. 125–146 (2017)

32. Nedelcu, S.: Mathematical models for financial bubbles. Ph.D thesis (2014)

33. Aamodt, A., Plaza, E.: Case-based reasoning: foundational issues, methodological variations, and system approaches. AI Commun. **7**(1), 39–59 (1994)

34. Kolodner, J.L.: Case-based reasoning. In: The Cambridge Handbook Of: The Learning Sciences, pp. 225–242 (2006)

35. López, B.: Case-based reasoning: a concise introduction. Synth. Lect. Artif. Intell. Mach. Learn. **7**(1), 1–103 (2013)

36. Cunningham, P.: A taxonomy of similarity mechanisms for case-based reasoning. IEEE Trans. Knowl. Data Eng. **21**(11), 1532–1543 (2009)

37. Ji, S., Park, M., Lee, H., Yoon, Y.: Similarity measurement method of case-based reasoning for conceptual cost estimation. In: Proceedings of the International Conference on Computing in Civil and Building Engineering (2010)

38. El-Sappagh, S.H., Elmogy, M.: Case based reasoning: case representation methodologies. Int. J. Adv. Comput. Sci. Appl. **6**(11), 192–208 (2015)

39. Marketos, G., Pediaditakis, K., Theodoridis, Y., Theodoulidis, B.: Intelligent Stock Market Assistant using Temporal Data Mining. Citeseer (May 2014), pp. 1–11 (1999)

40. Pecar, B.: Case-based algorithm for pattern recognition and extrapolation (APRE Method). In: SGES/SGAI International Conference on Knowledge Based Systems and Applied Artificial Intelligence (2002)

41. Iglesias, F., Kastner, W.: Analysis of similarity measures in times series clustering for the discovery of building energy patterns. Energies **6**(2), 579–597 (2013)
42. Sengupta, S., Ojha, P., Wang, H., Blackburn, W.: Effectiveness of similarity measures in classification of time series data with intrinsic and extrinsic variability. In: Proceedings of the 11th IEEE International Conference on Cybernetic Intelligent Systems 2012, CIS 2012, pp. 166–171 (2012)
43. Khan, R., Ahmad, M., Zakarya, M.: Longest common subsequence based algorithm for measuring similarity between time series: a new approach. World Appl. Sci. J. **24**(9), 1192–1198 (2013)
44. Lin, J., Li, Y.: Finding structural similarity in time series data using bag-of-patterns representation. In: Winslett, M. (ed.) SSDBM 2009. LNCS, vol. 5566, pp. 461–477. Springer, Heidelberg (2009). https://doi.org/10.1007/978-3-642-02279-1_33
45. Wongsai, N., Wongsai, S., Huete, A.R.: Annual seasonality extraction using the cubic spline function and decadal trend in temporal daytime MODIS LST data. Remote Sens. **9**(12), 1254 (2017)
46. Zhang, X., Liu, J., Du, Y., Lv, T.: A novel clustering method on time series data. Expert Syst. Appl. **38**(9), 11891–11900 (2011)
47. Phan, T.t.h., et al.: Dynamic time warping-based imputation for univariate time series data To cite this version: HAL Id : hal-01609256. Pattern Recogn. Lett. (2017)
48. Cassidy, S.: Speech Recognition: Dynamic Time Warping, vol. 11, p. 2. Department of Computing, Macquarie University (2002)
49. Xihao, S., Miyanaga, Y.: Dynamic time warping for speech recognition with training part to reduce the computation. In: ISSCS 2013 - International Symposium on Signals, Circuits and Systems (2013)
50. Levitan, B.M., Sargsjan, I.S.: Inverse Problems. Sturm-Liouville and Dirac Operators, pp. 139–182 (2012)
51. Tarantola, A.: Chapter 1: Introduction 1.1 Inverse theory: what it is and what it does, vol. 1, pp. 1–11. Elsevier Scientific Publishing Company (1987)
52. Barlevy, G.: Economic Theory and Asset Bubbles, pp. 44–59 (2007)
53. Asako, Y., Funaki, Y., Ueda, K., Uto, N.: Centre for Applied Macroeconomic Analysis Symmetric Information Bubbles: Experimental Evidence (2017)
54. Abreu, D., Brunnermeier, M.K.: Bubbles and crashes. Econometrica **71**(1), 173–204 (2003)
55. Lin, J., Williamson, S., Borne, K., DeBarr, D.: Pattern recognition in time series. Adv. Mach. Learn. Data Min. Astron. **1**, 617–645 (2012). https://doi.org/10.1201/b11822-36

The Development Trend of Intelligent Speech Interaction

Yishuang Ning[1,2,3,4(✉)], Sheng He[1,2,3,4], Chunxiao Xing[1,2],
and Liang-Jie Zhang[3,4]

[1] Research Institute of Information Technology, Beijing National Research Center
for Information Science and Technology, Tsinghua University, Beijing 100084, China
ningyishuang@126.com
[2] Department of Computer Science and Technology, Institute of Internet Industry,
Tsinghua University, Beijing 100084, China
[3] National Engineering Research Center for Supporting Software of Enterprise
Internet Services, Shenzhen, China
[4] Kingdee Research, Kingdee International Software Group Company Limited,
Shenzhen, China

Abstract. To make the computers have capabilities of listening, speaking, understanding and even thinking is the latest development direction of human-computer interaction. As one of the most convenient and natural ways for communication, speech has become the most promising way of human-computer interaction in the future, which has more advantages than other interaction ways. As one of the most popular artificial intelligence (AI) technologies, intelligent speech interaction technology has been widely applied in many industries such as electronic commerce, smart home and intelligent industry as well as manufacturing. It will change the user behavior habits and become the new mode of human input and output. In this paper, we state the current situation of intelligent speech interaction at home and abroad, take many examples to illustrate the application scenarios of speech interaction technology and finally introduce its development trend in the future.

Keywords: Speech interaction · Intelligent technology ·
Multi-modality integration · Development trend

1 Introduction

In recent years, with the increasing popularity of portable intelligent terminal devices, it has become a new trend to use mobile applications to perform human-machine instant messaging anytime and anywhere. As one of the most natural, effective and convenient ways to obtain information, speech has become an important tool for human-machine communication. For example, the "2012–2013 China Instant Messaging Annual Monitoring and User Behavior Research Report" [1] shows that speech accounts for more than 50% of the instant messaging functions that users frequently use. A large number of intelligent speech

© Springer Nature Switzerland AG 2019
R. Xu et al. (Eds.): ICCC 2019, LNCS 11518, pp. 169–179, 2019.
https://doi.org/10.1007/978-3-030-23407-2_14

interaction applications (e.g. Apple Siri, Google Now, Microsoft Cortana, Baidu and Sogou speech assistants, etc.) have sprung up all over the world. As one of the key technologies in these years, intelligent speech interaction which uses speech as the main information carrier has made machines to not only have the ability to listen and answer, but also be able to understand and learn. It also makes the human-machine interaction increasingly more harmonious. Currently the ultimate goal of speech interaction has become understanding the whole scenario more and more accurately.

With the continuous expansion of the demand for intelligent speech interactive applications, the intelligent speech industry supported by key technologies (e.g. big data, cloud computing and mobile Internet, etc.) has developed rapidly, attracting the continuous attention of domestic and foreign research institutions and enterprises.

In many business areas or industries, speech has become a new way of input and output in the future. With the significant progress of speech technologies, the speech interaction technology has gradually gone to the market from libraries. It is currently applied in many areas, including telecommunication, medical, automotive electronics, home services and consumer electronics products. For example, you can use your speech to control a machine to operate as what you want or make a machine start to speak. This is the input and output of speech, which will become an input and output mode for future calculations.

However, what are the most important things about speech interaction? What is its ultimate goal? What are the application scenarios for enterprise? In this paper, we will first briefly introduce the speech interaction supporting technologies, then give an introduction to the current situation and many real-world application scenarios, and finally investigate the development trend of intelligent speech interaction.

The rest of the paper is structured as follows. Section 2 makes a brief description to the speech interaction support technologies, including basic speech technology, intelligent technology and big data technology. Section 3 introduces the current situation of speech interaction industry. Sections 4 and 5 present the application fields and the development trend of intelligent speech interaction, respectively. Section 6 summarizes the paper.

2   Speech Interaction Supporting Technologies

Intelligent speech interaction mainly studies the processing and feedback of speech information between human and machine. Generally speaking, there are three supporting technologies for speech interaction, as can be shown in Fig. 1.

2.1   Basic Speech Technology

The basic speech technology includes speech recognition, speech synthesis, speaker recognition and emotion recognition.

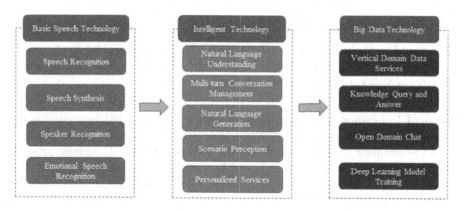

Fig. 1. Three supporting technologies for speech interaction.

Speech Recognition. Speech recognition is the ability of a machine or program to identify words or phrases in spoken language and convert them to a machine-readable format [2]. It is considered as the artificial ear. It uses acoustic model and language model to transcribe speech signals to texts. Acoustic model represents the relationship between linguistic units of speech and audio signals, while language model matches speeches with word sequences to help distinguish between words that sound similar.

Speech Synthesis. Speech synthesis, also called text-to-speech (TTS) is the technology that converts normal language text into natural and fluid speech [3]. It is the artificial production of human speech. Therefore, it is usually regarded as the artificial mouth. Currently the ultimate goal of speech synthesis has become synthesizing human-like speeches with high expressiveness.

Speaker Recognition. Speaker recognition or voiceprint recognition refers to the automated method of identifying or confirming the identity of an individual based on his or her voice [4]. It is the identification of a person from characteristics of voices. With the appearance of Amazon's smart speakers, this technology is rapidly used in many scenarios, such as public security, smart home and financial certification.

Emotional Speech Recognition. Emotion speech recognition is the process of identifying human emotion based on his or her speech [5,6]. Its main task is to analyze human expressions in multiple modalities such as text, speech or video and recognize the underlying emotions [7]. It is usually used in customer service scenarios to evaluate the quality of service (QoS) of agents.

2.2   Intelligent Technology

The second one is intelligent technology which includes natural language under-standing, multi-turn conversation management, natural language generation, scenario perception and many personalized services.

Natural Language Understanding. Natural language understanding is the process that converts human languages in to machine-readable, structured and complete semantic expression [8,9]. It is the subtopic of natural language process-ing (NLP) in artificial intelligence. It can be used in many commercial fields such as automated reasoning, machine translation, question answering and large-scale content analysis.

Multi-turn Conversation Management. Multi-turn conversation manage-ment plays an important role in the human-machine interaction systems [10]. Its main functionality includes two aspects. The first one is to maintain or update the dialog state while the second one is to generate dialog strategy based on the dialog state [10].

Natural Language Generation. Natural language generation is a technology that simply generates natural language from a machine-representation system [11]. With the development of deep learning technologies, this technology is adopted to help transform their business and innovate on how they better engage with their customers by enterprise organizations.

Scenario Perception. Scenario perception [12] is a technology the purpose of which is to perceive the current situation through sensors and related techniques. As an interdisciplinary concept, this technology has many in-depth researches in computer science, cognitive science, psychology and linguistics. With this tech-nology, intelligent devices can adaptively change with the current environment and push related services for users.

Personalized Services. The personalized services are implemented to provide or recommend related information to meet users' demand according to various channels and users' settings [13]. This technology breaks the traditional passive service model, can fully utilize various resource advantages to optimize the indus-trial chain and conduct all-round services for the purpose of meeting individual user demand actively.

2.3   Big Data Technology

The last one is big data technology [14,15], such as vertical domain data services, knowledge query and answer, open domain chat and large scale deep learning model training. In many real-world scenarios, users will use various of softwares or applications to understand the online speeches. All the speech data will be uploaded to the cloud and use the application programming interfaces (APIs) to transform speeches into texts. When the speech files are saved, they will actually be even larger than the text and image files. Therefore, speech is also a very important object based on the big data processing technology in the future.

3 The Current Situation of Speech Interaction Industry

In this section, we will introduce the current situation of speech interaction industry. As an important part of intelligent speech interaction, speech recognition or speech search has been widely used in many application scenarios. It has become the needs of mobile Internet times. Nowadays, in many applications (e.g. Baidu search or Google search, etc.), there is a speech search functionality. When users would like to buy a product or search a place, they just need to speak to the applications and then the applications will help them to find the corresponding information.

However, there are still many challenges for the speech interaction technology. (1) Although the near-field speech recognition has achieved significant improvements (can even reach 97%), the accuracy of the far-field speech recognition is still very low; (2) When there are many speakers, that is, when the speeches come from different directions, it will be difficult to give accurate response; (3) When the surrounding environment may have noise or reverberation, the technology is relatively less mature; (4) When the speech files are uploaded to the cloud through the Internet from different places, due to the differences of the speech quality, how to combine them for speech recognition is also a big problem.

4 Application Fields of Artificial Intelligence

To get good results in speech recognition, in addition to exploring application scenarios, many artificial intelligence (AI) [16] technologies should be introduced. In the AI industry, there are three application fields that can best bring value to people: speech, image, and natural language processing. Therefore, it will be natural to use the AI technologies in speech interaction, image processing and semantics understanding. In this section, we only discuss the application scenarios for speech interaction.

4.1 Smart Home and Intelligent Enterprise Fields

As is known to us that smart home [17] is still controlled by mobile phones currently. In this case, speech interaction can undoubtedly greatly enhance the operation experience of smart home. Amazon Echo is the first smart speaker that is made to play the role of controlling devices at home or offices. As one of the most successful products for speech interaction in foreign countries, Amazon Echo has become the best-selling electronic product in 2016. Relying on this product, Amazon gradually seized the information entrance of people's lives. They can use it to broadcast the daily news and weather forecast, schedule trips, or control the electrical appliances at home, etc. As a speech-based interaction controller, one of its core capabilities is to integrate various services on the Internet into the connector of the smart speaker. For example, the "IFTTT" is a function that can trigger events when conditions are met. For example, a photo will be posted to the Sina Weibo automatically after it has been taken. It turns such an "IF-THEN" condition and event-driven process into a rule which will fulfill the intention when the condition is met. As a matter of fact, such a process can also be controlled by smart speakers, which means that the future speech recognition will be seamlessly connected to the various services on the Internet with the mouse as we can see today. In addition, Google also launched the same device, Google Home, which has been maken as another input mode at home or in the office. Likewise, some Internet companies in China (e.g. Baidu, Alibaba, Jingdong and Xiaomi, etc.) have published their smart speaker products.

However, these products mainly focus on the personal consumption level entertainments, lacking of applications in enterprise scenarios. At present, the top international enterprise resource processing (ERP) vendors (e.g. Oracle, SAP, Salesforce and Acumatica, etc.) are building enterprise digital AI assistants and applying them in many enterprise fields, such as procurement, finance, human resource (HR), customer relation management (CRM) and distribution management. These AI assistants can be connected to a variety of back-end application systems, helping employees simplify user interaction, and improving efficiency and user satisfaction. In China, as the leading enterprise in the enterprise Internet, Kingdee also proposes the business digital assistant solution for enterprise users which takes smart speakers and chatbots as the product design, and takes financial office scenarios as the core businesses. It is actively deploying the AI scenarios to seize the industrial development opportunities. In the future, there will be increasingly more hardware devices that use speech as the new input and output.

4.2   Vehicle Field

With the development of speech technologies, the value of speech interaction is gradually transformed to the "big connection" stage. As one of the core connected hardware devices, the speech interaction platforms for vehicle are gradually applied in vehicle navigation systems. The entering of speech interaction technology cannot only free the drivers' hands to make convenient driving, but also make them concentrated on the surroundings to ensure the safety.

As the leading enterprise in the speech interaction field, Amazon has made great efforts to commercialize on the production vehicles of many global automobile companies (e.g. Ford, Volkswagen, Hyundai, BMW and Nissan, etc.) [18]. In the CES of 2018, Amazon has won the strong support of Toyota, Batten and Jeep. As a strong competitor, Google is relying on the high carrying rate of its Android Auto to upgrade the Google Assistant to make connection to a large scale of vehicles such as Ford, Nissan, Volkswagen and more than 40 brands of more than 400 models. In China, as the world's largest car ownership country, the speech interaction battlefield competition is also very fierce. Early In 2017, Baidu first released the conversational AI operating system, DuerOS, and has applied in vehicle scenarios. The speech synthesis technology of iFlyTek also successfully cooperated with many large automobile factories such as Volkswagen, Beiqi and Volvo [18].

4.3   Wearable Device Field

Compared with communication through text information, the universal applicability of speech recognition is much stronger. Depending on its inherent characteristics, the speech interaction technology has been applied in the wearable device field. More and more wearable devices (e.g. smart watch, smart glasses) have been implanted the speech interaction systems to make the interaction become much more convenient. Suppose when you are tired from overusing your eyes, smart glasses can scan the texts and help you "read" them out.

4.4   Customer Service Field

Whether it is a website, software, APP or other entity product, customer service is a always its important part. The huge number of repetitive human services have brought huge costs to enterprises. Faced with the trend of "user-centric" personalized service, how to effectively reduce customer service costs is a great concern for enterprises. Compared with traditional human services, there are many advantages for intelligent customer service: (1) the cost is much lower and the efficiency is higher; (2) it can be applied to various fields; (3) for user consultation, it can search information with the big data technology and respond to user quickly and accurately.

4.5   Electronic Commerce Field

This kind of speech technology can not only be used in hardware device systems, but also to redefine the software systems in electronic commerce field. To take an instance for example, Google's smart messaging system, Smart Messaging or Google Allo, which let you search what you are looking for through interacting with it via speech, such as display the restaurants nearby after hearing what we say.

So what's happening now? In fact, whether it is Amazon Echo or Google Allo, such messaging devices or softwares can be used in the enterprise softwares or each scenario of specific industries. Therefore, what's happening now is to solve the problems that exist in the real world, such as far-field speech recognition or speech synthesis with low quality speech samples. In this paper, we will give three examples to illustrate the application of speech input in electronic commerce scenarios (as can be seen in Fig. 2).

The first example is an Amazon application on the mobile phone. For example, when a user wanted to know the best-selling camera in the last month, the

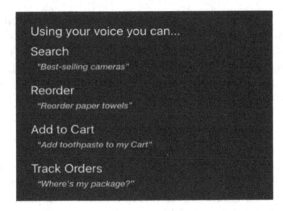

Fig. 2. Application of speech input in electronic commerce scenarios.

user would interact with the application via speech with the following three keywords: (1) the things that have been sold out; (2) camera; (3) best-selling. Then the application will try to understand the user intention and finally display the best-selling cameras on the Amazon website.

The second one is a repetitive order example. When a user told the application to reorder the hand sanitizer, it knows that the user has bought the hand sanitizer before, and will put it in your shopping cart automatically.

The last example is package tracking. When a user wanted to track where the package is, the application will check the orders the user has already placed, which of these orders have been shipped, and finally give the detailed information of the order.

From these examples above, we know that in a specific scenario, the keywords can be defined to form a thesaurus. After becoming a vocabulary of speech input and output in this scenario, the quality of speech recognition and speech synthesis will be improved significantly. It means that to use a new technology, it is best to find the application scenario first, then accumulate knowledge in the field, and then use the new technology to make better performance.

5   The Development Trend of Intelligent Speech Interaction

Finally, this paper will share four development trends of intelligent speech interaction.

5.1   Big Digitization

We are now in an digital economy era. There are almost 1.3 billion people who are using social media to communicate with each other on the Internet, and 9 billion sensors which have been adopted in the intelligent devices to obtain data every day. In these cases, as an asset with a huge amount of data, it is necessary to redefine the technologies of speech recognition, speech synthesis and speech understanding in the environment of big data. Therefore, instead of putting it on a stand-alone machine to investigate the capability of speech recognition or natural language understanding, the future speech interaction will definitely explore new technologies in a digital ecosystem.

5.2 Internet of Things Industrialization

In the future, almost all the devices will be connected to the Internet. When everything is connected, every connected object will generate data. Once the data is generated, we need to interact with it to demonstrate its value. Therefore, it is possible for the speech input, output and understanding capability to become an important supporting technology in the connected objects.

5.3 Multi-modality Integration

All the intelligence comes from the understanding of different data. Speeches, images and texts will coexist. When we are conducting speech interaction, the text information and the capability of natural language understanding will assist in improving the performance of speech recognition and the quality of speech synthesis. Therefore, in the future, the multi-modality data (e.g. speech, text, image, etc.) will be integrated to enhance the ability of creating values as a data asset.

5.4 Trusted Interaction and Record

Because of the probability of error in the speech interaction, speeches and the results of recognition are generally hard to be used as a reliable data resource, such as for auditing or judicial field. As an incorruptible digital ledger of economic transactions, the blockchain [19] can be programmed to record not just financial transactions but virtually everything of value [20]. Therefore, through the blockchain technology, the whole process of speech interaction can be recorded and traced in the blocks. Based on the feature of irreversibility, it is possible to realize the trusted interaction and record of the speech. Beside the advantage of logging and feedback of errors in the interaction and recognition process, it is more likely to innovate some new valuable business interaction modes, for example, the enterprises can discuss and sign contracts more quickly just by speeches.

6   Conclusion

In the era of digital economy, intelligent speech interaction will become the new way of input and output of equipment operation in the future. The future speech interaction will inevitably explore new technologies in a digital ecosystem.

With the expansion of the influence of intelligent devices, intelligent speech interaction can be popularized to a wide range of people and integrated into users' lives and work, thus satisfying both of their actual demand and psychological needs. On the one hand, it will become an effective way of replacing a huge number of repetitive, customized human services and work categories. On the other hand, it will create new scenarios and promote new technologies to provide better user experience. With its extensive application in medical, financial, education and other important industries, enterprises should grab this opportunity to achieve multi-win relying on their data centers and platforms.

Acknowledgements. This work is partially supported by the technical projects No. c1533411500138 and No. 2017YFB0802700. This work is also supported by NSFC (91646202). This work is also supported by NSFC (91646202), the 1000-Talent program and the China Postdoctoral Science Foundation (2019M652949).

References

1. 2012–2013 China Instant Messaging Annual Monitoring and User Behavior Research Report [OL], 25 December 2018. https://wenku.baidu.com/view/3eb4d4d6f90f76c661371a83.html
2. Speech Recognition [OL], 25 December 2018. https://en.wikipedia.org/wiki/Speech_recognition
3. Speech Synthesis [OL], 25 December 2018. https://en.wikipedia.org/wiki/Speech_synthesis
4. Speaker Recognition [OL], 25 December 2018. https://en.wikipedia.org/wiki/Speaker_Recognition
5. Petrushin, V.: Emotion in speech: recognition and application to call centers. In: Proceedings of Artificial Neural Networks in Engineering (1999)
6. El Ayadi, M., Kamel, M.S., Karray, F.: Survey on speech emotion recognition: features, classification schemes, and databases. Pattern Recogn. **44**(3), 572–587 (2011)
7. Wu, B.Y., Jia, J., He, T., Du, J., Yi, X.Y., Ning, Y.S.: Inferring users emotions for human-mobile voice dialog applications. In: Proceedings of IEEE International Conference on Multimedia & Expo (ICME), Seattle, America (2016)
8. Natural-language Understanding [OL], 25 December 2018. https://en.wikipedia.org/wiki/Natural-language_understanding
9. Green, G.M.: Pragmatics and Natural Language Understanding. Routledge, New York (2012)
10. Sarikaya, R., et al.: An overview of end-to-end language understanding and dialog management for personal digital assistants. In: 2016 IEEE Spoken Language Technology Workshop (SLT), pp. 391–397, December 2016
11. Natural-language Generation [OL], 26 December 2018. https://en.wikipedia.org/wiki/Natural-language_generation
12. Roesener, C., Hareter, H., Burgstaller, W., Pratl, G.: Environment simulation for scenario perception models. In: Proceedings of IEEE International Workshop on Factory Communication Systems, pp. 349–352 (2004)
13. Otebolaku, A., Lee, G.M.: A framework for exploiting Internet of Things for context-aware trust-based personalized services. Mob. Inf. Syst. (2018)

14. Kashlev, A., Lu, S., Mohan, A.: Big data workflows: a reference architecture and the DATAVIEW system. Serv. Trans. Big Data (STBD) **4**(1), 1–19 (2017)
15. Zhang, L.J., Zeng, J.: 5C, a new model of defining big data. Serv. Trans. Big Data (STBD) **4**(1), 48–61 (2017)
16. Russell, S.J., Norvig, P.: Artificial Intelligence: A Modern Approach. Pearson Education Limited, New Delhi (2016)
17. Stojkoska, B.L., Trivodaliev, K.V.: A review of Internet of Things for smart home: challenges and solutions. J. Clean. Prod. **140**, 1454–1464 (2017)
18. Vehicle Voice Interaction: Transition from Vase to Just Need [OL]. http://baijiahao.baidu.com/s?id=1598227749471529133&wfr=spider&for=pc
19. Zheng, Z., Xie, S., Dai, H.N., Chen, X., Wang, H.: Blockchain challenges and opportunities: a survey. Int. J. Web Grid Serv. **14**(4), 352–375 (2018)
20. What is Blockchain Technology? A Step-by-Step Guide For Beginners [OL], 2 May 2019. https://blockgeeks.com/guides/what-is-blockchain-technology/

Imagery Signal-Based Deep Learning Method for Prescreening Major Depressive Disorder

Hyunjin Kwon⬡, Jinhyeok Park⬡, Seokhwan Kang⬡,
and Youngho Lee$^{(\boxtimes)}$⬡

Department of Computer Engineering, College of IT, Gachon University,
1342 Seongnam-daero, Seongnam-si, Republic of Korea
euleekwon@gmail.com, rev.hyeok@gmail.com,
{shkang,lyh}@gachon.ac.kr

Abstract. Depression is a high-risk mental illness that can lead to suicide. However, for a variety of reasons, such as a negative perception of mental illness, most patients with depressive symptoms are reluctant to go to the hospital and miss appropriate treatment. Therefore, a simple prescreening method that an individual can use to identify depression is needed. Most EEG measurement devices that individuals use have few channels. However, most studies using EEG to diagnose depression have been conducted in a professional multi-channel EEG environment. Therefore, it is difficult for individuals to prescreen depression based on the results of the studies. In this study, we proposed a model that predicts depression by using EEG data measured by a few channels so that it can measure depression using the EEG data measured by an individual. In this study, brain waves measured in two channels were imaged using STFT transform and a spectrogram. The EEG image data was then used in a deep learning model. As a result of the performance evaluation, 75% accuracy was shown for the classification of image depression EEGs and normal image type EEGs. As a result, low channel EEG data for deep learning can be used as an auxiliary tool to proactively diagnose depressed patients.

Keywords: Major depressive disorder · Short-time Fourier Transform · Convolution Neural Network

1 Introduction

Major depressive disorder (MDD), which is usually called depression, is a very serious mental illness that can lead to suicide in severe cases. According to the World Health Organization (WHO), more than 300 million people worldwide suffer from depression, and about 800,000 people commit suicide each year [1]. In this situation, Korea has the highest suicide rate among OECD member countries, and the suicide rate is also continuously increasing [2].

Although early detection and appropriate treatment of a large number of mental illnesses, including depression, are very important, the mental health service utilization

© Springer Nature Switzerland AG 2019
R. Xu et al. (Eds.): ICCC 2019, LNCS 11518, pp. 180–185, 2019.
https://doi.org/10.1007/978-3-030-23407-2_15

rate in Korea is only about 22.2%, which is very low compared to the United States (43.1%) and Canada (46.5%) [3]. One of the biggest reasons for Korea's low utilization of mental health services is that the country's social perception of all mental illnesses is very negative [4]. Thus, the actual rate of patients experiencing depression is expected to be higher than reported.

Previously, the Hamilton Depression Rating Scale and the Beck Depression Inventory were used to diagnose depression. In recent years, however, several studies have been reported to analyze depression by analyzing brain waves as a result of the development of brain science. Since the field of brain science research became active, inexpensive and simple brainwave measuring devices have emerged to replace expensive conventional brainwave measuring devices. This makes it easy for anyone to measure brainwave data, and the field of brainwave research is no longer limited to specific experts. In other words, this means not only that public access to EEG measurement is improved, but also patients who have depression but refuse to measure EEG in a hospital can measure EEG individually.

An infrastructure where people who have symptoms of depression can simply measure their brain waves at home is gradually being built. However, most of the existing studies that diagnose depression have been conducted with professional brainwave measuring devices that have multiple channels. Therefore, it is difficult for individuals to diagnose depression at home based on the results of these studies. In this study, we proposed a model that can effectively diagnose depression based on the small number of channels of brainwave measuring devices commonly used in the home. In our model, we converted EEG brainwaves to image data and used it for classifying depressed patients and controls. Then we evaluated the performance of classification.

2   Method

2.1   Dataset

This study was conducted using a set of brainwave data measured in Wajid Mumtaz's study [5]. The data are measured on the brain waves of 34 depressed patients (17 males and 17 females) and 30 healthy controls (21 males and nine females). The brainwaves were measured in the state in which subjects closed their eyes (5 min), the state in which they opened their eyes (5 min), and the state in which certain visual contents were progressed (10 min). Brain waves were measured on 19 channels according to the international 10–20 system, where the 19 channels corresponded to the frontal (Fp1, F3, F7, Fz, Fp2, F4, and F8), the central (C3, C4 and Cz), the parietal lobe (P3, Pz and P4), the occipital (O1, O2) and left and right temporal regions (T3, T4, T5 and T6) [6]. In order to use the same number of EEG data, we used 30 brain waves from 30 depressed patients and 30 healthy controls. In addition, we used only Fp1 and Fp2 brainwave data among 19 channels, as low-channel brainwave measuring instruments (Muse and Neuro-Harmony) commonly measure brain waves on two channels (Fp1, Fp2). To minimize noise caused by blinking or external stimuli, we used EEG data measured with eyes closed.

2.2   Overview of Research Process

The flow of this study is as follows (see Fig. 1).

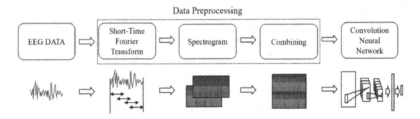

Fig. 1. Research flow

Short-time Fourier transform (STFT) was used as a method to simultaneously express both frequency domain analysis and time domain analysis. STFT is a method of performing Fourier transform on each part by shortening the time to analyze time and frequency simultaneously. The STFT transformation used the optimal parameter values presented in previous studies of the institution that provided this data. The optimal parameters proposed in the previous study are when the window length is 2 s, the hop size is 0.5 s, the FFT point number is 16 s, the sampling frequency is 256 Hz/s, and the overlap is set to 50% [5]. In this study, STFT conversion was performed for each channel using the corresponding parameters. We then used a spectrogram to image the results. The following figure shows the results of electroencephalogram (EEG) data obtained from a depressed patient measured on real channel 1 after performing STFT conversion and spectrogram (see Fig. 2).

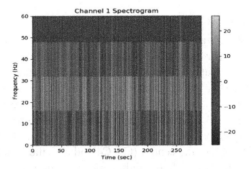

Fig. 2. Signal image of MDD patient

All patients' EEG data were imaged through the spectrogram and then combined into one for use as a single image. Therefore, the electroencephalogram image measured by one channel 1 and the electroencephalogram image measured by channel 2 were expressed as one image. Combined images were categorized as learning data and test data for use in deep learning. The data used for the study were 20 depressed EEG image data and 20 healthy EEG image data. The data used for the test were 14 pieces of data using seven pieces of EEG image data. Data were analyzed using the Convolution Neural Network (CNN) model as a deep learning model (see Table 1). Among the ways to classify brain waves, CNN is known to be very powerful in feature learning ability [7]. The CNN used in this study consisted of a three-layer convolution layer and used the ReLU activation function. We used max pooling with 3 × 3 spacing of 2 and soft-max as an activation function in the output stage.

Table 1. Convolution Neural Network model

Layer (type)	Out shape	Param #
Conv2d_1 (Conv2D)	(None, 62,94,32)	896
Max_pooling2d_1 (MaxPooling2D)	(None, 31,47,32)	0
Conv2d_2 (Conv2D)	(None, 29,45,64)	18496
Max_pooling2d_2 (MaxPooling2D)	(None, 14,22,64)	0
Conv2d_3 (Conv2D)	(None, 12,20,128)	73856
Max_pooling2d_3 (MaxPooling2D)	(None, 6,10,128)	0
Flatten_1 (Flatten)	(None, 7680)	0
dense_1 (Dense)	(None, 512)	3932672
dense_2 (Dense)	(None, 2)	1026
Total params: 4,026,946		
Trainable params: 4,026,946		
Non-trainable params: 0		

The image used for CNN was 64 × 96, which is one-hundredth the size of the original image. The batch size was set to 4, the steps per Epoch were set to 10, and Epoch was set to 35. The number of verification steps used was set to 2.

3 Results

We found that the model had a predictive accuracy of 75% for classifying image type EEG and healthy image type EEG in patients with depression. The following graphs show the change of performance according to the progress of Epoch. As can be seen in the graph of Fig. 3, the accuracy of the verification increases as the training accuracy

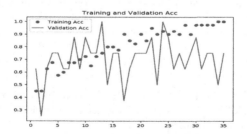

Fig. 3. Accuracy per Epoch

increases. In addition, in the graph of Fig. 4, the verification loss value decreases as the training loss value decreases.

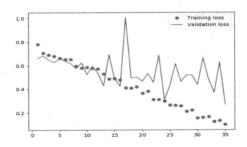

Fig. 4. Loss per Epoch

4   Discussion and Conclusion

It is very important to detect, treat and manage depression early. However, most patients with depression refuse to visit the hospital and are often reluctant to undergo a depression diagnostic test. Therefore, effective depression prescreening aids are needed to analyze depression using simple brainwave measuring device results without having to visit the hospital. In this study, we proposed a model that uses image-type brain waves to effectively distinguish patients with depression with data from a small number of channels. Brainwave data from two channels were imaged through a spectrogram after using STFT techniques. The imaging brainwave data were analyzed using the CNN model, which eventually showed a predictive accuracy of 75%.

In this study, we have shown that the method of classifying depressive patients using deep learning based on image EEG data can be used as a prescreening tool for depression. However, considering that the amount of data is one of the most important factors for the performance of deep learning, it is considered that the small number of EEG data used in this study has limitations in deriving the optimum performance of the model. Therefore, in future research, after acquiring a larger number of brain wave data, we will try to confirm its performance by using various deep learning models.

Acknowledgement. This research was supported by the Ministry of Science and ICT (MSIT), Korea, under the Information Technology Research Center (ITRC) support program (IITP-2019-2017-0-01630) supervised by the Institute for Information & communications Technology Promotion (IITP).

References

1. WHO. https://www.who.int/news-room/fact-sheets/detail/depression. Accessed 18 Mar 2019
2. Kwon, J., Chun, H., Cho, S.: A closer look at the increase in suicide rates in South Korea from 1986–2005. BMC Public Health **9**(1), 72 (2009)

3. Ministry of health and welfare. http://www.mohw.go.kr/react/jb/sjb030301vw.jsp?PAR_MENU_ID=03&MENU_ID=032901&CONT_SEQ=339138&page=1. Accessed 21 Mar 2019
4. Shin, K.: A study on the legal issues and challenges of insurance discrimination against the mentally Ill. J. Korean Neuropsychiatr. Assoc. **53**(2), 61–71 (2014)
5. Mumtaz, W., Xia, L., Yasin, M., Ali, S., Malik, A.: A wavelet-based technique to predict treatment outcome for major depressive disorder. PLoS One **12**(2), e0171409 (2017)
6. Klem, G., Lüders, H., Jasper, H., Elger, C.: The ten-twenty electrode system of the international federation. Electroencephalogr. Clin. Neurophysiol. **52**(3), 3–6 (1999)
7. Wen, T., Zhang, Z.: Deep convolution neural network and autoencoders-based unsupervised feature learning of EEG signals. IEEE Access **6**, 25399–25410 (2018)

Visual Cognitive Mechanism Guided Video Shot Segmentation

Chenzhi Shao, Haifeng Li$^{(\boxtimes)}$, and Lin Ma

School of Computer Science and Technology, Harbin Institute of Technology,
Harbin 150001, People's Republic of China
iamscz354@163.com, {lihaifeng,malin_li}@hit.edu.cn

Abstract. Shot segmentation of video sequences is one of the key technologies in video information processing, especially video retrieval. Traditional shot segmentation methods have low detection rate for the gradient shot and the abrupt shot, especially in a single scene. To deal with this problem, this paper proposes a video segmentation method based on visual cognition mechanism. This method proposes a block granularity color histogram to strengthen the visual salient area, and a highlight measure to describe the difference between the front and back frames. This brings great improvements to the accuracy of detecting shot switching in a single scene. In addition, based on the brightness visual perception in video, the difference between adjacent multi-frames in the sliding window is used to capture the brightness change for the gradient shots. Comparing with traditional methods, the proposed algorithm achieves better segmentation effect and has higher precision and recall rate.

Keywords: Video shot segmentation · Visual cognition mechanism · Block color histogram · Long time difference

1 Introduction

In the field of video retrieval, the accuracy of shot segmentation will directly affect the performance of video retrieval systems. Therefore, how to improve the accuracy of shot segmentation is one of the difficult problems in video analysis [1]. In multimedia information, videos can be divided into four different levels of frames, shots, scenes, and video streams according to different granularities. The shot refers to a set of consecutive frames of a camera that is continuous in time and space [2]. So the shot segmentation task is to divide a complete video into segments based on the shots. The shots can be mainly divided into the following two types: abrupt shots and gradual shots. An abrupt shot means that there is no obvious transition between two discrete frames; A gradual shot refers to a transition between two discontinuous frames, such as fade in, fade out, and dissolve. Therefore, our goal is to accurately find the boundaries of the two types of shot switching.

R. Xu et al. (Eds.): ICCC 2019, LNCS 11518, pp. 186–196, 2019.
https://doi.org/10.1007/978-3-030-23407-2_16

2 Related Work

The common shot segmentation method is mainly based on the difference value between two adjacent frames. Jinlai [3] used multi-feature fusion for video shot segmentation. Biswas [4] combined local similarity and global features, and used the method of matrix cosine similarity to detect the shot boundary. Mohanta [5] used the local feature-based frame transition parameters and frame estimation errors to achieve shot segmentation. In order to solve the copyright protection problem of multimedia video, Shang [6] proposed a motion vector based shot segmentation algorithm, and embedded the watermark in a suitable location to better protect the video. Chongke [7] proposed a shot boundary detection framework based on dynamic mode decomposition, which reduced the error detection rate. Baraldi [8] used hierarchical clustering for broadcast video for shot and scene detection. The above method has a high detection accuracy for shot switching in different scenarios, but the detection effect of the shot switching in the same scene is poor. In addition, the above methods have a low detection accuracy for the gradual shots, therefore, it is necessary to improve the accuracy of the shot segmentation.

As one of the most important channels of multimedia video, vision is also the main way of human cognition [9]. Under the constraints of visual physiology and visual sensitivity, the visual sensitivity of human eye to distinguish the details of the object is basically same for the similar things. The vision system is insensitive to absolute brightness, but is sensitive to color contrast. In the process of cognizing images, color plays an important role that can be directly perceived and conveyed by viewers [10]. According to the principle of visual continuity [11], vision tends to perceive continuous forms rather than discrete pieces. People use the same color to make visual recognition of continuous images. When the shot is switched, the color distribution of the video frame has a large difference, so we employ color as an important factor in the determination of the shot segmentation. In addition, according to cognitive psychology research, humans have different degrees of interest in different regions of the video, namely the visual attention mechanism [12]. In order to simulate the degree of interest of the biological vision system in different regions of the video image, this paper studies the influence of the video frame blocking strategy on the detection of the abrupt shots. For the detection of the gradual shots, a significant change occurs in the brightness of the video frame since the post-processing (fading, etc.) is added between the two discontinuous frames. Therefore, this paper studies the gradual shot detection method based on brightness information in view of human visual perception of brightness information [13].

The research content of the paper has the following aspects: 1. Research on the detection method of abrupt shot based on visual cognition mechanism. As for abrupt shot detection, this paper proposed a visual color block histogram detection method, which effectively solved the problem of low accuracy caused by shot switching in the same scene. 2. Research on the detection method of gradual shot based on visual cognition mechanism. In the aspect of gradual shot detection, the paper proposed a long-time difference detection method based on brightness information, which effectively improved the detection accuracy of the gradual shot.

3   Detection Method of Abrupt Shot Boundaries

3.1   Color Histogram Method

When detecting the abrupt shot, we can emply the difference of two continuous frames since the different shots are discontinuous in space and time, and there is no post-processing (fading, etc.) between the two frames of the abrupt shot. The abrupt shots in the video are shown in Figs. 1 and 2.

Fig. 1. Giagram of the abrupt shot A

Fig. 2. Giagram of the abrupt shot B

When we describe the difference between adjacent video frames, the common metric is the color histogram method [14], which is insensitive to camera shake and motion of objects within the shot. The color histogram is a statistical table reflecting the color distribution of an image pixel. The abscissa indicates the interval of each different size, and the vertical axis indicates the percentage of the total number of pixels in the image in a certain interval. It describes the proportion of different colors in the entire image, and does not care about the spatial location of each color. The HSV color space [15] is closer to the way humans feel color, encapsulating information about colors. Therefore, we first convert the original RGB color space to the HSV color space. The HSV model has three parameters: Hue, Saturation, and Value. The hue is the basic property of the color. The saturation refers to the purity of the color. The higher the value, the purer the color. The value means the brightness of the color. The conversion method from RGB color space to HSV color space is as follows:

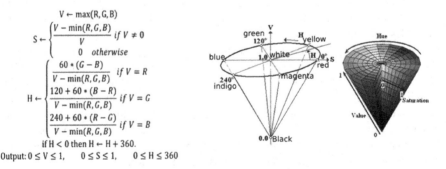

Fig. 3. HSV color model diagram

The formula for calculating the color histogram of an image is shown as follows:

$$H(k) = \frac{n_k}{N}, k = 0, 1, \ldots, 255 \tag{1}$$

In the above formula, n_k represents the number of pixels whose pixel value is k in the image, N refers to the total number of pixels in an image, and H(k) means the distribution of color histograms (Fig. 3).

3.2 Visual Color Block Histogram Strategy

Because of the frame images under different shots are similar in color in a single scene, people usually judge the situation by the region of interest rather than the overall color distribution of the image. Therefore, taking the color histogram of the entire image as a feature will result in a great error. Aiming at the situation, this paper proposed a segmentation method based on visual cognition mechanism, which is block color histogram. The block color histogram means that we divide the video frame firstly, and then compute the color histogram of each block. Finally, each color histogram is weighted to obtain the color distribution of the entire image. In order to highlight the main content of the image and reduce the influence of the background in the image, a larger weight is given to the main body region in the middle of the image, and the remaining background regions are given a smaller weight. In an image, since the four corners and the upper boundary are in the background area, a lower weight is given to the area. Sometimes the characters may occupy a vertical space in the multimedia video, so the left and right sides should be paid more attention. Therefore, the weights are assigned according to the scale shown in Fig. 4. The numbers in the rectangle represent the weight of each small block, while the 1:4:1 in the outer box represents the proportional relationship between the length and width.

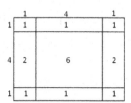

Fig. 4. Video frame block diagram

After the image frames in video are segmented, the color histogram difference of a small block of images in two adjacent frames on a single channel is calculated, as shown in the following formula:

$$d_m(i,j) = \frac{1}{2} \sum_{k=0}^{255} \left| H_{im}(k) - H_{jm}(k) \right| \tag{2}$$

In the above formula, $H_{im}(k)$ represents color distribution of the i-th frame image on the m-th block, $H_{jm}(k)$ refers to color distribution of the j-th frame image on the m-th block. Then, we calculate the color histogram difference of the adjacent two frames on a small block:

$$D_m(i,j) = \frac{1}{3}(d_{Hm}(i,j) + d_{Sm}(i,j) + d_{Vm}(i,j)) \tag{3}$$

Finally, the color histogram difference of the adjacent two frames is shown:

$$T(i,j) = \frac{\sum_{m=1}^{9} w_m * D_m(i,j)}{\sum_{m=1}^{9} w_m} \tag{4}$$

When the color histogram difference value $T(i, j)$ reaches a threshold, it is determined to be an abrupt shot. The choice of the threshold q is adaptive according to different types of video. The specific calculation method is as follows:

$$q = \alpha * \frac{T(1,2) + T(2,3) + \ldots + T(i,i+1) + \ldots T(N-1,N)}{N-1} \tag{5}$$

In the above formula, $T(i, i + 1)$ is the color histogram difference between video frame i and next frame. N refers to total number of frames, α is the coefficient and experiments show that α is suitable for $5 \sim 6$.

Algorithm 1. The Abrupt Shot Detection Algorithm

```
Input: A video to be detected containing N frames
Output: The abrupt shot frame number
1: Read original video frames
2: Convert each frame of RGB image to an HSV image, and
   scale the image proportionally
3: for i = 1 to N-1
     Compute T(i,i+1) according to formula 1~4
     sum = sum + T(i,i+1)
   end
4: q = sum/(N-1)*α
5: for i = 1 to N-1
     if T(i,i+1)>q, print i
   end
```

4   Detection Method of Gradual Shot Boundaries

In the detection of the gradual shot, since the transition forms such as fade in, fade out and dissolve are added between the two frames, the difference between their adjacent frames becomes smaller, which brings challenges to the shot segmentation. The gradual shots in the videos are shown in Figs. 5 and 6.

Fig. 5. Giagram of the gradual shot A

Fig. 6. Giagram of the gradual shot B

Since the brightness information changes between adjacent video frames are small when the gradual shot occurs, it is difficult for us to judge by the difference between the brightness information of adjacent frames. However, since the human visual system perceives regular changes in brightness information within a continuous number of frames, we can capture the change in brightness information. Based on this, this paper proposed a long-time difference method based on brightness to detect gradual shots. In this paper, a sliding window with a length of 6 frames is constructed, which slides from the front to the rear to observe the change of brightness difference of the video frames in the sliding window.

Similarly, we calculate the color histogram difference between adjacent frames:

$$d(i,j) = \frac{1}{2} \sum_{k=0}^{255} |H_i(k) - H_j(k)| \tag{6}$$

Since we only use the information on the brightness channel when performing gradual shot detection, the difference between adjacent frames can be calculated as:

$$T(i,j) = d_v(i,j) \tag{7}$$

It is assumed that successive frames in a sliding window in the video are frames $i-5, \ldots, i-2, i-1, i$, respectively. This paper first calculates the HSV color histogram of each frame image, and then computes the difference value $T(i, i-1)$, $T(i, i-2)$, $T(i, i-3)$, $T(i, i-4)$, $T(i, i-5)$. If the brightness of the image frames satisfied $T(i, i-1) < T(i, i-2) < T(i, i-3) < T(i, i-4) < T(i, i-5)$, and $T(i, i-1)$ is greater than a certain threshold, it is determined to be a gradual shot. The selection method of the threshold is as shown in the formula 5.

Algorithm 2. The Gradual Shot Detection Algorithm

```
Input: A video to be detected containing N frames
Output: The gradual shot interval (i, j)
1: Read original video frames
2: Convert each frame of RGB image to an HSV image, and
   separate the V channel
3: for i = 2 to N
     Compute T(i, i-1) according to formula 6~7
     sum = sum + T(i, i-1)
   end
4: q = sum/(N-1)*α
5: for i = 6 to N
     if T(i, i-1)<T(i,i-2)<T(i,i-3)<T(i,i-4)<T(i,i-5) &
        T(i,i-1)>q, print (i-5, i)
   end
```

5 Experiments and Results

5.1 Dataset and Evaluation Criteria

Videos to be detected are derived from TRECVID [16], which is the internationally authoritative dataset in the field of video detection. This paper used some of the videos published on the Open Video website. The following is the video information to be detected (Table 1):

Table 1. Test dataset information

Video name	Duration	Frames	Resolution	Shots	Abrupt shot	Gradual shot
anni005.mpg	6'19	11363	320*240	65	38	27
BOR08.mpg	28'07	50568	320*240	531	380	151
anni009.mpg	6'50	12307	320*240	103	39	64

In the task of shot segmentation, the evaluation benchmark is generally Precision and Recall. Precision refers to the percentage of the correct number of detected shots in the total number of detected shots, and the recall is the percentage of the number of correctly detected shots in the actual total number of shots. They are defined as follows:

$$P = \frac{TP}{TP+FP} \tag{8}$$

$$R = \frac{TP}{TP+FN} \tag{9}$$

In the above formula, *TP* represents the number of correctly detected shots boundaries, *FP* means the number of incorrectly detected shots boundaries, and *FN* refers to the number of undetected shots boundaries. In addition, *F1* value is defined as follows, which is the average of recall and precision.

$$F1 = \frac{2 * P * R}{P + R} \tag{10}$$

5.2   Results and Analysis of Abrupt Shot Detection

When detecting the abrupt shots, the paper compared the traditional color histogram method, the method of other paper and the histogram method based on visual color block proposed in this paper. The experiment results are shown in Tables 2, 3 and 4:

Table 2. Anni005 video abrupt shots results

anni005.mpg	P	R	F1
Traditional color histogram method	0.86	0.89	0.88
Other paper [17]	0.91	0.85	0.88
Proposed	**0.97**	**0.95**	**0.96**

Table 3. BOR08 video abrupt shots results

BOR08.mpg	P	R	F1
Traditional color histogram method	0.84	0.89	0.86
Other paper [17]	0.92	0.88	0.90
Proposed	**0.98**	**0.96**	**0.97**

Table 4. Anni009 video abrupt shots results

anni009.mpg	P	R	F1
Traditional color histogram method	0.64	0.64	0.64
Other paper [17]	0.84	0.76	0.80
Proposed	**0.83**	**0.90**	**0.86**

As can be seen from the above experimental results, video frames are segmented and given a large weight to the main area in the abrupt shot detection, which increase the difference between discontinuous frames and improves the effect of shot segmentation. Especially in the block before and after, that is, the traditional color histogram method and the method in the paper on the comparison of experimental results, we can clearly see the advantages of the block color histogram proposed in this paper.

5.3   Results and Analysis of Gradual Shot Detection

When detecting the gradual shots, the paper compared the traditional color histogram method, the method of other paper and the long-difference method based on brightness information proposed in this paper. The experiment results are shown in Tables 5, 6 and 7.

Table 5. Anni005 video gradual shots results

anni005.mpg	P	R	F1
Traditional color histogram method	0.62	0.48	0.54
Other paper [17]	0.64	0.53	0.58
Proposed	**0.82**	**0.67**	**0.73**

Table 6. BOR08 video gradual shots results

BOR08.mpg	P	R	F1
Traditional color histogram method	0.52	0.43	0.47
Other paper [17]	0.46	0.64	0.53
Proposed	**0.70**	**0.71**	**0.71**

Table 7. Anni009 video gradual shots results

anni009.mpg	P	R	F1
Traditional color histogram method	0.45	0.43	0.44
Other paper [17]	0.59	0.62	0.60
Proposed	**0.83**	**0.63**	**0.72**

As can be seen from the above experimental results, in the detection of gradual shots, due to the small difference between the two frames, it is difficult to detect shot boundaries and recognition rate is lower than that of the abrupt shots. However, the long-time difference strategy based on brightness information proposed in the paper has a significant improvement over the traditional color histogram method. In addition, the employment of brightness information can also have a good tolerance for camera shake and motion of objects within a shot. However, in the detection of gradual shots, the scenes (sunset, etc.) in which the brightness gradually changes are hard to detect, so there is still room for improvement.

6   Conclusions

Shot segmentation task is the premise of later video information retrieval, so the accuracy of shot segmentation will directly affect the performance of video retrieval system. The paper first introduced the visual cognitive mechanism and human perception of color. Then, based on the visual cognitive mechanism, a histogram method of visual color segmentation was proposed. This method strengthens the region of interest of biological vision system, weakens the influence of background, and improves the accuracy of abrupt shot detection. On the other hand, a long-time difference method based on brightness information was proposed to detect the gradual shots. The method improves the detection accuracy by capturing the perception rule of human vision for brightness. In addition, the paper used the method of window sliding, which is easy to achieve. Compared with other shot segmentation methods, the precision and recall are improved. The method can be used as an effective shot segmentation strategy. Due to the high computational complexity when comparing the difference between adjacent frames, variable step size method will be considered to speed up the shot segmentation in the future.

Acknowledgements. Our thanks to supports from the National Key Research and Development Program of China (2018YFC0806800), National Natural Science Foundation of China (61671187), Shenzhen Foundational Research Funding (JCYJ20150929143955341), Shenzhen Key Laboratory of Innovation Environment Project (ZDSYS201707311437102), Open Funding of MOE-Microsoft Key Laboratory of Natural Language Processing and Speech (HIT. KLOF.20150xx, HIT.KLOF.20160xx). The authors are grateful for the anonymous reviewers who made constructive comments.

References

1. Kumar, G.S.N., Reddy, V.S.K., Srinivas Kumar, S.: Video shot boundary detection and key frame extraction for video retrieval. In: Bhateja, V., Tavares, J.M.R.S., Rani, B.P., Prasad, V. K., Raju, K.S. (eds.) Proceedings of the Second International Conference on Computational Intelligence and Informatics. AISC, vol. 712, pp. 557–567. Springer, Singapore (2018). https://doi.org/10.1007/978-981-10-8228-3_51
2. Xing, Y., et al.: Multi-scale shot segmentation based on weighted subregion color histogram. J. Inf. Hiding Multimed. Sig. Process. **6**(3), 622–628 (2015)
3. Lv, J., Bai, H.: Research on shot detection algorithm of self-adaptive dual thresholds based on multi-feature fusion. In: Pan, Z., Cheok, A.D., Müller, W., Zhang, M. (eds.) Transactions on Edutainment XIII. LNCS, vol. 10092, pp. 247–261. Springer, Heidelberg (2017). https://doi.org/10.1007/978-3-662-54395-5_21
4. Biswas, S.K., Milanfar, P.: One shot detection with laplacian object and fast matrix cosine similarity. IEEE Trans. Pattern Anal. Mach. Intell. **38**(3), 546–562 (2016)
5. Mohanta, P.P., Saha, S.K., Chanda, B.: A model-based shot boundary detection technique using frame transition parameters. IEEE Trans. Multimed. **14**(1), 223–233 (2012)
6. Shang, G., et al.: Video watermark algorithm study of shot segmentation based on motion vector. In: Proceedings of the 2018 International Conference on Information Hiding and Image Processing. ACM (2018)
7. Bi, C., et al.: Dynamic mode decomposition based video shot detection. IEEE Access **6**, 21397–21407 (2018)
8. Baraldi, L., Grana, C., Cucchiara, R.: Shot and scene detection via hierarchical clustering for re-using broadcast video. In: Azzopardi, G., Petkov, N. (eds.) CAIP 2015. LNCS, vol. 9256, pp. 801–811. Springer, Cham (2015). https://doi.org/10.1007/978-3-319-23192-1_67
9. Monty, R.A., Fisher, D.F., Senders, J.W.: Eye Movements: Cognition and Visual Perception. Routledge, Abingdon (2017)

10. Schloss, K.B., et al.: Color inference in visual communication: the meaning of colors in recycling. Cogn. Res. Principles Implications **3**(1), 5 (2018)
11. Peteranderl, Sonja, Oberauer, Klaus: Serial recall of colors: two models of memory for serial order applied to continuous visual stimuli. Mem. Cogn. **46**(1), 1–16 (2018)
12. Li, N., Zhao, X., Ma, B., Zou, X.: A visual attention model based on human visual cognition. In: Ren, J. (ed.) BICS 2018. LNCS (LNAI), vol. 10989, pp. 271–281. Springer, Cham (2018). https://doi.org/10.1007/978-3-030-00563-4_26
13. Xing, D., et al.: Brightness–color interactions in human early visual cortex. J. Neurosci. **35**(5), 2226–2232 (2015)
14. Jeong, S., Won, C.S., Gray, R.M.: Image retrieval using color histograms generated by Gauss mixture vector quantization. Comput. Vis. Image Underst. **94**(1–3), 44–66 (2004)
15. Chen, T.-W., Chen, Y.-L., Chien, S.-Y.: Fast image segmentation based on K-means clustering with histograms in HSV color space. In: 2008 IEEE 10th Workshop on Multimedia Signal Processing. IEEE (2008)
16. Smeaton, A.F., Over, P., Doherty, A.R.: Video shot boundary detection: seven years of TRECVid activity. Comput. Vis. Image Underst. **114**, 411–418 (2010)
17. Li, Z., Liu, X., Zhang, S.: Shot boundary detection based on multilevel difference of colour histograms. In: 2016 First International Conference on Multimedia and Image Processing (ICMIP). IEEE (2016)

A Best Detecting Synchrony Method in Audio STROOP EEG Based on Wavelet Coherence

Kang Liu[1(✉)], Chunying Fang[1,2], Haifeng Li[2], and Tingpeng Li[1]

[1] Heilongjiang University of Science and Technology, Harbin, China
lksscl621@163.com, fcy3333@163.com
[2] Harbin Institute of Technology, Harbin, China

Abstract. Advanced brain function requires different levels of integration and coordination between multi-regional nervous systems, the underlying mechanism is the simultaneous oscillation of various neural networks. EEG is an increasingly method to detect brain function with high temporal resolution and low cost. How to analyze the synchronization phenomenon is the focus of cognitive neuroscience research based on EEG signals. Wavelet coherence is a classical method to evaluate EEG synchronization, but it is uncertain how to use. In this paper, this requires knowledge of the true relationship between signals, hence we compare different measures of functional connectivity on simulated data (unidirectional coupled Hénon maps, and the auditory Stroop EEG), including wavelet cross-spectrum, wavelet correlation, wavelet coherence and FFT coherence. To determine whether synchrony is detected, surrogate data were generated and analyzed, and FFT coherence measures performed best on simulated data. Above all, the parameter optimization method of the wavelet cross-spectrum is proposed with many samples. It is found that the optimized wavelet coherence performed most reliably than FFT coherence.

Keywords: EEG · Synchronous · Wavelet coherence · Shannon entropy

1 Introduction

Buzsáki proposed that neurons cause synchronous oscillations through conventional excitation and suppression in the network [1, 2], electroencephalograph (EEG), which is a very suitable activity for studying the human brain on the time scale of cognitive processes by covering a large number of the entire head sensors [3, 4]. Synchronization of EEG is thought to be an expression of brain function region integration or binding, time-varying brain activity makes the generated EEG be a non-stationary signal, an extremely complex non-periodic bioelectrical signal because of mutations and noise, how to deal with this signal is a huge challenge. Most signals have an energy distribution of 0.5 and 60 Hz, and their amplitude is usually 2 to 100 μV [5]. Therefore, the EEG signal overlaps many other biological signals and external noise in amplitude and frequency. Since synchronization can be expressed in different ways, various measures have been proposed to quantify the synchronization between signals. [4]. A good EEG synchronization measurement method should be insensitive to noise, robust and can detect linear and nonlinear relationships between signals.

© Springer Nature Switzerland AG 2019
R. Xu et al. (Eds.): ICCC 2019, LNCS 11518, pp. 197–204, 2019.
https://doi.org/10.1007/978-3-030-23407-2_17

Nolte et al. provides an imaginary part of coherency method to study brain inter-actions which is demonstrated for EEG measurements of voluntary finger movement. But nonlinearity not considered, imaginary part is mostly small, thereby risking to miss meaningful interactions [7]. Stam et al. propose a novel measure to quantify phase synchronization, the phase lag index (PLI), and compare its performance to the well-known phase coherence (PC), and to the imaginary component of coherency (IC). But Less sensitive to volume conduction, common sources, and montage [6], Vinck et al. [8] proposed phase leads and lags is weighted by the magnitude of the imaginary part of the coherency, but there is no evidence that the size of the phase difference is important for the coupling strength, Relative insensitive to phase differences around 0 and 180 degrees. The advantage of wavelet transform is that it has good time aggre-gation, high frequency resolution, phase information and its similarity with conven-tional signals, so it is used to identify the degree of association between two non-stationary time series and perform signal Spectrum estimation. However, there are many ways to use the wavelet transform to determine EEG synchronization. These methods have different advantages when dealing with different problems. But which is the best measure to use? How to use?

In this paper, unidirectional coupled Hénon maps and the auditory Stroop EEG are stimulated, which measure is best able to detect connections that do exist, hence we compare 5 measures of functional connectivity on simulated data and the degree of synchronization of the analog signal can be precisely adjusted. A variety of methods using wavelet synchronization signals and FFT coherence methods are used for comparison. For the problem of parameter setting in wavelet coherence process, the Shannon entropy method is used to optimize the parameters and more accurately detect the synchronization process of cognitive control EEG than FFT coherence. In a word, it is concluded that the wavelet coherence measures performed best on the auditory Stroop EEG.

2 Methods

2.1 Wavelet Correlation Analysis

2.1.1 Wavelet Cross Correlation

Wavelet cross-correlation is similar to classical signal cross-correlation, effectively quantization two signal correlations based on scale. Set two cross-correlation signals $x(t)$ and $y(t)$ at a given scale a and delay u, the wavelet cross-correlation of x and y is defined as:

$$WC_{XY}(a, u) = E[W_{XX}(a, \tau) W_{YY}(a, \tau + u)] \qquad (2.1-1)$$

In formula (2.1-1) $W_{XX}(a, \tau)$ and $W_{YY}(a, \tau + u)$ are the wavelet transform coeffi-cients of $x(t)$ and $y(t)$, respectively.

If the real part $RW_{XX}(a, \tau)$ and the imaginary part $IW_{YY}(a, \tau + u)$ of the wavelet transform coefficients are separated, the correlation between the two signals at a given scale a is quantified by the real part, then the wavelet cross-correlation is defined as:

$$WR_{XY}(a,u) = \frac{RWc_{XY}(a,u)}{\sqrt{RWC_{XX}(a,0)RWC_{YY}(a,0)}} \qquad (2.1-2)$$

2.1.2   Real Part Quantization Wavelet Cross Correlation

Sello and Bellazzini suggest that only the real part $W_{xy}(a,u) = \overline{W}_{xx}(a,u)W_{yy}(a,u)$ of the wavelet transform is considered, and the wavelet local correlation coefficient is defined by the wavelet cross spectrum:

$$WLCC(a,u) = \frac{RW_{xy}(a,u)}{|W_{xx}(a,u)||W_{yy}(a,u)|} \qquad (2.1-3)$$

2.1.3   Real and Imaginary Wavelet Cross-Correlation

If you consider the information provided by the real and imaginary parts of the wavelet transform, there is a certain relationship. Then the wavelet cross-correlation is defined as:

$$WR_{XY}(a,\tau) = \frac{\sqrt{|RWC_{xy}(a,\tau)|^2 + |IWC_{xy}(a,\tau)|^2}}{\sqrt{|WC_{xx}(a,0)||WC_{yy}(a,0)|}} \qquad (2.1-4)$$

where RWC_{xy} and IWC_{xy} are the real and imaginary parts of the cross-wavelet correlation function defined by Eq. (2.1-1), respectively.

2.1.4   Wavelet Coherence

Based on the above process, after calculating the cross-wavelet spectrum for the signals x and y and smoothing them, Wavelet Coherence (WC) is defined as.

$$WC_{xy}(a,b) = \frac{S(WCS_{xy}(a,b))}{\sqrt{S(|CWT_x(a,b)|^2)}\sqrt{S(|CWT_y(a,b)|^2)}} \qquad (2.1-5)$$

According to Schwartz's inequality:

$$\left(\sum_{I=1}^{n} a_i b_i\right)^2 \leq \left(\sum_{T=1}^{n} a_i^2\right)\left(\sum_{T=1}^{n} b_i^2\right) \qquad (2.1-6)$$

where $a_1, \ldots, a_n, b_1, \ldots, b_n$ are real numbers, and Schwartz's inequality guarantees that the value of WC is between 0 (the frequency component is completely unrelated) and 1 (the frequency component is completely correlated).

2.2   Fast Fourier-Based Coherence

In order to calculate the correlation of the two signals in the frequency domain, we define by crossover:

$$C_{xy}(f) = E[X(f)Y^*(f)] \qquad (2.2-1)$$

where $E[.]$ is the expectation operator, $X(f)$ is the (discrete) Fourier transform of $x(n)$, the asterisk indicates complex conjugation, and f is frequency. In practice, a finite number of samples will give a noisy estimate of (cross-and auto-) spectra. To reduce the noise, signals are segmented into equal length pieces, and the spectra of each segment is averaged.

The coherence function $c(f)$ is the square of the cross spectrum, normalized by the (auto-) spectra of the two signals:

$$C(f) = \frac{|C_{xy}(f)|^2}{C_{xx}(f)C_{yy}(f)} \qquad (2.2-2)$$

This measure is particularly useful when the correlation between signals is limited to a particular frequency band.

3   Experimental Results and Analysis

3.1   Generate Simulation Signals

We first use the chaotic system to obtain two simulation signals that can control the coherence. Here we use Hénon maps. We can simulate the generation of a pair of unidirectionally coupled X and Y signals,

$$x(k+1) = 1.4 + bx(k-1) - x^2(k) \qquad (3.1-1)$$

$$y(k+1) = 1.4 + dy(k-1) - [\mu x(k) + (1-\mu)y(k)]y(k) \qquad (3.1-2)$$

We analyzed the system in three different situations. One system is the same $(b = d = 0.3)$, the other two are different systems $(b = 0.3, d = 0.1)$ and $(b = 0.1, d = 0.3)$. The data is generated using the latter two cases. In general, we use μ to control the correlation and independence of the two signal data from $\mu = 0$ (completely independent) to $\mu = 1$ fully correlated with the simulation.

In order to confirm the relevant method we proposed. We propose that the signal using the chaotic system is superimposed with the real auditory Stroop EEG signal from literature [12]. The 2024 points are generated, and in order to avoid the instant start effect, we give up the first 1000 points. We selected an EEG signal and added it to the two signals generated by the chaotic system. Select 200–280 for display, as shown in Fig. 1, the result of $b = 0.3$ and $d = 0.1$ when $\mu = 0.9$.

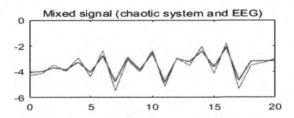

Fig. 1. Simulated signal synchronization

3.2   Comparison of related methods results

We used the simulated honen simulation signal to control the correlation to 0.9 to get several synchronization methods. The results of wavelet cross-correlation considering only the real part are shown in Fig. 2A, local wavelet correlation results are shown in Fig. 2B. The wavelet correlations considered in the real part imaginary part are shown in Fig. 2C, 4Wavelet coherence results D in the figure. Through comprehensive comparison we can see that the results of using wavelet coherence are better, indicating that the coherent method has a good effect on synchronous EEG signals.

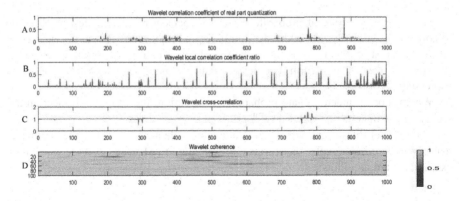

Fig. 2. Multi-method comparison results graph

Figure 2, the use of wavelet coherence works best. But it's hard to compare the methods that are intuitively better. Therefore, we have obtained the standard deviation of the results obtained by the two methods.

The red line in Fig. 3 shows the result of the difference between Fourier coherence and 0.9. The blue line shows the standard deviation of the results after wavelet coherence. We can see that the results of wavelet coherence are better than Fourier, but the results are not very obvious. We propose a method for optimizing wavelet parameters based on Shannon entropy.

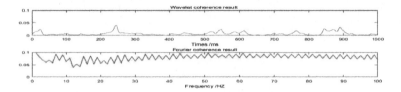

Fig. 3. Standard deviation result (Color figure online)

3.3   Optimization of Wavelet Parameters

In order to determine the Morlet wavelet shape, the Shannon entropy method is proposed to optimize the wavelet basis parameter β. When the EEG signal is similar to the Morlet shape, a high-amplitude band energy will appear on the time-scale phase plane, and thus the energy distribution can be used. "Sparseness" is used to evaluate the degree of similarity with the mother wavelet, and finally the Morlet wavelet that best matches the EEG signal is obtained.

$$H(p) = -\sum_{i=1}^{n} p_i \log P_i \qquad (3.3-1)$$

From the perspective of probability theory, "sparseness" can be described as the uniformity of probability distribution. Combining entropy to reflect the uncertainty of information distribution in information theory, Shannon entropy is used to estimate the sparsity of wavelet transform coefficient matrix. The Shannon entropy H(p) is expressed as follows:

Where: For an indeterminate probability distribution, the sum of all uncertainties satisfying the uncertainty is 1, i.e. $\sum_{i=1}^{n} P_i = 1$.

The wavelet transform coefficients at a certain scale are recorded as the coefficient matrix composed of wavelet transforms corresponding to M scales, and the calculation expressions are as follows:

$$P_i = \left| w_g\left(a_j, b\right) \right| / \sum_{j=1}^{M} w_g\left(a_j, b\right) \qquad (3.3-2)$$

The calculated results are shown in Fig. 4.

Therefore, by calculating the Shannon wavelet entropy corresponding to different shape Morlet wavelets, the Morlet wavelet parameters are optimized according to the principle that the mother wavelet with the smallest entropy is the most similar to the feature components. As shown in the figure, when the shape parameter β is 1.2.

We use Shannon entropy to optimize wavelet parameters. Select and compare 100 sets of real EEG signals. In Fig. 5, the red line indicates the optimized result, the blue line indicates the result before optimization, and the result show that parameter optimization is found to be better than the original result. We can easily see the difference between the results before and after optimization.

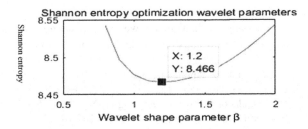

Fig. 4. Shannon entropy optimizes wavelet parameters

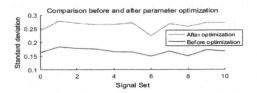

Fig. 5. One hundred groups of signal experimental comparison (Color figure online)

It can be seen that the synchronization effect of wavelet coherence is more precise than the Fourier coherence from Fig. 6 after the Shannon entropy optimization, the error is close to zero (blue line).

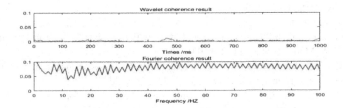

Fig. 6. After optimization with Shannon entropy (Color figure online)

4   Conclusion

In this paper, we address part of this question: which measure is best able to detect connections that do exist, in the non-stationary and noisy auditory Stroop EEG data hence we compare 6 measures of functional connectivity on simulated data (unidirectional coupled Hénon maps and EEG). No measure performed best in all tested situations. The FFT andwavelet coherence measures performed best on simulate data, and wavelet coherence performed most reliably on non-stationary data after Shannon entropy parameter optimization. From the perspective of brain network, the synchronization of brain cognition in different cognitive states is obtained more accurately. In the future, the dynamic evolution process of brain cognition can also be analyzed in detail through the method proposed in this paper. It can be seen that the neural network construction and analysis method based on wavelet coherence can be an effective tool to study the neural processing mechanism and we use the Shannon entropy to select the appropriate wavelet parameter to construct brain function connectivity.

Acknowledgements. Our thanks to supports from the National Key Research and Development Program of China (2018YFC0806800), National Natural Science Foundation of China (61671187), Shenzhen Foundational Research Funding (JCYJ20150929143955341), Shenzhen Key Laboratory of Innovation Environment Project (ZDSYS201707311437102), Open Funding of MOE-Microsoft Key Laboratory of Natural Language Processing and Speech (HIT. KLOF.20150xx, HIT.KLOF.20160xx). The Project of young talents of Heilongjiang University of Science and Technology of China in 2013 (Q20130106). Heilongjiang Provincial higher education reform general research project (SJGY20180453). The authors are grateful for the anonymous reviewers who made constructive comments.

References

1. Buzsáki, G., Wang, X.: Mechanisms of gamma oscillations. Annu. Rev. Neurosci. **35**, 203–225 (2012)
2. Buzsaki, G.: Rhythms of the Brain. Oxford University Press, Oxford (2006)
3. Schoffelen, J.M., Gross, J.: Source connectivity analysis with MEG and EEG. Hum. Brain Mapp. **30**(6), 1857–1865 (2009)
4. Bakhshayesh, H., et al.: Detecting synchrony in EEG: a comparative study of functional connectivity measures. Comput. Biol. Med. **105**, 1–15 (2019)
5. Nunez, P.L., Srinivasan, R.: Electric Fields of the Brain: The Neurophysics of EEG. Oxford University Press, Oxford (2006)
6. Stam, C.J., Nolte, G., Daffertshofer, A.: Phase lag index: assessment of functional connectivity from multi channel EEG and MEG with diminished bias from common sources. Hum. Brain Mapp. **28**(11), 1178–1193 (2007)
7. Nolte, G., et al.: Identifying true brain interaction from EEG data using the imaginary part of coherency. Clin. Neurophysiol. **115**(10), 2292–2307 (2004)
8. Vinck, M., et al.: An improved index of phase-synchronization for electrophysiological data in the presence of volume-conduction, noise and sample-size bias. Neuroimage **55**(4), 1548–1565 (2011)
9. Bowyer, S.M.: Coherence a measure of the brain networks: past and present. Neuropsychiatric Electrophysiol. **2**(1), 1 (2016)
10. Reid, A.T., et al.: A cross-modal, cross-species comparison of connectivity measures in the primate brain. Neuroimage **125**, 311–331 (2016)
11. Damoiseaux, J.S., Greicius, M.D.: Greater than the sum of its parts: a review of studies combining structural connectivity and resting-state functional connectivity. Brain Struct. Funct. **213**(6), 525–533 (2009)
12. Bo, Y., Xunda, W., Lin, M., et al.: The complex pre-execution stage of auditory cognitive control: ERPs evidence from stroop tasks. PLOS One **10**(9), 0137649 (2015)

Author Index

Printed in the United States
By Bookmasters